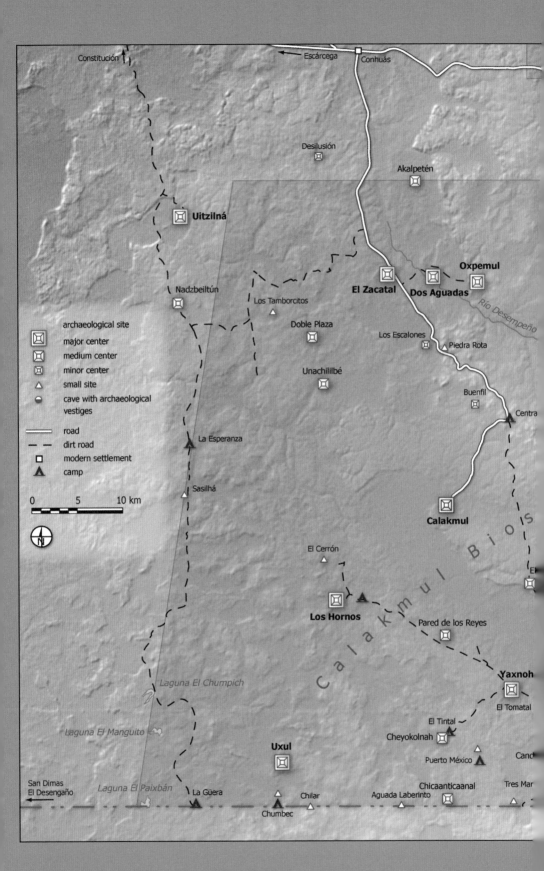

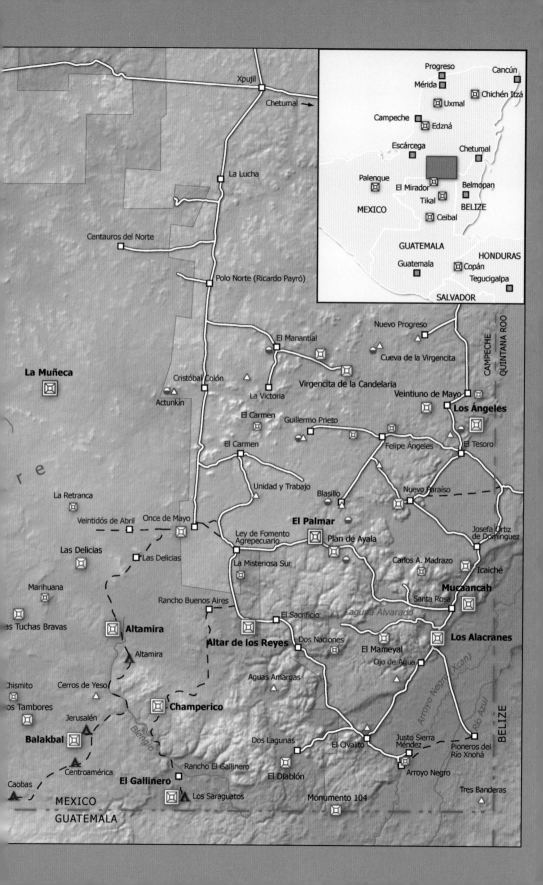

LOST MAYA CITIES

Publication of this book was made possible
by a generous gift from Ken Jones.

LOST MAYA
CITIES

Archaeological Quests in
the Mexican Jungle

Ivan Šprajc

Translation by Petra Zaranšek and Dean Joseph DeVos

TEXAS A&M UNIVERSITY PRESS
COLLEGE STATION

This paper meets the requirements of ANSI/NISO Z39.48–1992
(Permanence of Paper).
Binding materials have been chosen for durability.
Manufactured in China through Four Colour Print Group

Library of Congress Cataloging-in-Publication Data

Names: Šprajc, Ivan, author. | Zaranšek, Petra, translator. | DeVos, Dean, translator.
Title: Lost Maya cities : archaeological quests in the Mexican jungle / Ivan Šprajc ;
    translation by Petra Zaranšek and Dean Joseph DeVos.
Other titles: Izgubljena mesta. Slovenian
Description: First edition. | College Station, [Texas] : Texas A&M University Press,
    [2020] | Includes index.
Identifiers: LCCN 2019035609 | ISBN 9781623498214 (trade paperback) |
    ISBN 9781623498221 (ebook)
Subjects: LCSH: Šprajc, Ivan—Career in archaeology. | Šprajc, Ivan—Travel—Mexico. |
    Šprajc, Ivan—Travel—Yucatán Peninsula. | Mayas—Mexico—Antiquities. | Mayas—
    Yucatán Peninsula—Antiquities. | Excavations (Archaeology)—Mexico. | Excavations
    (Archaeology)—Yucatán Peninsula. | Mexico—Description and travel. | Yucatán
    Peninsula—Description and travel. | Mexico—Antiquities. | Yucatán Peninsula—
    Antiquities. | LCGFT: Autobiographies. | Travel writing.
Classification: LCC F1435 .S7913 2020 | DDC 972/.01—dc23
LC record available at https://lccn.loc.gov/2019035609

To Silvia

Contents

LOST MAYA CITIES

1

The Maya and Their Land

The tropical forest has a strange power. An endless green thicket obstructs one's view, hinders movement, and, with trouble and danger lurking at every step, makes one feel powerless. However, the unmistakable smell of moisture, the lush vegetation, the fluttering of birds whose variety and sounds are beyond imagination, the shrieking monkeys and their boisterous acrobatics up in the trees, even the buzzing of insects—all this imposes millions of stimuli that become lodged somewhere deep in one's brain, thereby leaving a powerful impression and stirring a desire to return. Blossoms, leaves, and fruit in the most varied shapes, colors, and scents; the rotting trunks of gigantic trees that have died naturally; animals of every stripe—all coalesce into natural beauty that is beyond compare, yet wild, untamed, and even belligerent. In 1937 the Mexican writer Ramón Beteta described it in his book *La tierra del chicle* in the following manner:

> Among the countless winding roots it is easy to overlook a snake; millions of insects, ants, and giant grasshoppers all defend themselves and attack; and even plants—those without thorns—excrete caustic juices, have poisonous fruits, cause a burning itching when touched, or their shade brings on drowsiness. Their defense is passive, yet frighteningly effective. Here, a human being is a slave and

an alien, an intruder and an enemy. The air is filled with an intense smell of fermenting organic matter; however, it is not clear whether the odor announces new life or is a symptom of continuous dying.[1]

So remains the tropical forest of the central and southern Yucatán Peninsula. The rainfall brought by the trade winds from the northeast increases from north to south, resulting in relatively low vegetation in the north, which gradually becomes taller and turns into tropical forest farther south. Nowadays, the lowlands stretching north from Belize and northern Guatemala into the Mexican states of Campeche, Yucatán, and Quintana Roo are quite populated, especially in the north, but significantly less so in the central and southern part of the peninsula. While the tropical forest in general seems rather unsuitable for mass colonization, the specific environment of the Yucatán Peninsula is particularly inhospitable because flowing surface waters are practically nonexistent, except in the south. Nonetheless—or perhaps precisely because nature itself was not too generous—it was in these lowlands that one of the greatest and most fascinating civilizations in human history reached its peak.

The origins of the relatively uniform culture created by the peoples now known collectively as the Maya go back to the second millennium BC. At first, the term "Maya" referred only to the language spoken at the time the Spanish conquerors arrived in the northern Yucatán Peninsula, where it is still in use. However, this term now has a broader meaning, as it designates the entire group of peoples who used to live in what is now southeastern Mexico, Guatemala, Belize, El Salvador, and western Honduras. The Maya culture developed within the broader cultural area known as Mesoamerica, which corresponds to the central and southern parts of present-day Mexico and the northern part of Central America and is characterized by numerous cultural elements that were common to the peoples living in this territory when the Spanish arrived. Such elements first began to develop in the second millennium BC with the emergence of the earliest complex, stratified societies along the southern coast of the Gulf of Mexico. Further developments led to the expansion of Mesoamerica and—despite the great linguistic diversity and significant regional

---

1. Ubaldo Dzib Can, *Sicté: La tragedia del chicle de los mayas* (Campeche, Mexico: Gobierno del Estado de Campeche, Instituto de Cultura de Campeche, 2000), 19–20 (extract translated from the Slovenian translation of Ivan Šprajc into English by Petra Zaranšek).

Figure 1.1. A typical landscape in the central Yucatán Peninsula.

and time-dependent variations—to increasing cultural unity. This unity, resulting from both common origins and a high degree of cultural interaction, can be seen in an economy based on intensive agriculture (particularly on the cultivation of corn as a staple crop), the similarities observed in monumental architecture (most notably in temples taking the form of stepped pyramids), and various aspects of the social organization, art, religion, and calendrical system.

The history of Mesoamerica is usually divided into three main periods or developmental stages: Preclassic (about 2000 BC–AD 200), Classic (about AD 200–900), and Postclassic (about AD 900–1521). The development of the first stratified, urban societies in the Preclassic period was followed by the florescence of the Classic period, which was noticeable particularly in art, architectural achievements, and the development of writing, while the main characteristics of the Postclassic period were intensive migrations, the spread of the new cultural elements, an emphasis on militarization, and—especially in the Maya area—increased political fragmentation.

The land of the Maya, encompassing approximately four hundred thousand square kilometers, consists of two essentially distinct geographical units: in the north, vast lowlands characterize the karstic and almost completely flat Yucatán Peninsula, while in the south mountain ranges of mostly volcanic origin stretch across Guatemala, El Salvador, Honduras, and the Mexican state of Chiapas. The two areas differ greatly in terms of climate, geology, vegetation, and available natural resources.

The American continent was initially populated by the end of the last Ice Age. The first people came from Asia, more specifically across the land bridge that—because of the lower sea level at the time—connected the two continents at the site of today's Bering Strait. In the millennia following the Ice Age, agriculture developed in the territory of the later Mesoamerica, and as it became an increasingly important subsistence strategy, it gradually replaced the previous hunting and gathering way of life and brought about permanent settlements. In the second millennium BC, the number of permanently settled communities in southeastern Mesoamerica increased, especially along the Pacific and Caribbean coasts, an environment where—aside from cultivating corn and other crops—fishing was possible. The favorable natural circumstances led to population growth, and when the most suitable locations were filled, communities had to improve how they organized the production, use, and exchange of goods in order to survive. These were the first steps toward the emergence of state-organized societies, which most likely arose independently in various places; however, commercial and other connections certainly played a role. The increasing social stratification is reflected in the ever-greater differentiation observable in residential structures and grave goods. Furthermore, certain major buildings, typically of a religious nature, bear witness to this fact, because their construction required organized work that could not have been carried out by egalitarian communities. In time, the ever-larger population on the coast was forced to colonize the hinterland, which was less hospitable and therefore required an even more efficient social organization. The more challenging conditions typical of these areas must have been the reason the first major centers arose alongside smaller ones in the first millennium BC, in the highlands to the south as well as in the lowlands of the Yucatán Peninsula. Certain characteristics of such centers demonstrate their increasingly complex political order. Besides architecture, which at that time became more monumental and diverse, the development of crafts, arts, trade, and script also reflects increasing specialization in individual activities—that is, a high level of division of labor, for which some manner of state order is necessary.

The largest cities of the Preclassic period, which were the centers of both large and small states, appeared in the second half of the first millennium BC in the lowlands featuring a tropical climate and flora. There, at the very heart of the Yucatán Peninsula in the northern part of modern-day Guatemala, are the archaeological sites of Nakbé, Tintal, El Mirador, and Wakná, the remains of extensive centers with magnificent pyramidal temples, palaces, and causeways. In the largest one, El Mirador, the Danta pyramid rises toward the sky, the most voluminous building the Maya ever built. Later, in the Classic period, their culture also reached its peak in the lowlands; but there it also experienced its greatest crisis and subsequent downfall at the end of the period. While the population in the southern highlands and the northern Yucatán Peninsula managed to carry on until the arrival of the Spanish conquerors—despite the varied fates of individual states—nearly all of the once-glittering cities in the central and southern lowlands were abandoned during the ninth and tenth centuries. The reason for their demise is still a subject of heated debate; however, it is certain that a combination of overpopulation, an increasing lack of agricultural land, and prolonged periods of drought in the Late Classic period had a decisive impact. General distress and the inability of the ruling structures to adapt appropriately to the new conditions led to growing social unrest and destructive wars between ever-weaker states and, finally, to the complete collapse of the institutions that made up the rigid social system.

The disintegration of the political structures that would have been essential for the survival of large communities facing difficult natural circumstances resulted in a drastic population decline. Abandoned cities were gradually swallowed up by the jungle, leaving extensive areas almost completely uninhabited. The rare settlements that the first Spanish colonizers stumbled upon in the central lowlands were mere villages, with a simple social order and barely noticeable traces of their former splendor. Because of their reserves of wood and other natural resources, these regions piqued the interest of the modern world only in the nineteenth century, which also witnessed the arrival of the first travelers and researchers.

2

Studying the Maya

The history of research into the Maya culture began in the early colo-nial period, with the first studies of written sources and the discovery of certain important archaeological sites. However, interest in the Maya increased only in the early nineteenth century, when the first reports of travelers and explorers revealed to the broader public the existence of monumental remains of an extinct civilization. The most important mile-stones were two books, *Incidents of Travel in Central America, Chiapas and Yucatan* and *Incidents of Travel in Yucatan*, published in 1841 and 1843 in New York by the American lawyer and diplomat John Lloyd Stephens. They included illustrations by the English architect and artist Frederick Catherwood. Stephens's stories are descriptive, devoid of unfounded speculation, and written in an attractive style, even for a modern reader, and Catherwood's illustrations are both very precise for their time and embellished with details that—following the spirit of the nineteenth cen-tury—imbue his artistic depictions of buildings and monuments with a distinctly romantic feel. For these reasons, Stephens's books, on one hand, demarcate the onset of the archaeology of the Maya as a serious field of study, while on the other they represent the most significant origin of the fascination with this topic still present today.

Of all the pre-Columbian peoples of the New World, the Maya were unique in numerous aspects. Although, technologically speaking, they lived in the Stone Age, as the rare metals they knew of did not play a significant role in everyday life, they reached a relatively high level of economic, societal, artistic, and intellectual development, comparable to that of ancient Egypt, Mesopotamia, and older periods in China, cultures in which the use of bronze and—in later periods—iron provided the foundation. Proof of the magnificence of Maya culture, which was achieved without draft animals or metal tools, as well as without knowledge of the plow or use of the wheel, can be found not only in their grandiose architecture, beautiful artwork, and diverse and elegant luxury objects; they also developed a true phonetic script, which was the most sophisticated of any in the pre-Columbian Americas. While the predecessors of the Maya, the Olmecs, created a system of writing numbers with place values, the Maya upgraded it and applied it in their complex calendrical system and astronomical calculations, thereby attaining the leading position among pre-Columbian peoples.

The great interest in the Maya can be attributed not only to these aspects but also to a sentiment that pervaded the study of this civilization for many decades, including a large part of the twentieth century: the Maya were considered to be essentially different from all other ancient civilizations; they were deemed to be a peaceful group of farmers and craftsmen ruled by a noble elite whose only concerns were religious matters, the observation of heavenly bodies, and the glorification of spiritual matters. So, what were the grounds for such a romantic view?

In the late nineteenth century, research was based largely on written sources such as the *Popol Vuh*, the holy book of the K'iche' group of the Maya, who live in the highlands of Guatemala; the *Relación de las cosas de Yucatán*, a report written by Bishop Diego de Landa in the sixteenth century containing abundant information on the Maya in the northern Yucatán Peninsula; and a small number of preserved codices or illustrated manuscripts. Such studies resulted in the first significant findings regarding the Maya numerical system, calendar, and astronomy. New data were also obtained in the first archaeological studies at the end of the nineteenth century; however, for many decades the results of attempts to decipher the Maya hieroglyphic script were limited to only numerical and calendar glyphs—despite an ever-increasing corpus of inscriptions discovered and documented at numerous archaeological sites. The lack of success in decoding other glyphs, the many calendrical and astronomical texts, and the seeming scarcity of other types of data that would have disclosed the warlike spirit and true nature of the Maya were the reasons for the romanticized opinion of them, which was—however unusual—deeply rooted and generally accepted. It was repeated even by scholars of such merit as the illustrious Sylvanus G. Morley, who in his book *The Ancient Maya*, published in 1946, wrote that Maya texts, being completely different from those originating in ancient Egypt, Assyria, and Babylon, contained neither the history of real conquests and military victories nor the glorification of certain individuals. In 1954, J. Eric S. Thompson—probably the greatest authority on the archaeology of the Maya at the time—expressed a very similar opinion in his book, *The Rise and Fall of Maya Civilization*.

This idealized picture began to transform only in the 1960s, principally because of progress in deciphering the Maya script, which showed that inscriptions were dedicated mainly to events from the lives of rulers and their families. It had once been believed that the lushly decorated figures depicted on stone monuments and the facades of buildings represented gods, but now real people from Maya history started emerging from the dark past: haughty lords celebrating their births, enthronements, victories in battles, and sacrifices of captives. What had been unfathomable for many decades became evident: the Maya were not essentially different from other peoples at a comparable level of development.

We must admit that the Maya, too, were just people, with virtues and vices, advantages and shortcomings. However, although we must deny their superhuman perfection, they are no less fascinating a subject of study than they once used to be. One reason is that the remains of numerous once-magnificent cities—ruins of glorious temples and palaces, and monuments with relief carvings and enigmatic hieroglyphic inscriptions—have either been discovered or still lie hidden deep in the jungle, overgrown with gigantic tropical trees and wrapped in vines. It is precisely this exotic environment, apparently hostile and unfavorable to the development of a civilization, that has remained one of the strongest reasons for the romantic allure that has surrounded the Maya ever since the time of the first explorers.

And it is precisely this fatal attraction that appears to be stronger than any difficulties an explorer is exposed to. It is quite surprising how varied the professional backgrounds were of many people who later became the most prominent experts in Maya archaeology. The interest in Maya ruins of Frans Blom, a Dane who originally worked in the Mexican oil fields, was first stirred during his jungle travels on which he met Sylvanus Morley, who later brought him to study at Harvard. The legendary Edwin Shook, in charge of or a collaborator on a number of archaeological projects at various sites, was first a student of technical sciences in Washington, DC. Gustav Strømsvik was a Norwegian sailor who one night, when his ship was anchored some kilometers from the northern Yucatán shore, jumped into the sea with his colleague and swam all the way to the town of Progreso; the following day the captain notified the authorities that two of his men had most likely drowned. In an interview in 1990, Ed Shook jokingly continued the story thus:

> Curiously enough, a body happened to be found on the beaches of Progreso the next day, and its features more-or-less matched those of Stromsvik: age so-and-so, blond hair, blue eyes. The body was buried in Progreso, a little cross placed on the grave, and the marker inscribed with Gus' name and his date of drowning. When Gus would "get in his cups," we'd go down and put flowers on his grave.
>
> As soon as Gus and his chum hit the beach, they went right into the bush and walked as far as they could, to get away from the coastal area. They ended up at a sugar *trapiche* and found a job, which paid them about a peso and a half a day. While they were working there, they kept hearing rumors of a bunch of Americans digging up old ruins in a place called Chichen Itza. So they got fed up with the sugar mill and walked into Chichen, which was in the middle of a field season. At the time, Earl Morris was on the Temple of the Warriors, and Morley was running around frantically trying to construct a chute for the backdirt. Gus and his friend were just a godsend. Gus was put on as a mechanic and the other fellow as a carpenter. They were a huge success because the archaeologists weren't very clever with that sort of thing.
>
> At the end of the season Gus' chum decided he was going back to Norway, and Gus offered to become a caretaker of Chichen during the off-season. This pleased Morley, for Gus was someone he could trust. And a remarkable thing happened: Gus had nothing to do the whole dry season, except take care of the camp. As a consequence, he decided to read the whole library of the Carnegie at Chichen—a pretty full field library. God, by the second season he knew more about

the Maya than most of the staff! Eventually, he became the head of the largest project going on at the Carnegie, the Copan excavations.[1]

This story concerns the years when Ed Shook, Gus Strømsvik, Eric Thompson, and many other famous archaeologists worked within the framework of a multiyear research program sponsored by the Carnegie Institution of Washington, which in the first half of the twentieth century probably played the most important role in Maya archaeology. The head of the program was Sylvanus Morley, the famous Vay, as everyone called him, a charismatic character with an extraordinary ability to acquire funds from sponsors yet also be a productive researcher and tireless field worker. Following his father's wishes, he too first studied construction engineering. He hated the conditions in the jungle, yet he kept returning, even though he was afflicted numerous times with malaria, amebic dysentery, and other diseases, to which he eventually succumbed in 1948.

Once, a colleague who was accompanying me said, "I don't know why I'm here again; I hate the jungle and the heat." Another mentioned, after an especially long field season, that for days he could not bear the color green and he would walk around dressed in a suit with a tie—attire hardly compatible with the personality of most archaeologists. (Not entirely without reason, the witty Paul Bahn wrote: "Archaeologists are therefore the precise opposite of dustmen, though they often dress like them.")[2] I, too, have said to myself numerous times that a certain season would be my last, and yet just as many times I have broken this promise. And the return is always exciting, even before reaching the destination. On several occasions while driving from Mexico City, my colleague and friend of many years, the surveyor Pepe Orta, would point at a large road sign hanging above an intersection in the town of La Tinaja, where we would get off the highway to Veracruz and turn right to head southeast, and say: "Look, magical words!" The sign stated in large block letters: AL SURESTE (TO THE SOUTHEAST).

This must be some kind of addiction. But is it not the same with alpinism, for instance, or other extreme activities? The greater the effort and difficulty, the more satisfaction one feels once the objective is achieved.

---

1. Edwin Shook, as recounted to Stephen D. Houston, "Recollections of a Carnegie Archaeologist," *Ancient Mesoamerica* 1 (1990): 250.

2. Paul Bahn, *Bluff Your Way in Archaeology* (Horsham, UK: Ravette Books, 1989), 5.

Figure 2.1. The nearly forty-meter-tall Structure 1, the second tallest in Calakmul, still rises magnificently above the expanse of tropical forest, which more than a millennium ago overgrew the once-flourishing metropolis, possibly the largest city the Maya ever created.

Many times we would fruitlessly wander around in the forest for days or even weeks, getting pricked by thorns, tripping over vines and roots, and fixing chain saws and vehicles. Yet we felt rewarded for all the trouble once we finally laid our eyes on a magnificent pyramid or an inscribed monument.

I cannot be certain how far back the beginning of this story of addiction goes. Does it go back to 1974, when I enrolled in archaeology and ethnology studies at the University of Ljubljana, quietly hoping for such adventures? I first set foot in a tropical forest only in 1977, during a short trip to Mexico, and some years later in South America. Or did it all start later, in 1985, when I received a scholarship for postgraduate studies in Mexico and for the first time set off for the jungle to carry out research? Or even later, in 1992, when I secured a position at the Mexican Instituto Nacional de Antropología e Historia? At that time, I was in charge of the demarcation and mapping of sites that were to be protected by presidential decree. I was often sent off to remote areas in the southeast of the country; in order to determine the extent of archaeological sites, we had to examine the area, making our way through the jungle that had overgrown once-flourishing Maya towns.

Without a doubt, all these experiences were important, but a true challenge presented itself only some time later.

3

A Meeting

In 1992, an amendment to Article 27 of the Mexican Constitution enabled the privatization of communal land—*ejidos*—which had been established by an agrarian reform following the revolution in the early twentieth century. Within the scope of a broader governmental program aimed at transferring ownership, the National Institute of Anthropology and History (Instituto Nacional de Antropología e Historia, hereafter referred to as the INAH) was assigned certain special tasks. This enormous institution comprises a number of administrative bodies, departments, and regional centers. In 1995, at a meeting of researchers from the Department for the Public Registry of Archaeological Monuments and Sites (Dirección de Registro Público de Monumentos y Zonas Arqueológicos), our director outlined the upcoming work within the scope of the program. It included a field inspection of archaeologically less well-known areas of Mexico; the reason was that once communal lands became private property, this work would be much more difficult. Among the regions the director listed was the southeastern part of the state of Campeche, at the heart of the Yucatán Peninsula.

Southeastern Campeche? I knew that was the territory with the largest blank areas on the archaeological map of the Maya. In the 1930s the American archaeologist Karl Ruppert led four expeditions into this vast expanse and recorded several important archaeological sites, but no one now knew exactly where many of them were. Aside from that, in his monumental work *Archaeological Reconnaissance in Campeche, Quintana Roo, and Peten*, published in 1943 with John Denison, a specialist in Maya writing, Ruppert mentioned that his expeditions had managed to document only some of the largest sites. Since Ruppert, other than a few rare exceptions, no archaeologist had journeyed into this area, mostly because of the difficult access: just as in Ruppert's time, it was still largely covered by tropical forest. Despite all that, the likelihood that the jungle was still hiding many secrets was very high.

"Does this mean that money is available for such research?" I asked.

"Money will be available," the director assured me. "The head office has notified us that anyone willing to assume responsibility for one of the regions listed should submit a research project proposal. If it is approved, funding will be provided."

That was all I needed. Only a couple of days later I submitted my project proposal. Some time passed, and then one day the secretary entered my office, visibly excited.

"You have a phone call. It's Doctor Nalda—he wants to speak with you."

I was startled as well. Enrique Nalda was the technical secretary, number two in the hierarchy of the INAH, just below the director general. I picked up the receiver.

"Hello. I've read your project for Campeche. I can see that some people at our institute still know how to write."

"Thank you so much," I replied, relieved.

"Very good. But, are you familiar with the conditions? Are you sure you want to do this?"

"Of course."

"Very well. It won't be easy, but you'll certainly find things you haven't even dreamed about. Not just mounds, ruins; there will be stelae, inscriptions . . ."

Nalda knew what he was talking about. He had done archaeological research in neighboring regions for many years.

"I hope there will be something interesting indeed," I answered cautiously.

"The project is yours, then. You'll receive the money once next year's budget is approved."

After thanking him and saying goodbye, I hung up, feeling victorious.

The money did arrive, but not until June 1996. I set off in July, in the middle of the rainy season, the consequences of which were extremely unfavorable. However, the work had to be done. I still needed someone to assist me. Florentino García Cruz and Héber Ojeda Mas, my colleagues at the regional INAH center in Campeche, were the right people for the job. Although they were younger than I was, they had enough experience in fieldwork, and above all, a willingness to cooperate. Florentino spent an entire season with me, from the beginning of July until the end of August, while Héber joined us later, after seeing to other obligations.

4

Becán

Almost exactly in the middle of the Yucatán Peninsula in southeastern Campeche lies Becán, a small village that came into existence only about five decades ago. Prior to that, the area had been covered by vast tropical forests, almost completely abandoned for more than a millennium—ever since the demise of the Classic Maya culture. It was not until the beginning of the twentieth century that people began to arrive in the area in greater numbers—not, however, with the intention of settling down. The forests piqued the interest of chewing gum producers, especially foreign ones, because the basic ingredient of chewing gum is chicle—a sappy gum contained in the *zapote* or *chicozapote*[1] trees, which grow in great abundance in the central and southern lowlands of the Yucatán Peninsula. Thus, within a few decades *chicleros*, collectors of this sappy gum, had scored the forests with mule trails. They would set up camps along small lakes called *aguadas*, where they would collect chicle, boil it, and shape it into bricks, which they would then sell in larger camps, or *centrales*, where stores sold food, clothing, tools, and other necessary equipment.

It was the chicleros who were the first to come across the ruins of Maya cities in these hitherto abandoned regions, and by spreading the word they inspired the first archaeological explorations. Thus, in 1931 Cyrus Lundell, an American botanist who worked for a chicle-collecting com-

---

1. *Manilkara achras.*

Figure 4.1. *Zapote* trees featuring characteristic incisions made by collectors of chicle sap for the production of chewing gum.

Figure 4.2. Water is especially good and fresh in aguadas covered by water lilies and other floating plants. These small lakes have muddy banks and bottoms; bridges such as the one in the photo enable the collection of water where it is deeper and clearer.

pany, discovered Calakmul, one of the largest Maya cities of all time. After Lundell informed him of his discovery, the famous Sylvanus Morley, who at that point was leading excavations at the site of Chichén Itzá in the northern Yucatán Peninsula, came to Calakmul. Enraptured by its grandeur and the many stone monuments with relief images and hieroglyphic inscriptions, he organized several expeditions to discover and document other archaeological sites in the central peninsula. He led the first one himself in 1932, while the following three, in 1933, 1934, and 1938, were directed by his colleague Karl Ruppert. The expeditions relied on the infrastructure of the camps and trails used by the chicleros, as well as on their knowledge of the terrain. These men, who most certainly boasted the most profound knowledge of the tropical forest, were (and still are) a great help to archaeologists. Although collecting chicle has remained somewhat alive to the present day, in the second half of the previous century it saw a steep decline because of the introduction of synthetic materials in the production of chewing gum, while the exploitation of precious varieties of wood, especially mahogany, became more widespread and led to the first permanent settlements. In the 1960s, when the Mexican government began to promote the colonization of the area, new settlements were established by people who came from other parts of Mexico where there was insufficient agricultural land. In 1972, an asphalt road was completed that crossed the Yucatán Peninsula approximately in the middle, thus connecting the cities of Escárcega in the west and Chetumal in the east. A number of settlements sprang up along this road, including Becán.

The village of Becán gained its name from a large archaeological site nearby, which is now open to visitors but was discovered and named in 1934 by Ruppert's expedition. Some sites were simply named after a nearby chiclero camp, while others were newly christened with names that are often in a Mayan language, usually Yucatec. Although the latter is only one of some thirty languages belonging to the Mayan linguistic family that are still spoken by the natives of southeastern Mexico, Guatemala, Honduras, and Belize, it is the most widespread. Numerous settlements and archaeological sites in the northern Yucatán Peninsula have preserved their names in this language since pre-Hispanic times. This was also the language of many of the chicleros who helped Ruppert's expeditions, which must be yet another reason it seemed especially suitable for naming ancient sites. The names typically allude to a certain characteristic of the place or the special circumstances of its discovery. Calakmul, for

Figure 4.3. The remains of a two-tower palace at Becán, with the modern town in the background.

instance, got its name from the two great pyramids presiding over the ruins of the former metropolis: *ca* means "two," *lak* means "neighboring," and *mul* can be translated as "artificial hill." The latter term is still used by Yucatec-speaking locals to refer to the ruins of pre-Hispanic buildings, which now look more or less like pyramidal mounds. Uxul, the "end," was the name Ruppert gave to the last site found in his 1934 field season, while Becán, a "defensive ditch," was named after an artificial moat encircling the core of the ancient city.

That day in July 1996, when I walked down a muddy street in Becán, was very special. No, it was not my first visit there; it was, however, the beginning of an exciting story, which it seems is still not finished.

Following the path, I arrived at the house of the guard responsible for the archaeological site nearby. This was the legendary, now-deceased Juan Briceño, who had worked as a guard for many years. As a young man, while working as a chiclero in the vast Yucatán forests, he had met the American archaeologist E. Wyllys Andrews IV, who asked him for help in searching for archaeological sites. Juan proved himself to be a gifted guide; thus other archaeologists who came to the area afterward would seek out his help as well. In the end he was employed by the INAH. I became acquainted with him in the early 1990s while leading survey work in Becán and at the nearby archaeological sites of Chicanná and Xpujil. Although I was familiar with them from the literature, determining the extent of these ancient settlements in the actual forest terrain was anything but easy, and Juan's help was welcome at every step. As it turned out, he more than deserved the nickname that everyone knew him by: Juan Ruinas (Ruins).

I found Juan in his cabin.

"Good day," I said loudly, standing in front of an open door. A graying but still strong man rolled out of his hammock and looked toward the door, his mouth expanding into a broad smile.

"Iván!" In Mexico, my first name is not problematic (unlike my surname), although they stress the last syllable.

He spread his arms, I did the same, and we hugged like old friends. I opened my backpack to pull out a few ice-cold beers. I knew his (and my) weakness.

"So, how's your *colmoyote* doing?" he grinned.

A *colmoyote* is the larva of a kind of bot fly[2] that gets under the skin of a person or some other mammal in order to feed on its flesh; at first it is as thin as a thread, but eventually it becomes egg shaped and can grow to a length of more than one centimeter. A few years prior, a little before the end of the survey work, one such specimen chose me as its host and made its way in at a most unpleasant spot. The first sensations felt like ant bites, but since they persisted I took a closer look and discovered the real cause. These larvae need to come out to get air, so it is possible to see them with a magnifying glass. The doctor in Xpujil was a very pleasant fellow; what he did, however, was less pleasant. While I felt as if I had nearly been castrated, he told me in a victorious voice that he had managed to extract the animal. But only a few minutes later I could feel the same biting as before. I returned to his office, where he told me that we were obviously dealing with two animals. He tortured me some more and then gave up, telling me to try solving the matter with chicle, which is the preferred remedy of the locals. My colleague, a surveyor who was practically a local, drove me to Becán, found a *chicozapote* tree, and cut into it with his machete to collect some sap onto a leaf. Thus, the parasite was "sealed in" and could no longer breathe. Luckily, these insects do not carry any disease.

"All is good," I answered, laughing; the memory was funny, but the experience not so much.

---

2. *Dermatobia hominis.*

As we sat on the doorstep, I explained to him what had brought me to the area this time. Since our task was to discover archaeological sites in remote places to the south, Juan was the right person to come to for help or advice.

"I'd join you, but I can't. I have to be here, we have workmen on the job." An archaeological project involving the restoration of certain buildings in Becán was under way, and Juan was very busy. "But I'll find someone to help you."

The following morning, he found me in the cabin of the archaeological camp where Florentino and I had spent the night.

"One of my workmen is from the village of Justo Sierra. He knows the ruins near his village and is willing to help. This afternoon I'll send him to you."

The village of Justo Sierra Méndez is one of the southernmost settlements in the territory we had set out to examine.

Indeed, that afternoon, a young man showed up; he approached us rather slowly, revealing the insecurity of someone not used to talking to people, and certainly not about the unusual intentions of such so-called learned people.

"Hello." I squeezed his hand and explained to him what it was all about. He listened carefully and said there truly were many ruins near his village. He agreed to take us to all he knew about, and to talk to some people from his village who surely had knowledge of some others as well.

We set off the next day. First we drove our Dodge pickup, which my institute had loaned me for fieldwork, down the main road to Xpujil, which lies seven kilometers east of Becán. Like Becán, Xpujil was named after the nearby archaeological site, which Ruppert had recorded and described during his final expedition in 1938. In this case, too, the modern settlement was founded a little over five decades ago when the road connecting the eastern and western coasts of the Yucatán Peninsula was being built. Since two roads heading north and south from this point were also constructed, leading to other recently established villages, Xpujil became the center of a newly founded municipality (Municipio de Calakmul) in 1996 and has subsequently grown into a fairly large settlement boasting approximately five thousand inhabitants.

Thus Xpujil served as our main supply center. Florentino and I bought food, machetes, and other provisions, and later that afternoon we set off to the south.

5

Justo Sierra Méndez

The Yucatán Peninsula is dominated by lowlands and gently undulating hills that only seldom exceed a height of four hundred meters above sea level. Because of its limestone bedrock, the peninsula is replete with karst features such as intermittent lakes, sinkholes, and caves, as well as flat-bottomed basins created by long sedimentation processes; these are known as *bajos*, or *akalché* in the Yucatec language, and during the rainy season they become swamped and transform into nearly impassable areas with thick layers of sticky mud. In the northern peninsula there are no surface waterways; the groundwater is fairly close to the surface and accessible in natural wells known as cenotes, which are essentially water-filled sinkholes. To the south, the level of the groundwater declines, and it is not until the southern end of the Yucatán lowlands that streams and larger rivers become more common. Annual rainfall increases from north to south as well, resulting in gradually changing vegetation, from thicket and low forest in the north to tall rainforest in the south.

A large portion of the extensive area south of the road that juts across the Yucatán Peninsula via Xpujil and Becán, all the way to the border with Guatemala, is presently a protected and entirely uninhabited national park, which was founded in 1989 and named the Reserva de la Biósfera de Calakmul (Calakmul Biosphere Reserve). A stretch of land to the east, about thirty kilometers across and extending south of Xpujil along the border with Belize, is dotted with numerous small villages settled as part of a government colonization program initiated after Xpujil and other settlements along the main road were founded. It was here that I had been tasked to do surveys and record as many archaeological sites as possible.

Here, at the very heart of the Yucatán Peninsula, the tropical humidity and abundant rainfall have produced lush and diverse vegetation. Higher ground is dominated by tall trees, while the bajos are home to dense and mostly thorny, low vegetation, which even in the dry season, when the ground is not flooded or swamped, is very difficult and time consuming to cut through. The area is teeming with insects; there are wild turkeys, pheasants, and many other birds, jaguars and other wild cats, deer, tapirs, peccaries, crocodiles, lizards, and scores of other reptiles, including venomous snakes. At the heart of the peninsula, the groundwater is typically deeper than one hundred meters. Surface waterways are infrequent, and even these are mostly torrential and limited to the wet season, which starts in May or June and lasts through October or November. The only more or less reliable sources of fresh water are small lakes, or aguadas, which are common but frequently dry up in the dry season. Just as the Maya would typically build their cities adjacent to these lakelets, often reinforcing the lake bottoms with stone slabs to retard the water from seeping underground, centuries later, the chicleros were forced to set up their camps next to the aguadas. In recent decades, after the development of Xpujil triggered the colonization of the area to the south, many settlements sprang up on the same sites for a similar reason. Their residents live almost exclusively off the land, using simple slash-and-burn farming techniques. This has resulted in the destruction of huge swaths of the forest, and it was not until the Calakmul Biosphere was created and government restrictions were adopted several years ago that the deforestation largely stopped.

Today, these settlements south of Xpujil are reasonably well connected by road, and most have electricity; in 1996 the situation was very different. Most villages were connected by dirt roads that became practically useless for vehicles in the wet season. Supplies from the civilized world were severely limited, and electricity was available only in villages along the first few dozen kilometers of the only southerly gravel road that was passable year round.

Because the first assistant Florentino and I hired was from the village of Justo Sierra Méndez, we decided to start working right there, at the southernmost end of the area we had been sent to reconnoiter. Even though the village was no more than ninety kilometers from Xpujil, it took us over five hours on the horribly rutted gravel road to get there. This gave us plenty of time to talk while we were driving.

Miguel Cruz Montejo, our twenty-two-year-old assistant, had arrived in the area as a child almost twenty years before, from mountains about four hundred kilometers to the southwest in the state of Chiapas. A lack of arable land, which large-scale ranchers voraciously claimed for themselves, had forced many indigenous people to flee the area, and social tensions resulted in the Zapatista guerrilla insurgency starting in the 1990s. Many immigrants from villages that spoke Chol, one of the Mayan languages, found a new home in southeastern Campeche, in lowlands overgrown with jungle that had not seen a permanent population for about a thousand years, ever since the demise of the Classic Maya culture. Like all other immigrants, Miguel's family was allotted a piece of land sufficient to eke out a modest living.

As we came to a turn, Miguel motioned with his hand. "This is where last year the police intercepted some drug smugglers who had several hundred kilos of marijuana next to the road ready to be shipped. When the shooting broke out, one of the smugglers was killed, and one of the cops too."

"And how did the police learn about it?" Florentino asked.

"Many farmers plant marijuana around here and the smugglers sometimes come to pick it up. Everyone knows that; somebody must have ratted them out."

"But is there no danger for ordinary people minding their own business?" I ventured.

"Oh yes, there is," Miguel said. "Sometimes armed bandits attack. They'll throw a log over the road or large rocks so the car has to stop. They prefer to ambush trucks that deliver goods to the stores, which have money; sometimes they'll also target a poor soul who has hardly anything on him."

Florentino and I exchanged looks. The feeling was anything but pleasant, but the fact was that we were in an area far outside the reach of the law—which also made it ideal for smuggling hard drugs from South America. The smugglers occasionally find intermediaries in this area and airdrop their cargo at a remote location, from where it is then shipped onward. *Narcotráfico*, the illicit drug trade, is one of Mexico's most intractable problems.

Figure 5.1. Miguel's house in Justo Sierra Méndez. The authorities equipped villages with solar panels like the one in front of his house. In 1996 there was no electricity in these villages.

At around ten in the evening we arrived in Justo Sierra, our backs aching from the drive. Many settlements in the area are named after important personalities from Mexico's history. Justo Sierra Méndez was a writer, poet, and historian who was born in Campeche, the capital of Campeche state, and spent most of his life in Mexico City, where he held a series of high political positions in the education sector around the turn of the twentieth century.

Miguel said that Florentino and I could spend the night at his house, where he lived with his wife and two-year-old daughter. It was a simple rectangular shack with walls made of wooden posts flush against each other and a roof thatched with *guano* palm[1] leaves. The house had a single room with a stone fireplace that sat on a sand-filled structure of wooden boards supported by four legs. Such fireplaces are common in the area: since they are lifted off the ground, cooking does not require bending down too much. The smoke escapes through the roof, which is made of folded palm leaves and is just like roofs thatched with straw: porous but watertight. In addition to a wooden table and two chairs, there was a sim-

---

1. *Sabal* sp.

Figure 5.2. Florentino inside Miguel's house.

ple bench along the wall consisting of two tree stumps and a board placed on top. Smaller boards affixed to the walls with rope acted as shelves, whereas the few pieces of clothing in the house were hung on a string attached to adjacent walls. People around here typically use hammocks for beds, and Florentino and I hung ours as well.

Houses like the one Miguel Cruz and his family lived in are the simplest dwellings in these areas. Their walls are more commonly made of wooden boards, and they typically have tin roofs instead of palm thatch. Tin roofs offer better fire protection, and they are also cheaper since guano palms do not grow everywhere and often have to be transported from afar, not to mention the time-consuming thatching. However, palm leaves offer superior heat insulation, whereas the temperature in houses with tin roofs is scorching during the day, unless the ceiling is tall enough or there is a layer of wooden boards beneath the tin roof.

Miguel's wife prepared breakfast and dinner for the three of us the next few days, while we took our lunch in the field. For most people, the staple is very simple: *tortillas y frijoles*, tortillas and beans. All households have chickens, but since families tend to be large, meat is rarely put on the table.

Tortillas, arguably Mexico's signature dish and one that has been around for many centuries, have a role similar to that of bread in countries where wheat is as important as corn in Mexico. In the countryside many make them at home, and Miguel's wife baked them as well. She would first soak the corn in a bucket of water, to which she added a spoonful of slaked lime. After the corn soaks overnight, the skins peel off and can be drained, while the soaked kernels are ground in a manual corn grinder. In some areas they still use quern stones, whose shape, the archaeological record shows, has hardly changed over the last several millennia: a flat and slightly concave smoothed stone serves as a base on which grain is ground with an elongated and equally smooth hand stone, which is used like a modern-day rolling pin. The dough is then shaped into tortillas by hand—although special presses are available nowadays—and grilled on an iron griddle or ceramic plate over an open fire.

Just like corn, which was domesticated approximately nine thousand years ago in present-day Mexico, beans are native to the area. They are either cooked whole or mashed and fried. Today rice is also a staple, along with corn and beans.

Justo Sierra is situated along one of the few creeks in the area, the Arroyo Negro. Lack of water is therefore not a problem for the locals, especially in the rainy season; hence there was plenty even for regular evening bathing, an elixir after the excruciating fieldwork. But the water is also home to crocodiles,[2] and it was not advisable to just swim in the creek; we would instead scoop up the water with buckets and "shower" on the banks.

In the subsequent days we thoroughly crisscrossed the area by foot. Miguel knew of multiple sites with ancient Maya ruins and helped us forge contacts with other locals; he was also more than happy to help us trudge and hack our way to sites and clear the areas that needed to be surveyed in greater detail. Not that it was difficult to find workers to do that; the locals appreciated any kind of odd job that provided occasional income, but Miguel stood out in every way, so he accompanied us everywhere in the following weeks as we continued surveying sites around other villages, even though we always had to hire additional workers from the settlements nearest to the sites we were exploring.

Archaeological reconnaissance, as ground surveys are sometimes called, can produce significant findings in the Maya area because most of the buildings are made of stone. Maya architecture is very diverse, reflecting

---

2. Morelet's crocodile (*Crocodylus moreletii*) is the dominant crocodile species in the interior Yucatán Peninsula.

the complexity of their feudal-like society. In cities, where the highest nobility and the priesthood lived alongside important artists and craftsmen, they built pyramidal temples, residential palaces, and buildings for administration and public events. These were made almost entirely of stone; the roofing was made of perishable materials in the early period, but in the Classic period vaulted ceilings were widespread, meaning that entire buildings, roofs included, were made of stone. One typical feature of Maya architecture is the corbel arch, which was also used in the Old World until it was replaced by the true arch, most extensively by the Romans. Whereas true arches have stones arranged in a semicircular design and can bear a significant amount of weight, corbel arches are built virtually the same way as the walls, the difference being that the stones are placed on the support walls slightly offset from the bottom course of stones and project toward the center of the archway; the distance between courses of rocks decreases progressively toward the top of the arch, and when the two sides are close enough, large capstones top it off, bridging the final gap.

The houses of commoners, who lived on the periphery of cities and in smaller settlements, were not as large as the buildings in city centers and were thatched with degradable materials, but many still had stone walls or at least stone foundations, as is evident from numerous remains. Aside from houses whose ruins can be easily detected by surveying the surface, people also lived in homes like the one that Miguel and many others in his village built. They were, and still are, particularly common in the northern Yucatán Peninsula: a single rectangular or oval room circumscribed by wooden poles, sometimes daubed with mud, with an entrance in one of the long walls and a roof thatched with palm leaves. Nowadays, hammocks are a common fixture in homes, but it is questionable whether the Classic Maya had them; they seem to have arrived later from the Caribbean islands.

Miguel and other villagers knew the locations of many ruins, and Florentino and I wanted to see every single one. This was no simple endeavor, for the territory of Justo Sierra was quite expansive and the archaeological remains scattered, in forests as well as in fields that were either planted with crops or left fallow and were covered in secondary vegetation. We recorded the geographic coordinates of the remains with a handheld global positioning system (GPS) device; for the remains of larger buildings, we also sketched how they were arranged. We did not find any standing walls. There were only stone mounds, but they clearly represented distinct groups: the Maya typically built their houses around rectangular courtyards. We picked up any pieces of ceramics we came across, for analysis of ceramics provides the first clue about the time a settlement was in use and its connection with neighboring regions.

Florentino and I surveyed the terrain in the neighboring villages of Arroyo Negro and El Civalito just as thoroughly, but over time we started to doubt whether this strategy made sense. We had been in the area for two weeks and walked many kilometers, but we had yet to find anything of significance. There was a mound several meters tall every now and then, no doubt a pyramidal temple, but there were no major buildings.

One thing was clear: during the heyday of Maya culture the area was settled as densely as other, better explored parts of the lowlands. But Maya settlements were not as compact as the contemporary settlements we are used to. They had cities, but only the city centers with the most important buildings were densely built, whereas the surroundings were dotted with simple clustered dwellings with open spaces between them, probably gardens or fields. Such an arrangement of buildings makes it very difficult to determine where a city or a territory that belonged to a city ended and another began. What is more, searching for ruins scattered across a large territory required significant time and effort. If we continued like that, Florentino and I thought, the work would progress at a snail's pace, and thoroughly surveying the entire territory to Xpujil would take several years, an undertaking for which funding was not available. True, it was necessary to record as many archaeological remains as possible, but the most important sites needed to take precedence since they offered a wealth of information: the buildings were larger, they had more prominent architectural elements that could be of particular interest, and we could expect to find stone monuments with inscriptions. So, we would have to be more selective in our reconnaissance; we would no longer visit every small ruin that someone mentioned.

Engrossed as we were in these thoughts in Miguel's house, where we were still staying, we had no way of knowing that an event the same day would vindicate our decision to focus on major sites. That day we had come back from our fieldwork in the early afternoon. A neighbor came by and mentioned that a truck had brought beer to the store in the neighboring village of Arroyo Negro. The footpath there, along Arroyo Negro Creek, was only about a kilometer long.

6

Defilers of Tombs

The owner of the shop in Arroyo Negro was a corpulent man, an immigrant from the city of Tapachula at the southernmost tip of Chiapas. He confirmed that indeed he had beer. Florentino and I realized that after two weeks of drinking tepid water, even unchilled beer would hit the spot. Miguel smiled and cast his eyes down, as if to say: "Here we can rarely afford even warm beer." Naturally, he did not have to pay for his beer this time.

Sitting against the shopkeeper's house, which doubled as the shop itself, were two men in tall boots of the kind that chicleros wear. They had been observing us with curiosity since we had greeted them upon arriving. I must have been the one piquing their interest, a fair-haired "paleface" who came from who knows where to this remote area. Finally, one of them built up the courage and asked, "Did you come for a trip?"

I thought to myself: Who would possibly want to make a trip to such a godforsaken place?

"No, no, we're here on business." I explained briefly what we were doing. They listened attentively.

"We're interested in ruins as well. We've dug around many places and found lots of nice things."

"Ah, so you've worked with archaeologists," Florentino remarked, although the tone of his voice did not indicate belief.

"No, we did it alone. Some people collect antiquities, they buy them and pay good money," he said frankly, with some naiveté, confirming our suspicions. So they were looters, predators of archaeological sites.

Figure 6.1. A looters' tunnel into a building with a sculpted stela, one of many that looters dug at the major site of Uxul, not far from the Guatemalan border.

I nodded, took a sip of beer, and asked indifferently, "So where are you digging now?"

"No, no, we stopped doing that a long time ago. The laws are strict, and it is too dangerous. We're from Guatemala and collect chicle, right here over the border. We've just come here for the beer."

There was no way of telling how sincere their answer was. True, it was easy to cross from Guatemala. The border separating Campeche state from Guatemala is little more than a ten-meter clearing running through the forest along the 17°49' north parallel, just five kilometers south of the village of Arroyo Negro. Nobody protects it; they just cut back the border slash occasionally so it does not become overgrown. But five kilometers was the distance to the border as the crow flies; it would be significantly longer if you had to take the trails, and there was no way the two men came just for the beer—they could not be sure they would indeed get it, as the supply of beer was occasional rather than regular. Still, I did not want to put myself in the role of investigator; my goal was merely to obtain more information.

"And how would you do that? What would you actually look for?" I said, trying to come across as genuinely curious.

"Graves. There are many ruins in these forests. These used to be houses, palaces, and temples made by the people who lived here. The Maya, right? And they buried their dead in them as well. The big ruins have the tombs of the nobles, and they contain painted vessels, necklaces, jade masks."

One of the men was particularly talkative, and he turned out to be very good at his business. He was quite didactic, as if he were not talking to two archaeologists. It was just as he said: the Maya buried their dead under their houses and did not have designated burial sites. The dignitaries and rulers were buried along with their ceremonial gear and ornaments, with painted pottery and other personal artifacts placed in the tombs as well. The highest-status individuals were buried in residential palaces and temples, quite often adorned with jade necklaces, earrings, and masks.

"But you can't sell every object. To have some value, a clay plate or vase must have at least one Indian painted; if there are several, the price rises, in particular if it has a legend as well."

True, artfully made ceramic vessels found in elite tombs are painted with mythological scenes, including human and animal figures and depictions of deities. By "legend," the man meant the hieroglyphs frequently accompanying these scenes.

"But jade has the highest value: necklaces, earrings, figurines, masks."

Although there are no jade deposits in the Yucatán lowlands, the Maya often put artifacts made of this stone in the graves of dignitaries. They procured jade through well-organized trade networks from the Motagua River valley in the Guatemalan highlands to the south. Just as jade used to be the most precious material for the Maya, their jade products have the highest value on the black market today. Whereas a well-preserved and richly painted ceramic plate can reach a price—for example at an auction in the United States—of roughly $30,000, jade artifacts are much more valuable. Naturally, it is the intermediaries who take the biggest cut in this illicit trade; the grave robbers get much less.

"And how do you know where to dig?" I continued to inquire.

"Every chiclero knows the forest that he works in and knows where the ruins are. There are plenty of small mounds everywhere, it makes no sense to dig those up. But if you come across ruins that are high and there are many clustered together, you know that you've hit a *reinado*, that's where it pays off to dig."

This was the first time I had heard this romantic-sounding word that is used mostly by chicleros. *Reinado* is Spanish for "rule" or "reign," although the more appropriate translation in this context was "kingdom," since it clearly referred to major archaeological sites, the remains of Maya cities with tall pyramidal temples and imposing administrative and elite residential buildings.

"Years ago, I worked at Las Gardemias. That was a *reinado grande*: big ruins everywhere, you could see walls in some places, the tomb walls were painted."

Las Gardemias! That was the name the locals used for the famous archaeological site now known as Río Azul, which lies in northeastern Guatemala, less than ten kilometers from where we were having this conversation. The American archaeologist Richard E. W. Adams headed a multiyear research project there after finding out in 1981 that looters had come across several unique tombs with walls that had paintings and hieroglyphs. Was this man among the robbers who had been chased away?

"Once," the man continued enthusiastically, "as we were gathering chicle, we came across a group of huge ruins. Some were very high, and there were a lot of stelae, a true *reinado*."

So, this man also knew what stelae were—stone slabs erected on the buildings or plazas of ancient cities, many decorated with relief images and hieroglyphic inscriptions. They celebrated important events and glorious acts by rulers and their families: war victories, the capture of prisoners, rituals they had performed, births, enthronements, weddings to brides from noble families, and other notable occasions.

"You found stelae as well?"

"Of course. Stelae sell well too, as long as they contain images and letters."

"And how did you take them away? The stones are big and heavy."

"We didn't take the whole stones. We just sawed off the decorated sections."

Florentino and I stayed calm, even though the story made us quite queasy. Of course we knew about the practice of sawing off stelae. Since they are typically made of soft limestone, this is not very difficult. At many archaeological sites you can still see stone slabs with cleanly sawed-off surfaces, a depressing result of the actions of looters who sell their finds to God knows whom and for who knows how much money. Thus, we now have no clue where many of these monuments are, and valuable information that could have been gleaned from the images and inscriptions has been lost.

"Still, these are big pieces. They had to be brought to the customer somehow?"

"That wasn't a problem. Someone came from Ciudad de Guatemala, a *gente de collar blanco*; nobody inspected him."

So "a man with a white collar" came; he must have been someone important. Given the rampant corruption, legislation outlawing activities such as *profanación de tumbas*, or the desecration of graves, does not help much.

The looting of archaeological sites is unfortunately very widespread. In just the first few days of fieldwork we had seen many places that had been dug up, and later we realized there was hardly a major archaeological site that remained untouched. Hoping to find a tomb, the looters typically dig a trench or tunnel from the base of the building into the interior. The damage they cause is not confined to extracting grave goods with high aesthetic value. For archaeologists and anyone interested not only in the artifacts as such but in understanding the lives of the people who used to live in the area, the greater damage is that for such artifacts—which surface in private collections around the world—it is no longer possible to determine where they came from and in what context they were uncovered. What is more, the looters usually tear down any walls or other architectural elements in the way, thus causing irreparable damage to buildings and further accelerating their decay.

In the past, most of the looters were chicleros, who were also often *ruineros* (ruiners), as someone once designated them. While collecting chicle, which had to be done in the wet season, they became familiar with the forests they worked in and came across ruins; in the dry season this allowed them to dedicate themselves to looting. Today, many villagers from the area we were surveying dabble in looting as well. In numerous places we found old ditches and tunnels that were already caving in, and in other places they had clearly been dug not long ago.

Mexican law prescribes stiff prison sentences for looting and unlicensed possession of archaeological artifacts, but the arm of the law rarely reaches these remote places. Over the years I have talked to many people who I know have at least occasionally looted ruins, even if hardly any admitted it. In Guatemala this business is much more widespread and destructive than in Mexico, and it is also more aggressive: some groups of looters are armed, and people have been killed in clashes. The looters I have met personally can hardly be described as evildoers, however. They are mostly ordinary people, some of them very hard working, reliable, and honest; many took to looting because of financial problems. Digging up ruins is not an easy task; on the contrary it is backbreaking and dangerous. I have heard of people being buried alive deep underground because of tunnels collapsing; instead of finding a rich ancient interment, they dug their own grave. What is more, the middlemen reap the biggest gains, so the hardest aspect of the work yields only modest profit, not unlike in many other industries. That is why I have never entertained the idea of reporting any looters. I have chosen instead to try to convince them that it would be much better for them in the long term for the archaeological sites to be preserved: rather than engage in illicit activities, they could expect that they or at least their children would sooner or later get a job with archaeological excavations, which typically last several years and often result in the development of local tourism and other commercial activities.

Darkness fell as our conversation over beer in Arroyo Negro expanded. Florentino and I had mixed feelings when we shook hands to say goodbye. The two men were perfectly congenial, and they had said that looting was a thing of the past for them, which is perhaps why they talked so candidly about it. Nevertheless, two days later when we checked out a site south-

Figure 6.2. Pieces of polychrome ceramics left by looters at the Monumento 104 site on the Guatemalan border.

west of Arroyo Negro, right on the Guatemalan border, we came across four freshly dug trenches. In three of them it seemed that the diggers had not found anything, but in one they must have hit a rich tomb, for they left behind a large cache of ceramics, including painted fragments.

My stomach knotted up when I saw the trenches, which looked like painful, gaping wounds through which the formerly glorious palaces and temples had been eviscerated. Was this the work of the two men we had met?

Whatever the truth, this was yet another reason Florentino and I had to focus on major sites henceforth: it was precisely such sites that were the main target of looters, and it was paramount that we inspect as many as possible and survey them as best we could before the looters damaged them. One thing we expected to find at major sites was sculpted stone reliefs—not just stelae, but also the circular altars that were frequently paired with stelae. Both may contain depictions of people and events, as well as hieroglyphic inscriptions that recount important historical happenings. Since these monuments are highly prized by looters and could sooner or later disappear, it was advisable that we precisely photograph and draw them if we could not prevent their disappearance or destruction.

Such finds must also be published immediately. Looted antiques often end up abroad and appear at auction. The sellers typically try to prove that they inherited them or that the items were brought from the country of origin a long time ago, before that country adopted laws prohibiting the sale or export of archaeological artifacts. If a published report shows that an artifact for sale was until recently at a certain archaeological site, such claims can be rejected. It can thus be proved that the import was illegal; legal action against the perpetrators can then be taken, and the artifacts can be returned to the country of origin.

7

High-Level Security Detail

After we had finished working on plots around the villages of Justo Sierra, Arroyo Negro, and El Civalito, Florentino and I had to get to Xpujil to resupply and pick up our colleague Héber Ojeda, who was supposed to come up from Campeche. It was already the second half of July, deep into the rainy season, and the downpours were gathering strength. We told Miguel we would return in a couple of days and headed out. But after just a few hundred meters, the pickup got stuck in the mud of the sodden road. I turned on the four-wheel drive without worrying too much, but the vehicle would not budge. Florentino got out and watched the wheels while I tried to get the car to move.

"The front wheels aren't spinning," he shrugged.

But why not? They had told me at work that the car was perfectly fine! So far, we'd had neither the need nor the opportunity to test the four-wheel drive, but now, when we most needed it, it turned out it was not working.

Fortunately, help was at hand. Offering to double their pay, I enlisted eight people from Justo Sierra. The only solution was to push the truck and cut out bypasses in order to avoid the worst stretches of the dirt road to El Civalito, where a gravel road began. It took us six hours to get through just five kilometers! When we arrived in the afternoon a local

Figure 7.1. Pushing a car over such mud is futile. Where would the best bypass be?

stumbled out of the store, a man who had worked for us a few days before when we were surveying the area around his village. He stepped closer, his eyes hazy from a significant quantity of beer, and patted me on the shoulder. "Come during the dry season next time! It's impossible to work now."

I already knew that. Even Ruppert had always worked between February and April. But how could I explain that the national budget had its own logic and that I simply had to come whenever I got funding?

Late in the evening Florentino and I arrived in Xpujil. Héber was already waiting for us, but aside from purchasing provisions, we had to do something very important: get the truck's four-wheel drive repaired. It took me two days to find a mechanic willing to accept the job, but Martín Yamá, from the nearby village of Zoh Laguna, proved that competent rural people can improvise their way through problems that city mechanics would not even begin to tackle, even with all the parts, tools, and devices they could possibly need. From then on, the truck's four-wheel drive worked for years, and Don Martín thereafter helped us with numerous quandaries of every stripe.

When we returned to El Civalito the owner of the local store offered us a place to stay. In this village and several villages around it we continued working the next few days without finding anything noteworthy. Our faithful companion Miguel was with us, as were several locals.

One day we heard there were big ruins in Los Alacranes, a village not far from us. Arriving there by a dirt track that led through several smaller settlements, we agreed with the locals that they would take us to the ruins the next day. When we returned to El Civalito, we stopped at the village of Ojo de Agua, where I asked some locals standing by the road whether they knew of any ruins. I asked them to inquire with other villagers as well and to let me know the following day, when we would be passing by again.

As I drove off, their curious eyes remained fixed on us until we disappeared around the first bend. A few moments later Miguel, who was sitting in back on the side of the truck bed, leaned toward me and remarked through the window, "That wasn't good."

"What wasn't?" I asked, without averting my eyes from the huge potholes in the dirt track ahead.

"You told them you were willing to pay for work and that we would be driving by tomorrow. Now they know that you have money. This is precisely the village where they attack and hold up travelers."

I really had acted like a complete novice, I thought to myself angrily. I did not say anything, but I tormented myself considering how I should resolve the situation. We had to return to Los Alacranes the next day, since we had already made a deal with the locals.

In El Civalito I turned toward the military camp instead of the cottage where we were staying. Florentino looked at me in puzzlement. I drove up to the guard without saying a word.

"Good day. Is the lieutenant here?"

"He is."

"May I talk to him?"

"I'll see if he can receive you."

He left and returned a few moments later with the commander, whose bed head, T-shirt, and sweatpants revealed that I had interrupted his afternoon nap.

"How are you, archaeologist? How can we help you?"

I explained that we had to be in Los Alacranes by the following morning, which meant passing through Ojo de Agua, a place infamous for its road bandits.

"Oh, so you want a security detail?" the lieutenant interrupted me.

"Well, if it's possible."

Figure 7.2. The ruins of buildings rising from the hill west of Los Alacranes, overgrown with sparse trees and low vegetation, are visible from a distance.

"No problem. When do you head out?"

"Would seven be OK?"

"We'll wait for you at seven," the commander said tersely.

When we arrived at the camp at the agreed time the next morning a Hummer was already roaring, ready to head out.

"You'll drive in front," the commander said.

And off we went. Our Dodge rocked in the deep mud like a boat on choppy seas, while the wide-wheeled Hummer behind us swayed lightly and elegantly as if it were an ocean liner impervious to such small disturbances. Even more importantly, there were nine armed soldiers in its cargo bed ready to fire their guns. Who would possibly want to attack us?

When we arrived in Los Alacranes, the locals we had agreed to hire were waiting for us at the side of the road. Seeing us, they jumped to attention.

I stopped the car and thanked the commander.

"You know, you can always count on us," he said when bidding farewell, adding, "I'll see you in the evening. There should be no further danger."

I saw Miguel's concurring glance in the background. Of course, now that the bandits had seen us with the soldiers, we were safe. Even if they reasoned that we would be returning via the same route in the evening, nobody would dare touch us. It was now clear to everyone that we had the support of the federal army, and they are not people you want to have a beef with. Even the well-armed *narcotraficantes* are loath to fight the army.

We made an impression on the Los Alacranes locals as well.

"The army is protecting them," they murmured, but they soon changed the topic.

"Where are we going first?" asked a boy named Esteban, the first to snap out of his awe. "This hill or that one?" he indicated.

"Let's see the eastern one first," I said.

This time we were in for a surprise. On the hills east and west of the village there were large complexes of ruins with clearly visible remains of pyramidal temples and other buildings on plazas at several different levels.

8

Los Alacranes

The following day we returned to the eastern hill to sketch the site. Héber, Florentino, and I divided the work and each headed out to our own part of the complex with tape measures and compasses.

As I was standing on a small ruin trying to figure out the shape of a building as it had existed about a millennium and a half ago, before being disfigured by the destructive forces of the tropical rainforest, I suddenly heard someone screaming, "Don Iván, Don Iván!" Leaves rustled and twigs cracked under the feet of a man who was approaching quickly but remained obscured by the thick undergrowth. He finally wheezed up: it was Miguel.

"We've found a stela," he said, visibly excited.

"How do you know?" I asked, trying to remain calm, refraining from clinging to false hope even as my heart started pounding.

"It is a big stone, the kind we saw at El Palmar, with letters on one side."

That was all I needed to hear. I dashed after Miguel, who was running back the way he had come. At that point I did not suspect how important July 29, 1996, would be, but his words had to be taken seriously. A few days before, we had visited El Palmar, a major site about twenty kilometers to the northwest that Eric Thompson had discovered in 1936. Because colleagues from our institute were soon to start detailed research there,

Figure 8.1. At the East Complex of Los Alacranes, Miguel Cruz (*right*) was the first to notice Stela 1.

we had not paid much attention to it, but we had seen almost forty stelae; although many were eroded, some still bore clearly visible carved images and hieroglyphs. Miguel, who had accompanied us, had shown great interest in the stone monuments and the carvings and paid close attention to our commentaries. When he mentioned "stela" and "letters," he must have known very well what he was talking about.

This went through my head as I trotted after him. We stumbled over roots and branches, which the workers had cut to clear the terrain so we could make a map of the site. A few moments later we arrived, sweaty and short of breath.

"It's here," Miguel fired off and pointed his machete at a stone with a relatively flat upper surface slanting out of the ground. A few other workers had already cleared off the vegetation covering it.

"And the letters?" I asked anxiously.

"They're on the other side," he said.

I crouched to look at the downward-facing side of the flat rock. Near the rounded upper edge I saw several well-preserved hieroglyphs carved in relatively high relief.

There was no longer any doubt. What we were seeing was a Maya stela; it was at the western foot of a fairly large building whose ruin was now an elongated mound about eight meters high, which had probably been a ruler's residential palace. The centuries showed: the once-upright stela was tilted forward, almost completely covered with stones from the ruin, soil, and vegetation. Although excavations had not been planned, I decided we should remove the rubble and dig away the dirt so we could at least lift the stela and document it. This was an impulse born not of impatience, but from fear of looters. We could not leave the stela without meticulously photographing its carved side, which undoubtedly contained important historical information. It soon turned out I was right, and about a year and a half later my fear of looters would also be proven prescient.

The task was by no means simple. We needed to find an appropriate tool to lift the heavy rock, and that was after we carefully removed the material covering it. We decided to do the job in a few days; we would first finish the sketch maps of the complexes on the eastern and western hills.

The western hill site was overgrown with dense, low vegetation, as just a few years before this had been a pasture belonging to Rafael Castán, an elderly farmer from Los Alacranes. Don Rafa, as everybody called him, mentioned that he had once seen a flat stone with letters in front of a ruin on his property. Another stela? He led us to the place he thought he had seen the stela, but there was nothing there.

"I saw it here," Don Rafa motioned. "It was standing here, I remember it well."

"Perhaps it fell and has been covered over with ruin debris," Héber ventured.

Some of the locals who were helping us stepped up and started to clear debris from the area Don Rafa indicated. The relatively smooth surface of a large, clearly carved stone soon emerged, and within a few minutes the slab was completely uncovered. It was indeed a stela, but there were no "letters" or other signs of relief on the upper surface. It appeared to be turned face down. Yet another stela to be lifted.

Figure 8.2. Stela 2, at the West Complex of Los Alacranes.

Figure 8.3. Lifting Stela 1 at Los Alacranes.

We decided to procure foam rubber mats and blankets in Xpujil to protect both monuments during the lift, and we borrowed log skidding tools in Los Alacranes.

We started with the stela on the eastern hill, which we labeled Stela 1. As we carefully removed the debris, the carved surface on the bottom side gradually came to light. We were able to make out the headdress of a central figure, undoubtedly a ruler, bookended by well-preserved hieroglyphs, including calendrical information with numbers. After enough material had been removed, we protected the stela, lifted it into an upright position with the help of a skidding device equipped with a lever and pulley system, and leaned it against the ruins of the building in front of which it had once stood. Compared to most Maya stelae, it was very large, standing almost four meters tall.

It was only then that we could clearly see all the details of the carved surface. The central part depicting the ruler was severely damaged, but the feathered headdress was quite visible; a mask in the shape of a human face carved in side view was hanging along the right side of the body, and at the bottom were two sitting human figures, most likely captives, as one of them appeared to have his hands tied behind his back. There were two

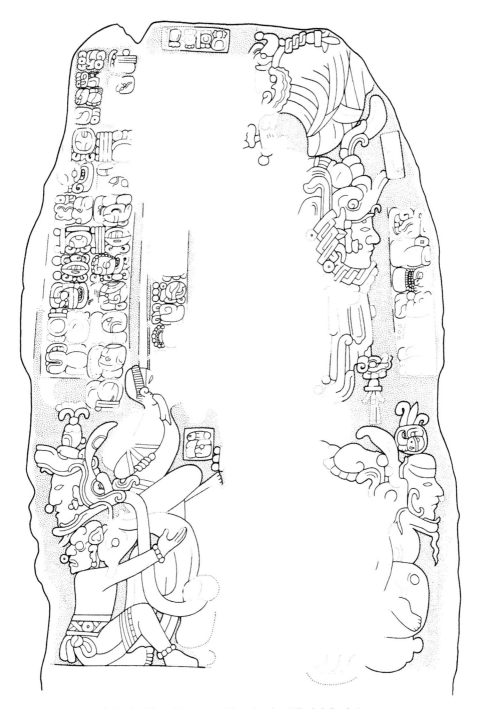

Figure 8.4. Stela 1 of Los Alacranes (drawing by Nikolai Grube).

mythological scenes on the sides, human faces in gaping snake maws. We could also see that the hieroglyphic inscriptions along the central figure were very well preserved.

We conducted a similar maneuver with Stela 2 on the western hill. Don Rafa was right. Although this one was not as well preserved, when the light was right it was possible to make out the remains of a hieroglyphic inscription and a carving of a ruler brandishing a luxurious feathered headdress.

Both monuments were photographed and drawn in minute detail, although it was clear that detailed drawings would additionally have to be made by an epigrapher, a specialist in Maya writing. Both stelae, which were returned to their original position after the work had been completed, were undoubtedly significant, which is why I proposed to my institute at the end of the fieldwork season that we should relocate both monuments to the present-day village, where they could be exhibited and appropriately protected. This was also the wish of the people of Los Alacranes. I would come back in two years, after funding for the salvage operation had been approved. But I will return to that later.

9
Buried City

The 1996 season was capped by another major discovery. In the village of Santa Rosa, Heladio Peña Silva told us that there were two groups of ruins on his property, and that the tallest building was approximately fifty meters high.

We knew from experience that such statements could not be relied on. The locals were not very good at estimating how tall things were and had previously sometimes mentioned heights of up to one hundred meters. Although such statements were not to be believed—the tallest Maya building, Temple IV in Tikal in Guatemala, is only about seventy meters high—we did not expect the actual height to be just ten or fifteen meters, as often turned out to be the case. But this time it seemed that the man was not exaggerating. Don Heladio was an enterprising farmer who specialized in cattle breeding, a rarity in the region, and he also owned a small shop. He was congenial and open, typical of immigrants from the state of Veracruz, as he was. We were to frequently encounter him in the future and accept his hospitality: his wife was an excellent cook and he occasionally had beer in his shop.

Don Heladio first took us over the fields east of the village and into the high forest. We passed several small ruins and were greeted by frolicking monkeys, when all of a sudden the outline of a huge pyramidal mass appeared before us. We measured the pyramid with a tape measure and clinometer and calculated that it was around thirty meters tall! This was the tallest building we had yet found, and it must have been a mighty temple in its day.

Pyramids are probably the most distinct and imposing remains of Mesoamerican peoples. Everyone who has ever heard anything about the Aztecs or the Maya will surely know about the pyramids, which usually have several superimposed platforms receding from the ground up. The Aztecs, although they were merely the last heirs of the millennia-long Mesoamerican tradition, having arrived from the north or northwest fairly late, are the most well-known Mesoamerican people aside from the Maya. In as little as one hundred years they developed into the imperial superpower that the Spanish conquerors found themselves up against in the early sixteenth century, which is why they feature so prominently in written sources from the time of the conquest and the Early Colonial period. Obviously, pyramids were not built just by the Maya and Aztecs but also by other Mesoamerican peoples.

Was it the Egyptians who brought pyramid building to the Americas? This is a question I have heard countless times. Given that a huge number of archaeological studies have been conducted in all corners of the New World without producing any compelling evidence of ancient transoceanic contact, it is remarkable how strongly these conjectures still excite the imagination. As if there were nothing as straightforward as coming among a foreign people and imposing your habits on them, including nothing less than the construction of pyramids. One cannot imagine doing such a thing without a strong organization or an outright conquest. But armies that could employ such force simply did not cross oceans at that time; and supposing they had had vessels capable of doing so, even the most ambitious ruler of Egypt or any other ancient state would not have known where or why to mount such an expedition. And if that were to have happened against all odds, such expeditions would have left irrefutable traces: the sudden occurrence of pyramids and other completely foreign artifacts. The reality is different: the development of pyramidal structures in Mesoamerica—as well as of the culture in general—can be traced through time, from the earliest small and simple earth mounds to elegant, tall, and ornately decorated temples. Of course, it is not impossible that the occasional castaways or adventurers might have wandered across the ocean, but if they were to survive in the new environment they would surely have been subdued and assimilated. Just imagine living in a village on the coast when one day a group of strange and most definitely thirsty and hungry foreigners comes ashore. Let's assume you help them survive—and then, in return, they start to impose their views and try to convince you (assuming you had overcome the language barrier with the help of a talented linguist) that you should build some kind of pyramid. How would you and your compatriots react, having been the masters of your domain your entire lives and accustomed to doing things your own way? Would you obediently start cutting stones and stacking them toward the sky, or would you adopt a different approach to the strangers? We know that the Vikings reached the northeastern shores of North America around AD 1000; there is even archaeological evidence to support this, and yet their visit did not leave a trace in Native American cultures, even in legend.

Why do people still entertain this notion that only Old World people were smart enough to invent anything? Why is it that we want to explain any similarity we notice between ancient cultures with intercultural transmission? Humans are simply humans, no matter where they live; as a biological species we function in the same way and therefore find similar solutions to similar challenges in similar circumstances. Pyramidal structures have been built in many places around the world, not just in Egypt and Mesoamerica. In early states the easiest way for rulers to show their power was by means of monumental architecture: the mightier the building, the more obviously the ruler showed how many people he had under his sway. Given enough people and appropriate coordination, a big structure can be built by simply stacking material of some kind, which is the simplest form of construction. And if the building is to be tall and imposing, the result of such an endeavor, considering the limitations of rudimentary technology, will always have a conical or pyramidal shape. At its core, the pyramid is one of the simplest forms of monumental architecture, while its different versions observable in various parts of the world resulted from differences in the available natural materials, local traditions, technology, and overall cultural development. Whereas the pyramids in Egypt are built of blocks of quarried stone, Mesoamerican pyramids have stone walls and cores made of rubble and earth. In Egypt they were designed to be tombs; in Mesoamerica, including the Maya area, they were primarily substructures for temples accessible by means of steep staircases. True, many contained tombs, but except in certain cases this was not their primary function. Also in Europe, kings and other dignitaries used to commonly be buried in churches. The Maya did not have special burial places: they buried their dead under their homes, and for the ruler, who was a deity personified, a temple was surely the most suitable final resting place.

The pyramid we found was in the middle of a large plaza flanked on the eastern and western edges by oblong mounds, and dominated on the northern side by a huge acropolis, a square platform whose sides were about 150 meters long; it was approximately seven meters high and contained several buildings arranged around courtyards. These must have been elite residences and buildings designated for public events such as meetings with the nobility of neighboring cities or states. Over the centuries the tropical vegetation had transformed the formerly glorious buildings into ruins of various shapes and sizes, but it is worth pointing out that only the top sections of buildings are typically ruined: the falling debris that piles up at the foot of buildings protects the lower parts, where sizable and well-preserved segments of facades are often unearthed by excavations.

To the east and west of the acropolis were other groups of larger and smaller structures. There were no exposed walls, nor were there any stelae, but the impression created by the mighty albeit decayed and overgrown architectural complexes was magnificent. Even though the largest buildings were only two kilometers from the village of Santa Rosa, the lush tropical forest hid them so well that it gave me an idea: we would name the site Mucaancah, which in the Yucatec Mayan language means "hidden" or "buried city."

The second complex was approximately 2.5 kilometers to the southwest, but this was where Heladio's ranch was and the ruins were mostly covered in tall grass and shrubbery. The vast plaza had two acropolises with multiple buildings on its east and west sides, and several pyramidal and oblong ruins along its southern flank.

In the middle of the plaza were two elongated and parallel mounds. We immediately suspected that this was a ceremonial ball court. Using latex from rubber trees growing in the tropical rainforest, the Maya and other Mesoamericans made solid balls weighing several kilograms and used them for a game that was widespread across Mesoamerica beginning in the Preclassic period. They played the game on special ball courts, which vary significantly in size and a number of other details but share a distinctive feature: they are flanked by two buildings with abutting slopes facing the playing field. We do not know the details of the rules of the game, which were probably not uniform, but in the most widespread version, which is documented in early colonial sources and confirmed by many depictions, the players were allowed to strike the ball only with their hips, which is why they were equipped with strong hip guards. The two-team game was actually a magical ritual act: in accordance with the principles of imitative magic, the ball continuously moving over the court was intended to maintain the most important celestial bodies, particularly the sun, the moon, and Venus, in constant and regular motion, whereas the orderly sequence of celestial cycles was believed to ensure the proper alternation of the seasons and, thereby, abundant water and

Figure 9.1. A view to the south along the remains of a staircase that led to the eastern structure of the ball court in Mucaancah. One of the two blocks with reliefs concludes the bottom stair at the lower right corner; the other is in the background on the left.

Figure 9.2. Reliefs on the stone blocks discovered in the ruined ball court of Mucaancah depict players with typical attire.

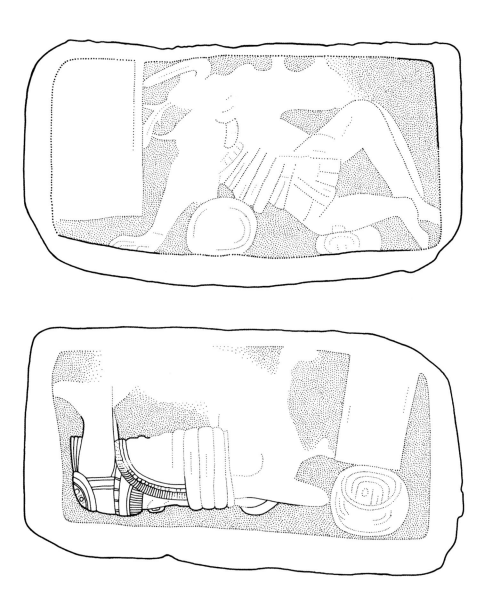

Figure 9.3. Reliefs of ball players of Mucaancah (drawing by Nikolai Grube).

crops. Mythological narratives and depictions testifying to the purpose of the ball game and its interrelation with the celestial bodies, rain, maize, and fertility in general also reveal that the game was associated with human sacrifice by decapitation. That sacrifice ensured fertility and the continuation of life is very clearly seen in depictions showing plant motifs and snakes—a symbol of fertility—spewing forth from the necks of decapitated individuals in place of gushing blood. But despite these primary goals, the ball game represents yet another example of religion being abused for political ends. At least for the Maya, we know that victorious rulers liked to stage a ball game against their captured enemies; the fact that those vanquished in war were also always defeated in the game and ultimately sacrificed raises justified doubts as to the sportsmanlike behavior of the participants and referees.

Miguel soon confirmed our conjectures about the two long ruins in the middle of the plaza. As he was carving out a path through the thick bush, he noticed a stone block with a relief on the upper surface, and we soon found another one nearby that was only partially sticking out of the ground and whose eastern side was decorated with a relief. At a higher level behind it were two more partially exposed, undecorated blocks of roughly the same dimensions, clearly part of a stair. Both carved stones must therefore have formed a portion of a staircase that led to the ball court from the eastern side, even though one of them was no longer in its original position, or in situ, as we say in archaeological jargon.

The reliefs on both blocks confirmed beyond a doubt the function of the original building. The block that appeared to have been lying for centuries with the relief side up was badly weathered, yet it was still possible to make out the image of a player with one arm and one leg against the ground and a ball under his waist and hip guard. A rectangular, slightly elevated surface to the left of the player may have had a hieroglyphic inscription, which was not preserved. The relief on the second block was badly damaged, but removing the dirt covering the bottom part revealed a prone human figure stretching for a ball in the bottom right corner. Its head was virtually invisible, but the hip guards, the decorated loincloth, and the right leg, bent up and with a knee guard, were clearly visible. Just as before, the right side had a rectangular surface where there once may have been a hieroglyphic inscription.

Depictions of players with typical hip and knee guards and in distinct poses that reflect the rules of the game, in which players were allowed to hit the ball only with their hips, are common on major Maya sites. Fearing that they might disappear, we precisely documented the position of the two blocks and transported them to Santa Rosa to officially hand them over to the local authorities, who took responsibility for their safekeeping and protection.

This was an important find. Courts for the ceremonial ball game are found almost exclusively at major archaeological sites, which were once important political centers. At this point, it was already clear that this architectural complex and the one not far to the northeast had been parts of a single large settlement. Between them we found a number of smaller ruins—remains of simple residential buildings—as well as openings to underground chambers, which are very common on Maya sites in the Yucatán lowlands and are normally referred to by the Mayan word *chultun*. Some of them may have served as storage facilities and been used for other purposes, but many were used for collecting rainwater. They are carved into bedrock and look like a bell-shaped bottle with a narrow neck: a vertical cylindrical shaft about a meter in diameter leads into a much larger space whose walls used to be plastered to make them impermeable. Around the circular mouth, which was covered with a stone lid—these are often found as well—was a funnel-like surface that channeled rainwater into the cistern. Most *chultuns* are now filled with debris, and few hold water since the plaster has peeled off, allowing water to permeate the porous limestone.

Judging from the architectural features and the ceramics found on the surface, we estimated that the earliest buildings had been constructed in the Late Preclassic period, during the last centuries BC, while the city reached its apex in the Classic period. The shape and spatial distribution of some of the buildings also suggested that the builders followed contemporary trends from the east, in present-day Belize, as well as those in vogue at the heart of the Yucatán Peninsula, especially in Guatemalan Petén.

10

Snakes Aren't Only in the Jungle

It took us a few days to elaborate sketch maps of both groups of monumental architecture. When we took a break from sketching the North Complex, I tried to explain to the workers what the acropolis buildings had probably looked like. Suddenly we heard the rustling of leaves in the treetops above us, as happens when a dry branch falls. Only this time what landed on my extended arm, which was pointing toward the slope of the acropolis, was not a branch—but a snake! I noticed it only after it had slid onto the ground. Everyone, including me, instantaneously leaped a few meters away, realizing only after the fact that the snake, which swiftly slithered away, was not poisonous. In the jungle the following principle applies: first move away and then figure it out!

Generally, 1996 was the year of snakes; however, not all were as timid and harmless. Only a few days earlier, workmen had killed a rattlesnake while examining another site, and one day later another unpleasant encounter awaited us. While I was taking measurements and sketching one of the two acropolises in the South Complex of Mucaancah, a local named Cristóbal who was clearing the undergrowth ahead of me suddenly darted backward, cursed through his teeth, tossed his machete aside, and wiped the sweat from his forehead.

"Una nauyaca," he said, pointing to the ground. A few meters ahead of us lay a curled-up snake with a lance-shaped head and an unmistakable triangular pattern on its back. Predominantly brown, it was barely noticeable among the dry leaves.

This was my first encounter with one in the flesh, although I had learned quite a lot about the species already. Because of its appearance, it is also called *barba amarilla* (yellow beard) and *cuatro narices* (four noses). The latter name refers to the four nostril-like features on its head and

Figure 10.1. A fer-de-lance.

Figure 10.2. Cristóbal killed this rattlesnake too.

is merely a translation of the term *nauyaca*, which stems from the Aztec language of Nahuatl. Although this snake does not live in central Mexico, the Aztecs clearly must have been familiar with it; because of the extent of their political control at the time of the Spanish conquest, the Spanish language adopted many more words from Nahuatl than from other Mesoamerican languages.

The central Yucatán Peninsula is the home of numerous snakes harmless to humans, including the boa. However, it also boasts four poisonous species, with the *nauyaca*, or fer-de-lance[1] (the English language uses the French term), undoubtedly the most dangerous of all. Another snake that is difficult to notice, like the *nauyaca*, is the *cantil* or moccasin snake, which is also known by its Yucatec name *wol poch*.[2] Rattlesnakes[3] are somewhat easier to spot, and they also draw attention with their characteristic rattle. The venom of the fourth, the *coralillo*,[4] is strong as well. However, this snake is easily noticeable thanks to its colorful ring pattern. It has a small head with relatively short fangs, which mostly cannot penetrate footwear. The fer-de-lance, though, has excellent camouflage in a range of colors and is unwilling to move out of people's way. Upon sensing danger, it is extremely swift and belligerent, and its strong fangs can penetrate leather. Sometimes it will raise itself off the ground high enough to bite a person above the knee. Its venom is fatal: it attacks primarily blood cells and causes tissue mortification and heavy internal bleeding, accompanied by a whole series of dreadful symptoms that are apparent externally. This snake is responsible for the highest number of deaths from snakebites in southeastern Mexico. Even the antivenin, which we did carry with us, is not always effective.

Cristóbal picked up his machete and looked around for a tall sapling about five centimeters in diameter in order to make a stick about three meters long. Then he cautiously approached the balled-up snake and struck with full force. The snake, which up to that point had lain perfectly still, began to squirm and wriggle frantically, albeit hopelessly. Striking a few more times, Cristóbal ended its suffering. A dangerous reptile like that certainly could not be granted a reprieve.

---

1. *Bothrops asper.*
2. *Agkistrodon bilineatus.*
3. *Crotalus durissus.*
4. *Micrurus diastema.*

Figure 10.3. A boa.

His answer when I asked why he had not used his machete was something I had heard before: "With the machete, you'd have to get too close to it. Besides, with some bad luck, you might even cut it in half in such a way that the head would fly off and possibly still bite you. If there's really nothing else at hand, you could hit it with the blunt side of the machete, but the most reliable thing is a long, strong stick. The strike has to break its spine such that it can no longer move and chase you."

With the 1996 field season drawing to a close, I was already alone and getting ready to return to Mexico City. One night in Xpujil I had dinner at a restaurant called El Mirador Maya. The restaurant was a space with tables out in the open covered by a huge cone-shaped roof made of palm leaves. At the table next to me a young couple was absorbed in romantic conversation, when suddenly the young man leaped to his feet and cried out to the two waitresses leaning on the bar, "What the hell! Is this thing here for decoration, or what?"

Their table obstructed my view of the chair the young man was pointing at. I was eating my dinner and not especially interested. The two must have been city folk on a trip, making a short stop here, and such people might easily make a fuss over a large beetle or moth.

"What's the matter?" a bored voice asked from the other end of the restaurant.

"A snake, here, on the chair!" the man exclaimed.

At that point I finally got up and stepped closer. On the chair, between the vertical rails of the back, was a smallish snake, curled up and motionless, but probably not dead. But who could have put it there?

"A rattlesnake!" said an older man approaching the scene. He was the driver of a large tractor trailer parked outside the restaurant. He was clearly clueless regarding snakes.

"No, it's a nauyaca," I said, feeling it necessary to correct him. The pattern on the snake's back left no room for doubt.

"Does anyone have a machete? Bring a machete!" ordered the truck driver. I glanced at the few other guests, expecting some local to step up and take matters in hand. But everyone just mumbled incomprehensively and exchanged glances, while the waitresses watched helplessly from a safe distance. Naturally, I had some machetes in my pickup. I grabbed the longest one and slowly returned to the table, deliberating how to tackle the situation. Only the head was sticking out of the bundle on the back of the chair, which was very close to the table.

"Let's move the chair away," someone suggested.

"Absolutely not!" I exclaimed in alarm. "This snake is too fast."

"So, it'll run away?"

"No, it will attack the first person that comes near."

Thus, instead of the chair, we carefully moved the table slightly. Everyone stepped away. Suddenly there was complete silence. The suspense was palpable. Could I do it? After all, I had never killed a snake before. But there was no time for hesitation. The words of the experts came to mind. I turned the machete blunt side down, lifted it, aimed it, and struck right along the back of the chair. As I hit the motionless snake on the neck, right behind the head, it suddenly sprang to life. It fell to the ground, where its desperate winding and wriggling made it clear that the blow had been successful. I finished the unpleasant job and cut off its head.

The snake was less than one meter long; it was a fer-de-lance, however, and dangerous despite its youth. It must have come from the forest behind the restaurant. I picked up the snake's dead body and threw it into a garbage can. I put away my machete and returned to the table. The truck driver was telling his neighbor about poisonous snakes and the dangers of being bitten, but I was no longer interested in the topic. In semidarkness I could see the waitresses smiling, and a tequila awaited me on the table.

11

The King Is Coming

In the 1998 field season we worked during a more appropriate time, from March until May. We focused on salvaging the two stelae from the Los Alacranes site and transporting them to the nearby village. This time I was accompanied by my colleague Vicente Suárez Aguilar, an archaeologist from the INAH center in Campeche. We were joined by Ian Graham, an eminent archaeologist from Harvard University, who had read the first report on our discovery and wished to make detailed drawings of the images and inscriptions on the stelae. Graham was certainly the right person for the task, having been the initiator and leader of the extensive, years-long Corpus of Maya Hieroglyphic Inscriptions project, within the scope of which a great many monuments from various sites had been documented and published. Unfortunately, on the eastern hill we were in for a disappointing surprise: the stela was in two pieces. Over the previous months someone must have attempted to hoist it, possibly in order to saw it apart, but broke it in the process. For whatever reason, the scoundrels then gave up on their objective. Luckily, the stela did not crumble further, and the surface with reliefs and inscriptions remained intact. Transportation, however, was consequently more difficult, and it was even more

Figure 11.1. The two stelae of Los Alacranes were drawn in 1998 by the renowned Mayanist Ian Graham. The Mexican army occasionally helped with work on the site. Stela 1, the lower part of which is visible in this photo, was broken in half by looters.

trouble putting the two pieces back together and lifting the entire thing into an upright position.

We used a bulldozer to move both stelae into the village, where we had prepared a special spot for them. Local authorities from Xpujil had arranged a two-day bulldozer loan from a construction team building a road not far from Los Alacranes. Everyone from the village knew what the motifs on the stelae represented: I had explained to our local workers that monumental ruins, like the ones on both hills next to their village, were the remains of ancient cities once inhabited by the Maya but abandoned more than a thousand years ago. Furthermore, I had told them that the rulers would often be depicted on the flat stones erected on the buildings and plazas, their glorious deeds made immortal by inscriptions. As most of the current inhabitants of Los Alacranes originate from the state of Chiapas, they were particularly impressed that the hieroglyphic texts were written in a language virtually identical to their own—Chol. They finally understood that these curious stones with images on them, at first so utterly incomprehensible, were the work of their ancient forebears and therefore deserving of their utmost respect. Thus it was a great occasion for the villagers when, after many days of preparation, the vehicle carrying the first stela finally came down the hill. As the day drew to a close and the roar of the engine of the approaching caterpillar grew ever louder, cries of joy and excitement could be heard throughout the village: "The king is coming, the king is coming!"

Chol is one of the Mayan languages still spoken today. In Mexico, schools and centers exist where Mayan and other indigenous languages (there are more than fifty in the whole country) are taught and transcribed into written form in order to be preserved. Nevertheless, most people are ashamed of their indigenous language, and many do not use it even to communicate with their children. This is due to the contempt shown by those whose mother tongue is Spanish, especially by schoolchildren, who typically look down on speakers of indigenous languages and treat them as country bumpkins. On numerous occasions I have attempted to convince people that it would be more useful for their children to know two languages instead of just one. Spanish is a requirement at school—but why not speak another language? Later on, such knowledge could help them learn even more languages. Many of them would agree that it is an advantage to be able to communicate with close friends in a tongue no one else understands.

The inhabitants of Los Alacranes became further convinced that the Chol language was not something to be scorned in the year 2000 when I brought in plaques explaining what the images on the stelae meant. The INAH provides such information at every archaeological site open to the public, typically in Spanish, English, and the most widespread local language. Thus, in this case, I suggested that Chol be used. Most people from the village can read and write at least somewhat, but this was the first time they realized that not only Spanish but also their own language could be written in Latin script.

The stelae stirred the interest of not only Ian Graham but also Nikolai Grube from the University of Bonn, one of the leading authorities on Maya script. He, too, made precise drawings of the motifs and inscriptions on both monuments. Once he had deciphered them, we learned what they were about. Nikolai, who continued to collaborate regularly with us thereafter, found some especially interesting information on the stela from the eastern hill.

The date on the stela corresponds to November 8, AD 504, the birthdate of the ruler Sak Witzil B'aah (White Hill Top), ruler of the city of

Figure 11.2. Prior to being attached to the plow of the bulldozer for transport to Los Alacranes, the stelae needed to be protected by blankets, hardwood sticks, and old tires, all in order to prevent direct contact between the stone slabs and the plow and to absorb shocks during transport.

B'uuk. As this name also appears at certain sites in neighboring Guatemala, the city must have been an important center, although politically not completely independent: farther down, dated April 30, 561, an enthronement is mentioned "under the auspices of Sky Witness, ruler of the Kaan dynasty." So the ruler depicted on the stela must have been a vassal of another, mightier lord. We know that in the Late Classic period the Kaan dynasty had its seat in Calakmul, which at the time was the capital of a vast and extremely powerful Maya state. Calakmul is some sixty kilometers west of Los Alacranes and is the largest Maya archaeological site. Thus far, more than one hundred stelae have been discovered there, and about six thousand structures. However, in the sixth century the Kaan dynasty did not yet rule from Calakmul but rather from the city corresponding to the archaeological site of Dzibanché, some fifty kilometers northeast of Los Alacranes, in the neighboring state of Quintana Roo.

Another interesting detail of the inscription is the earliest known mention of the king whose name epigraphers usually translate as "Sky Witness." He is famous primarily because in 562, soon after supervising the accession of his vassal in Los Alacranes, he attacked and defeated Tikal, another powerful Maya metropolis, in today's northeastern Guatemala. Thereafter Tikal had a subordinate position for almost one and a half centuries. Its revenge began only in 695 with the victory of King Jasaw Chan K'awiil over his rival Yuknoom Yich'aak K'ak' of the Kaan dynasty, which at that time ruled from Calakmul. The vendetta continued with wars in the first half of the eighth century, which irrevocably weakened Calakmul.

12

State and Federation

At the preprepared spot in Los Alacranes we hoisted both stelae into an upright position with a digger, which, like the bulldozer, had been lent to us by the road team. The placement of the smaller Stela 2 was not especially complicated. The larger one, though, which was in two pieces, first had to be reassembled on a bed of thick boards. We applied a special two-component epoxy cement to the contact surfaces of the stela and then brought the heavy stone slabs as close together as possible by means of levers and wooden wedges. Just as we were about to tie the wooden bed supporting the stela—now pieced together—onto the shovel of the digger in order to lift the entire construction, one of its tires burst and it could not come close enough. As we were not skilled in ancient Maya techniques and did not have time to experiment, the entire maneuver had to be postponed until the following day. Although by that point the glue had somewhat dried, there was no turning back. Fortune was with us, and in the lifting process the upper part came to rest on the lower one so well that the stability of the monument was not in danger. Once the stela was standing, we propped it up further with wooden posts. The wooden bed used for support was lowered back into a horizontal position and dragged away by a military Hummer that happened to be passing by. The two pits in which the stelae were standing had to be filled in with concrete, but in

Figure 12.1. Erecting Stela 2 in Los Alacranes; the simple village church is in the background.

Figure 12.2. Lifting Stela 1, reassembled on a bed of strong boards, in Los Alacranes.

order to prevent the concrete from coming into contact with the stelae and thus becoming irreversibly adhered to them, we first placed a layer of stones and limestone sand around the bottom of the slabs.

With the task completed and the stelae firmly in position in their spot by the road, Vicente and I were relaxing that afternoon in our hammocks in a cabin the locals had hospitably provided. Then we heard some noise down by the road. We stepped outside, only to see a police car and two policemen standing next to it. They were talking to two villagers. One of them turned around and called out to us, saying they would like to have a word with us.

We went over to them. A skinny policeman sporting a bushy mustachio and sunglasses approached.

"We've been wondering who brought these stones here," he said, pointing to the stelae, "and were told that it was you."

"That's right," I responded.

"Where are you from? And what are you doing here?"

"We work for the National Institute for Anthropology and History," I said and explained our task to him.

"May I see your ID, please? Do you have a permit? Who is the person in charge?"

I introduced myself, and both Vicente and I handed him our institute IDs. I went to the cabin to fetch our travel order and an official note for civil and military authorities containing our names and a short description of the project. The institute provides such a note to every person doing fieldwork.

The policeman went back to the car, where the two examined the documents, murmuring incomprehensibly. A few moments later he came back and handed us the papers.

"OK," he said tersely, his unfriendly expression never leaving his face.

After they left, Vicente and I got into our truck and went to Heladio's in the neighboring village of Santa Rosa for a beer.

It was approaching dusk when we returned, and to our great astonishment, the two policemen and their vehicle were again waiting for us.

As before, the mustachioed one approached, this time appearing more confident. He looked as if he had obtained some information that had changed his opinion. Self-importantly, he positioned himself in front of us, took off his sunglasses, and began.

Figure 12.3. Stela 1 standing in Los Alacranes.

"Your permit states that the work is to be limited to the state of Campeche, while Los Alacranes falls under the jurisdiction of Quintana Roo."

Aha! It dawned on me why they were giving me trouble. Quintana Roo is the youngest of the Mexican states. It was named after Andrés Quintana Roo, a fighter for Mexican independence at the beginning of the nineteenth century. In the second half of the nineteenth century the eastern Yucatán Peninsula was shaken by the so-called Caste War, which was an uprising of the Maya against the whites and embodied their struggle for independence. After the war ended, in 1902 the Mexican dictator Porfirio Díaz established the federal territory of Quintana Roo, which in 1971 was awarded the status of a federal state. The state inherited the demarcation problem originating from the unclearly defined border between the state of Campeche, established in 1863, and the newly founded territory of Quintana Roo. In 1997, this issue, which has persisted for decades, turned into a constitutional dispute triggered by the then-governor of the state of Quintana Roo. From the point of view of Campeche, which maintains that the border runs along the 89°09' meridian as an extension of the northern segment of the border between Belize and Guatemala, Los Alacranes lies six kilometers west of the border. However, as long as the problem remains unresolved, Quintana Roo will not recognize this border and has made repeated attempts to move it westward by establishing new communities and offering various services in the existing ones. Because I was familiar with all that, I was well aware that for Los Alacranes the situation was not perfectly defined. Naturally, the policeman's position was understandable: the license plates on his vehicle were from Quintana Roo.

I attempted a calming attitude. "I know about the border dispute. I don't know why the permit states Campeche, but in fact, this is quite irrelevant. You know that we do archaeology, and archaeological artifacts are part of the national heritage, patrimonio de la nación."

"No, I have been ordered to take you to Chetumal, the capital. I was told that the director of the INAH center there wants to speak to you."

"Adriana Velásquez Morlet?" I had spoken to her only a few days before. She knew very well what we were doing there. "Why on earth does she want to speak to me again, and so urgently, for that matter? She knows I'm not exactly around the corner. Chetumal is at least four hours away."

"I don't know, but I was told to bring you."

"I'm sorry, but this won't be possible. It's already late and tomorrow the work has to continue."

"Again, I'm telling you that you have to come with me. That's the order I've received," the officer insisted, shooting me a piercing look.

"Look. I have orders as well. Tomorrow, my boss is visiting from Mexico City. He's coming to check how the work is going. I have a hard time believing that going to talk to the director in Chetumal could be more important. I know her and she is familiar with our work."

"Lo siento," he said, the expression on his face not in the least confirming his regret. "You have to come with us!"

"With all due respect," I said, using a well-known Mexican phrase to express politeness, "I'm here in an official capacity and cannot do that. Unless, of course, you take me away by force. If you think that you have the authority to do so, I won't resist, but it might have consequences. I work for the Instituto Nacional de Antropología e Historia, which is a federal institution. Therefore, my authority exceeds that of individual states."

As expected, this worked. Anything *federal* will always invoke great respect among civil servants from local institutions.

The man shifted his weight from one foot to the other, his arrogant stance somehow deflating. He stepped closer to his colleague and the two murmured something between them. Vicente and I exchanged a glance and tried to remain serious. The policeman approached us again, his look noticeably less confrontational.

"All right." He looked down, stroking his mustache. "All right, but could you at least come with us to the police station here in Dos Aguadas, so we can make a record of this?"

That sounded much better. Since he had taken a step back, I had to do so as well. The village of Dos Aguadas was less than twenty kilometers away, and friendly relations with the police could never be a bad idea— even though they had never been of any great help to us.

"That I could do, I suppose. If you take me, could you bring me back later?"

"Certainly, certainly." He was almost friendly now.

About a half-hour drive on a bumpy gravel road later, we arrived in Dos Aguadas. It was already dark when we stopped in front of a wooden cabin that served as the police station. We entered a small room illuminated by the simplest—yet very practical—light, of a type that could be seen around here and that we also used in our camps: an old jam or mayonnaise jar filled with diesel fuel, with a piece of fabric—maybe from an old shirt—rolled and pulled through the perforated metal lid, serving as a wick. The flame of this modern oil lamp provides more light than a candle; it also emits more smoke, but then there are fewer insects around.

Half sitting, half lying on a wooden bench were two law officers, who could not be bothered to change their position when we arrived. In one of the corners stood a table piled high with documents, with a couple of chairs around it. The police officer who had been and remained the only one to talk to me offered me a seat. He sat down as well and pulled a typewriter closer, which under different circumstances would have been considered a rather valuable museum artifact. From the mountain of paper on the table he remarkably managed to pull out three blank sheets, carefully placed two sheets of carbon paper between them, and fed all of them into the typewriter. It took him a good ten minutes to type up the heading. Then he asked me to dictate a report regarding our work. After a few more questions, I finally grasped what he wanted of me and began to dictate. Intently, he searched for the right keys with creased forehead and, after every three strokes of his extended index fingers, carefully checked the results on the paper. Amused, I recalled an occasion many years ago when I myself had fought a similar battle against a typewriter with keys that kept hiding from me. My mother, having noticed this struggle, brought me a cup of water and explained gently in answer to my questioning glance that at that speed my fingers must need some cooling off. The policeman was typing so slowly that I kept losing my train of thought and forgot what came next. Some long minutes later I finally suggested to him, "May I? Perhaps I could type this up myself."

His face lit up as he pushed the typewriter over to me and said, gesturing courteously as he spoke, "Please, here you are."

I cleared my head and wrote a short summary of our work. In doing so, I did not forget to demonstrate an appropriate level of humility, asking him every now and then to look at this or that formulation and give me his opinion. He was pleased with everything I wrote; he even went to get me a *refresco* (soda). When the document was ready and signed, he loosened up and started talking, his previous officiousness completely gone. We were chatting away pleasantly, but it was getting late and the following day my boss really was arriving from Mexico City. I reminded him of that and asked to be taken back to Los Alacranes. He got up immediately and we left. We parted like true friends, but I never saw him again.

Figure 12.4. Construction of the protective shelter for the stelae in Los Alacranes.

The following morning after a breakfast prepared by Doña Miquelina, the owner of the house where Vicente and I were staying, we went over to the stelae. But none of our workmen were there at the agreed time. Soon thereafter, just as I had decided to go check at the nearest house of one of them, Aurelio Castán, among the handiest and also most influential villagers, came walking down the road.

"Don Iván!"

"Don Aurelio, buenos días."

"We saw the police take you away and said to ourselves: who knows Don Iván's business, but if the police have taken him away, he's certainly not coming back."

"Now, Don Aurelio, what's this!? You do know me, you know who we are and what we are doing. I would not allow some policeman to just take me away like that."

"Even the army supports us, as you saw. Éstas son cosas federales! (These are federal matters!)" Vicente added.

"Yes, yes. I saw you two from the house. And I said to the others: Don Iván's back already. They'll be here in a minute."

And so they were. With the stelae now standing, the next task was to set up a protective roof. Beforehand, we had agreed that a circular structure would be most appropriate for this purpose, with wooden posts encircled by wire mesh and topped by a cone-shaped construction covered with *guano* palm leaves. The locals were naturally quite skilled in such constructions. Before all the poles could be erected, a car arrived with D.F. license plates, which revealed that it was from the Distrito Federal, the administrative entity encompassing the greater part of the Mexican capital. My boss Pedro Francisco Sánchez Nava and his assistant Mario Córdova Tello, both experienced archaeologists, stepped out of the car. I summarized for them the events of the past few days, including the anecdote from the night before, which amused everyone. In the afternoon as they were leaving, my boss said with a trace of sarcasm in his voice: "We've got to hurry, there's cold beer waiting for us in Xpujil." I responded that when Vicente and I got there after all this work, we would undoubtedly enjoy it even more; but that was hardly any consolation.

A few days later, the protective shelter for the stelae was completed, which we celebrated with a simple yet solemn formal opening organized by high officials from the municipality of Xpujil. We even had a microphone and a battery-powered sound system.

Figure 12.5. The official inauguration of the shelter with the two stelae in Los Alacranes on April 5, 1998.

However, I never uncovered the reason for that incident with the policemen or who was behind it. Later I spoke to Adriana, director of the Chetumal INAH center, but she naturally knew nothing about it. Had someone called the police and fed them false information? In any case, if someone had been hoping to make my life difficult, he or she must have been disappointed.

13

El Comandante

Oftentimes, our team received help from the Mexican army, which was always very effective. Aside from serving as a defensive force, the military has an important role in civil society in Mexico, especially in rural areas. It performs various tasks aimed at preventing or eliminating the consequences of hurricanes, which often sweep across the southeastern part of the country; it also helps fight forest fires, and even provides medical care in remote areas. Furthermore, it tackles crime, especially the illegal drug trade.

As an authority capable of effectively intervening in numerous situations, the army is held in high regard by the local population. We had already witnessed this in 1996, when soldiers had accompanied us from El Civalito to Los Alacranes to protect us from road bandits. From that point on, we would always notify the Mexican Secretariat of National Defense (Secretaría de la Defensa Nacional) of our fieldwork and ask for assistance should we need it. As all our work was done under the auspices of the INAH, which is a federal institution, the Secretariat took us extremely seriously. While the military headquarters in charge of the area where our explorations were conducted was in Xpujil, there were smaller operational bases in other places; one of them was in the village of El Civalito, where we had sought help in 1996. In 1998, upon a directive issued by the secretary of defense, my colleague Vicente Suárez and I were provided lodging at the base in El Civalito. We stayed there for several days, before the salvage of the two stelae in Los Alacranes began, because we wanted to examine a few archaeological sites in the vicinity. The soldiers often accompanied us, and later they also assisted in erecting the stelae in the village.

The military camp, too, was full of adventure. One night, while half asleep, I tried to rub something off my face a couple of times, assuming that a gnat or mosquito was bothering me. When the annoyance would not stop, I finally got up and turned on my flashlight, only to see a convoy of ants making their way right across my pillow. "Leave them alone, they'll go away eventually," the soldier on the bunk bed next to me said in a sleepy, calming tone. But the column was so long I could not see its beginning or end. They were marching across the floor, crawling up the bed, and disappearing into the cracks between the wooden boards of the wall beside the bunk bed. To my good fortune they did not bite, and my presence did not in the least upset them. Such certainly does not hold true regarding certain other species, for instance the aggressive *xulab*,[1] which come out in great numbers before rain and can make life in a forest camp quite unenjoyable. In this case, even though it had not looked possible at first, the parade ended soon after.

One morning the driver of the military Hummer that belonged to the camp came rushing up to me, complaining about the battery being dead. As a visit from the general was expected at any moment and there was no time to charge it, he asked me to lend him the one from our truck. Naturally, I did as he asked and he swiftly installed the battery in the Hummer. As the general walked past, reviewing the troops with soldiers standing at attention, the flawless rumbling of the Hummer could be heard in the background. As in every army (I remembered my own military service), everything had to be perfect, even if only in appearance.

In the year 2000 I returned to Los Alacranes to mount the information plaques next to the two stelae. Again, the Secretariat of National Defense was notified of our intentions; however, I saw no need to report to the commander of the military base in Xpujil. One afternoon Aurelio Castán invited me for lunch and offered me the use of his bathroom. I was just

---

1. The Mayan name for the ant species *Eciton burchellii*.

Figure 13.1. For a military Hummer, most obstacles on the trails do not cause major problems.

pouring water on myself in a wooden shed adapted for this purpose when I heard Don Aurelio calling me in a somewhat worried voice: "Don Iván, the army is looking for you!"

I quickly dried myself, got dressed, and stepped outside. A military jeep and a Hummer were parked in the yard, some soldiers in front of them with weapons ready. The imposing commanding officer approached me. He was about my age and dressed in an impeccable uniform with epaulettes indicating the rank of lieutenant colonel.

"Doctor Iván Šprajc?"

"Yes, what can I do for you?" I grasped his hand.

"Soy Teniente Coronel Alfonso Cristóbal García Melgar, comandante de la 25 Compañía de Infantería No Encuadrada en Xpujil."

He was the commander of the infantry unit in Xpujil responsible for our region.

"I've been informed that you are carrying out archaeological explorations in this territory and have been ordered to offer you help, should you need it."

"Thank you so much, Commander!" I answered, sincerely astonished. "I apologize for not having reported to you, but on this occasion my task is solely to place information plaques next to the stelae here in the village. Therefore, I didn't think it necessary to trouble you."

"It is no trouble at all."

I briefly explained what our research was all about. He listened with interest and invited me to stop by his office at the headquarters in Xpujil when I had a chance, especially if I ever needed anything.

After the soldiers left, Don Aurelio, having carefully followed the conversation from a polite distance, adjusted his hat and gave me a nod of approval:

"Muy bien, Don Iván, muy bien."

The task completed, I indeed stopped by the military base in Xpujil and was warmly received by the commander. We had a long conversation about our work and about his unit's tasks. The impression Lieutenant Colonel García Melgar had made on me at our first meeting was reinforced, and more so during our encounters in the following years, as he remained in command of the Xpujil unit until 2004. He was a true soldier, a man of honor and discipline, committed to his job and demanding of his subordinates, but also fair and understanding. He would accept and carry out orders without hesitation yet still maintained a critical stance toward the politics and situation in his country. He would not strictly limit himself to his official duties, tasks, or specific orders. Within the scope of his authority, he would often act on his own initiative, simply because his conscience and humanity told him to. In 2001 he invited me to join him on one of his routine flights across the territory under his jurisdiction. In the helicopter, he spoke of the search for marijuana fields—one of his unit's tasks was to locate and destroy them—as well as about a much more serious problem the Mexican army had to struggle against, namely the trafficking of hard drugs from South America, especially Colombia. Occasionally, drug traffickers would transport their contraband by small aircraft and attempt to land on old runways that had been used by chicleros.

Naturally, I would also report to the commander on our work, informing him of our finds and the location of important archaeological remains. I would also tell him where the locals complained of road bandits, because in such cases the army can intervene and often does so very effectively. However, the commander did admit to a certain helplessness in this regard. As I had seen myself, it was not rare for the military to capture an offender; however, after two days it would have to hand him over to the civilian authorities, who unfortunately often released him because of insufficient evidence or corruption. Nevertheless, this would not in the least diminish the high regard the local people had for the army, as the army would also help them with quotidian matters such as fires, medical care, and similar issues. The police, on the other hand, do not enjoy the trust of the people, and we could confirm the commander's opinion that they were rarely of any help. In such circumstances it is naturally good for the federal army to have greater authority than the local police; as early as 1996, I witnessed soldiers mercilessly disarming some disgruntled policemen who were carrying weapons they were not permitted to.

I have often been asked whether we walk around armed. Such a question generally stirs up an image of romantic adventures and remarks along the lines of "You're like Indiana Jones." My friend and colleague Vaquero, of whom I will relate more later, once responded to such a comment: "Wrong. Indiana Jones is like us. He is fictitious, while we are real. It feels rather good to be a source of inspiration for Hollywood."

As paradoxical as it may be that the most famous archaeologist of all time is a product of fiction, he was indeed modeled on certain real people who lived in an era when a gun was quite a common tool of archaeologists, at least in the American tropics and other remote places; but this naturally does not mean that guns were actually used to resolve conflicts. Under the current Mexican legislation, carrying firearms is prohibited. There is no denying that we could easily hide a weapon among all the other equipment; however, using one in an actual conflict would not be the slightest bit cinematic, but rather utterly counterproductive. Nowadays, local people in rural areas are allowed to possess a hunting rifle if they register it with the army; along these lines, I asked the commander whether our local help were allowed to carry such rifles while accompanying us into the biosphere. Although it is true that jaguars will typically not attack a person, it could happen; tapirs, too, can be fairly unpleasant, as they may decide to trample anything that comes in their path. The lieutenant colonel's response was: "Regarding weaponry, I am at the moment the highest authority in the region and can thus grant you such permission. But do not kill any animals or else you will have to deal with the environmental police. If that happens, not even I can help you."

14

Run Out of Bush

I was mad and tired as I wielded my machete, clearing the bush and hop-ing to finally set my eyes on something real, like a pyramid or a stela. A few meters away, Pepe Orta was doing the same. We had been at it the whole day, blazing a trail through the forest on the westernmost edges of the territory of El Tesoro. The name of the village may sound nice, but the treasure (*tesoro*) was nowhere to be found. We had heard rumors from several locals that there were big ruins, Los Charros, somewhere in these woods, but we could not find anyone who would show us the way. We even had the feeling that they were refusing to show us the site, perhaps because they were busy digging up the ruins themselves. Using nothing but vague clues, we could only speculate where the site might be; we studied the map and decided to go it alone. We traversed all elevations, covering the most likely sites of major Maya settlements. Having trudged since morning, we had found only a few meager remains of small houses scattered around typical courtyards.

That is how the 2001 season began. By then I was already an employee at the Research Center of the Slovenian Academy of Sciences and Arts

(ZRC SAZU), but naturally I still maintained contact with my Mexican colleagues. I was accompanied by the land surveyor José Orta Bautista, my former colleague from the INAH, a great friend and an excellent field worker. The archaeologist Pedro Francisco Sánchez Nava, my former boss and an otherwise true friend, had allowed Pepe to accompany me. And as always, he supported the project and arranged a vehicle for us, the trusty gray Dodge. The financing this time came from the Foundation for the Advancement of Mesoamerican Studies, based in the United States.

It was already late afternoon and Pepe was still spouting his off-the-cuff remarks, but his signature wit, which rarely dried up, was wearing thin. His face was dripping with sweat and we were both soaking wet and starting to become moody, me especially. It was clear that the locals were taking us for a ride. They were hiding something; they must have been digging around in the ruins themselves while mocking us behind our backs. We had come across a densely overgrown section that we had to cut through; I was chopping like a madman and my anger was boiling up. That was when I received a valuable lesson: never, even if the situation is hopeless, lose your head and surrender to despair. One of my wild machete swings was ever so slightly too strong: the branches intended to receive the blow offered less resistance than I expected and the machete hit my left knee. Actually, it felt as if it had barely sunk into my flesh, but the sharp blade opened my knee like a mushy pear, and blood started gushing. Pepe leaped to help me, pulled out a first aid kit from his backpack, and dressed my wound as best he could.

We had to walk another hour to get back to the truck so we could drive to El Tesoro and find the clinic there. The village is small and there was no doctor, but we did find a nurse, a young woman who sutured my wound. That would have to do for the time being. When we were done, we drove to Josefa Ortiz de Domínguez, a village named after an early nineteenth-century Mexican independence fighter. The site used to be a chiclero camp, Icaiché, bearing the name of a former Indian village abandoned in 1933. We lodged at the village's community center. We knew the local doctor, Osvaldo, whom we almost considered a friend. Pepe found him on the football field, engaged in what must have been his second-favorite activity after medicine, and brought him to see me.

"Let's go to the clinic," he summoned, bursting with energy, as if he were about to take a shot at the goal.

"Hold on, Osvaldo," I said, trying to stop him. "Let me finish my beer."

"By all means do that, because afterwards—who knows."

Osvaldo was a dedicated doctor and even had decent equipment, but there was no electricity. Pepe directed a flashlight while Osvaldo poked around in the wound; the sheets and floor became drenched in so much blood that it looked as if a hog were being butchered. He finally had to admit he could not stop the bleeding. He sent me to Xpujil in the village ambulance, but even there they admitted defeat and sent me on to Chetumal. Pepe got a hotel room while I waited in the hospital a few hours for the doctor. When he finally arrived, he turned out to be far from a role model for his noble profession. Wearing a ho-hum expression, he asked me why I had been brought there. I summed up the whole story, the guy unwrapped the bandage and looked at the wound, which by then had miraculously stopped bleeding, and all he did was reinforce the suturing and send me on my way.

Pepe took me "home" to Josefa Ortiz de Domínguez. Despite the seriousness of the situation, the locals did not shy away from humorous remarks; in general, they tend to downplay the gravity of events with a joke, even when they are the victims themselves. Somebody asked me, "What happened, did you run out of bush?"

The following day Pepe made the rounds by himself. I was not worried. Even though he was a surveyor, he had experience in archaeology. But more than that, he had a feel for the terrain and the people: he was able to recognize and sketch ruins and the elements of individual buildings, and he always won people over with a perfect combination of hard work, indulgence, and wit. What concerned me more was that my wound opened up the second day and half-coagulated blood started oozing out, causing me significant unease.

The subsequent days were exhausting—torturous, in fact. The doctors, whom I visited several times, diagnosed an infection and prescribed drugs along with instructions to rest. Yet I was not—at least as I saw it—injured so badly that I was justified in interrupting my work. I thus spent days and weeks in the field, shuffling around on my injured leg. The wound would not heal, and the pain was excruciating whenever I stumbled against anything. After a while, a yellow liquid started seeping from the wound. Was it pus? Synovial fluid? I still don't know. It was only several weeks later that I groaned about my problems to the lieutenant colonel, the commanding officer in Xpujil, who immediately sent me to his military doctor. A young man, he convinced me from the get-go that he knew his profession. He gave me a chance to explain the whole story and all the treatments I had received before he looked at the wound, whereupon he concluded that it was not a bacterial infection but a mycosis, a fungal infection. He was a practical man, which was not surprising given the circumstances in which he worked. He said, "I understand you cannot interrupt your work, just try to bend your knee as little as possible; the wound wants to heal, but every time the movement is too intense it is torn open, creating a hypertrophic scar."

His medicine and instructions helped. When we met toward the end of our field season at a village where soldiers from Xpujil were offering medical assistance, he was able to conclude that the wound had healed despite everything. But many other things happened before that.

15

Pyramid of the Sorcerer

One of the main aims of the 2001 season was to precisely examine and map a large archaeological site we had briefly visited in 1998. It is right on the border with Guatemala, and we named it after the nearby ranch, El Gallinero, the former home of Alfredo Díaz Torres, a cattle breeder we had met who later moved to another property near the village of Ley de Fomento Agropecuario.

Many villages south of Xpujil developed on the sites of former chiclero camps. The proximity of aguadas made them ideal places for permanent settlements, but the picturesque names of these camps and aguadas were often replaced by less imaginative or outright prosaic denominations. For example, the abandoned camp next to Aguada La Misteriosa (Mysterious Aguada) made way for a settlement called Ley de Fomento Agropecuario (Law on the Promotion of Agriculture), an unwieldy toponym that is usually abbreviated as Ley de Fomento or simply Ley.

We found Alfredo Díaz at his Buenos Aires Ranch a few kilometers southwest of Ley de Fomento. He mentioned that he knew of another major complex of ruins adjacent to Aguada Champerico, which he said was on the way to El Gallinero. The only way to get to either place was via an old trail that led deep into the Calakmul Biosphere. Thus far, we had been working near settlements, where we were offered accommodation in community centers; the roads and trails were more or less passable, and there were shops in the larger villages where we could stock up on basic supplies. In the biosphere the situation was completely different. There used to be a whole network of trails there, used by loggers and chicle collectors, but these were now mostly abandoned and overgrown; only a few occasionally used by the Mexican army and park rangers were traversable—to a limited extent. The expedition to the biosphere therefore required special preparations. Don Alfredo offered to accommodate us at his abandoned El Gallinero Ranch (he had had to abandon it precisely because it lay deep in the biosphere), but for the time being, the only thing we had agreed on was the day of departure. Before we left, Pepe and I had to buy food and water as well as a chain saw, which was indispensable for removing fallen trees. In the meantime, Pascual Medina and the geographer Rubén Escartín, my former colleagues from the INAH, arrived from Mexico City to help with the surveying and mapping. This time we carried an electronic theodolite, which enables precise 3-D mapping of terrain; the device, sometimes referred to as a total station, emits a laser beam into a prism held by an assistant at a certain point. The ray is reflected back into the device, and based on the angle of its path and time delay, the position of the point is calculated.

Before departure, I stopped by the Xpujil barracks to talk to the commander and explain our plans. He said a group of soldiers needed to make the rounds in that area anyway and that they were bound to find us at El Gallinero; if I needed any help, I should turn to the officer in charge. I also visited the administration of the Calakmul Biosphere, whose director, the engineer José Rodríguez de la Gala, supported our expedition with an additional truck and a few of his men.

On the agreed day, Don Alfredo took us toward El Gallinero. The first surprise was a stela lying next to the trail close to Aguada Champerico. As soon as we removed the fallen leaves covering the stone slab, which was around two meters long, we saw the image of a Maya ruler flanked by hieroglyphic inscriptions. Since there were no archaeological remains nearby, it was immediately clear that the stela had been dragged there in modern times, almost certainly from a nearby hill that Don Alfredo said contained the main complex of the ruins. The work had not been easy; they must have dragged the stela some seven hundred meters. Why did they leave it on the side of the trail? The puzzle would remain unsolved for now as we continued toward El Gallinero to set up camp at Alfredo's abandoned ranch.

The dirt trail Don Alfredo took us on the following day brought us to Aguada Saraguatos, the site of a former chiclero camp. From there we headed west through the forest. The area was densely scattered with smaller ruins, and after only a few hundred meters we arrived at the urban core, barely a kilometer north of the Guatemalan border. My colleague Nikolai Grube would later tell me about having visited a site known as La Toronja years before, at virtually the same longitude just south of the border, so it likely pertained to the same city, which must have been very large. On the Mexican side we found not just the remains of simple houses but at least five expansive complexes of monumental architecture. Over the coming days we mapped four and named them after the animals that kept us (not always nice) company.

The first group was christened Abejas (Bees) because we came across a hollow tree that housed a colony of wild bees. In Mexico, wild bees have been strongly Africanized. They are sensitive and aggressive, which made surveying in their vicinity quite unpleasant: we tried to do everything with silent hand gestures; when we did use words, they were whispered.

Figure 15.1. A spider monkey.

While working on the second complex, we ran across a fer-de-lance and two rattlesnakes, which inspired the name Víboras (Snakes) for this architectural group. Fortunately, the meeting with all three reptiles ended unfortunately for them.

The animals that greeted us in the third group were friendlier. They were black howler monkeys that the locals call *saraguatos*.[1] This was also the name of the abandoned chiclero camp in the area and what we dubbed our architectural complex. Unsurprisingly, the howlers got their name from their loud howls, which scare the bejesus out of the uninitiated: they sound more like the screams of a monster than the howls of a harmless monkey less than a meter tall. Another species of monkey living in the Mexican southeast is the black-handed spider monkey,[2] which is slightly smaller but much more animated and even pestilent. They dislike intruders and bombard them with branches, which can be dangerous, or with their own excretions, which is not so dangerous but not exactly pleasant, especially if the stuff splatters over a meticulously drawn sketch map or a total station.

In the fourth complex we were greeted by swarms of much smaller animals, which were mostly harmless but all the more annoying: we called it Moscas (Flies).

As we were mapping the area, we gradually realized that El Gallinero was an exceptionally expansive site. The stelae and altars were testimony to its importance. The carved reliefs were badly worn down, but in the past there must have been at least a few that were better preserved: in front of one of the buildings we found several stone slabs with smooth surfaces produced by a modern steel saw. Professional looters had visited El Gallinero before us, just as they had many other sites, with the trenches dug into all the major buildings signifying their handiwork.

After wrapping up work at El Gallinero, Don Alfredo took us to Champerico, which is about ten kilometers to the north. We headed west from the stela that looters had dragged onto the trail. The terrain started to gently slope, and individual remains of buildings started popping up before we finally reached the eastern edge of a compact complex of ruins on the flat summit of a low hill, parts of which had been artificially leveled: this was the administrative and religious center of the old settlement. Don

---

1. *Alouatta pigra.*
2. *Ateles geoffroyi.*

Figure 15.2. Stone slabs whose carved relief surfaces have been cut off by looters lie at the foot of one of the many pyramids in El Gallinero.

Figure 15.3. An overgrown stela in front of a building at Champerico.

Alfredo stopped before a large mound and cleared the dirt off a flat stone slab with a bunch of twigs: another stela with a well-preserved relief. But like the stela left on the side of the trail, this one had been moved. Beneath and scattered around it were dried poles that someone had used to move it before abandoning the undertaking for reasons unknown. In the upper part of a ruined building nearby we found a third stela, which was still standing upright and had a well-preserved hieroglyphic inscription. Looters had damaged parts of its carved surface but fortunately had failed to finish the job here too.

Having spent well over an hour wading through the vegetation growing over the densely scattered ruins of buildings large and small, we suddenly noticed the outlines of a mighty pyramidal shape. Don Alfredo stopped. "This is the tallest building in Champerico. They tried to loot this one too, but they didn't succeed."

When I gave him a questioning look, Alfredo approached me and whispered with a grave expression on his face, "This place is haunted."

"True," added Javier, Alfredo's twenty-two-year-old son. "Years ago, while passing by in broad daylight, I heard some horrible banging behind me, as if empty metal barrels were rolling down the slope of the pyramid. I instinctively ran away, but the banging stopped as mysteriously as it had started. When I looked back, I couldn't see anything out of the ordinary."

At twenty meters high, the pyramid on the southwestern end of the city center is the biggest building in Champerico. A fairly shallow trench on one slope revealed that looters had had a go at it but did not get very far. There are stories of how trenches dug during the day would fill up overnight, of how looters would wake up in the dead of night to the sound of horrible screams, of how they had to jump away to avoid falling rocks, and so on.

"They say a shaman with great powers is buried here," Don Alfredo said. "I knew several people who dug here: they all died in just a few years."

Who knows what prevented the looters at Champerico from carrying out their misdeeds? No matter what the truth, it seemed appropriate to honor the presumed guardian of the impressive building: we called it the Pyramid of the Sorcerer.

We have often heard hair-raising stories about uncanny phenomena at archaeological sites. People have reported seeing lights, or hearing voices when there was no one around. Too bad most looters either do not believe these tales or do not have the grit to overcome their fears.

Even though I still have no idea what happened at Champerico, something must have thwarted the looters at this Maya site. They moved the stelae but did not manage to transport them very far, at least not all of them. One of them was missing the bottom section, and it later turned out that a very similar stela was kept by the museum in Campeche without a precise indication of its origin. Our epigrapher, Nikolai Grube, who visited Champerico in August 2001, discovered that the images were very similar, and the inscriptions even contained the same dates and fragments of names. Some sources suggest that the stela arrived at Campeche from Zoh Laguna, a village north of Xpujil that used to be a major logging and sawmill hub. If that was true, the stela was likely brought there by loggers working in the Champerico area, and it somehow wound up in the museum in Campeche. As Nikolai explained, the hieroglyphic inscriptions on the stelae in Champerico mention the name of the ancient city, its seventh-century rulers, and their rituals, enthronements, and connections with the fourth-century founders of the dynasty.

When we returned to El Gallinero, a group of soldiers who had set up camp nearby were already waiting for us. On orders from the commander in Xpujil, the lieutenant in charge offered to help. The next day his men cleared the undergrowth in Champerico, making it significantly easier for us to do our surveying work.

16

In the Underworld

One characteristic trait of the karstic Yucatán Peninsula is its underground caves, many of which hold archaeological remains. We have visited many such places during our fieldwork, in particular in the 2001 season. They are mostly inaccessible and unfit for habitation, and many were used for ceremonial purposes, as evidenced by archaeological remains.

Near Blasillo the villagers took us to a wide fissure in the limestone. It was the entrance to a voluminous underground chamber with a partially preserved stone arch. In narrow passageways leading in various directions we found significant quantities of ceramic fragments. The descent to a second cave near the same village was more difficult: squeezing through a narrow shaft, we barely made it into the cramped interior, where our anxiety was exacerbated by the fluttering of bats: their feces are a breeding ground for a fungus that causes the dangerous lung disease histoplasmosis. But curiosity trumped fear. With damp neckerchiefs covering our noses and mouths, we were soon in for a surprise that made the effort worthwhile. After a few turns, the narrow passage brought us into a small space where the beam of the flashlight afforded us a view that left us gasping: the ground was nearly covered by almost perfectly preserved ceramic

Figure 16.1. Ceramic vessels in a cave near the village of Blasillo.

pieces and mounds of sherds, which must have been lying there for centuries. Some of the vessels would have been toppled and broken by animals seeking shelter in the cave, but it looked as though human scoundrels had not yet set foot there. The boy who brought us there said that he had stumbled upon the cave some time ago when he was hunting, and that probably no one else knew it existed. We tried to convince him that its whereabouts should remain a secret until an archaeologist, lured by our report, could embark on a detailed study of the cave. We did not collect anything; excavation was not within our domain.

We made similar findings in other caves, although the artifacts were typically fragmented and scattered, probably by the action of water. Aside from ceramic sherds, we found arrowheads and spearheads of chert and obsidian, as well as human bones. Chert, the material of choice for many tools, is abundant in many places in the Yucatán Peninsula lowlands, especially in the bajos. Obsidian, however, is volcanic glass, typically black, and was brought to the peninsula via trade routes, mostly from the Guatemalan highlands.

Caves had great religious importance. Not only the Maya but also other Mesoamerican peoples deemed them to be entryways into the underworld of the dead, known from stories in the *Popol Vuh*, the collection of ancient Guatemalan myths. The underworld was also the abode of the rain and fertility deities. Such beliefs are not surprising, as they can be found around the world. Water comes from the ground, and its frequent presence in caves was particularly important in the karstic environment of the Yucatán Peninsula, where surface sources of water are rare and irregular. This is why caves took on significant symbolic importance. They were preferred places for carrying out fertility rituals, with offerings of vessels and other objects, and even for burying the dead, probably people who died in special circumstances related to water in some way. Even today many descendants of the Maya go to caves to collect "virgin water" (*zuhuy ha*), so called because it comes straight from the rock and has not had contact with the surface and living things, leading to the belief that it holds special power.

It is therefore no surprise that many caves have been found in settlements, sometimes under very important buildings. Their significance in the Mesoamerican worldview, in particular their connections with water

Figure 16.2. A chert spearhead found in a cave near the village of El Manantial.

and fertility, gave them an important place in geomancy or sacred geography, the set of beliefs involved in architectural and urban planning. Caves were one of the main factors in the selection of sites where settlements were to be founded or buildings of special significance constructed. If there was no natural cave near a site that was otherwise particularly suited to human habitation, an artificial one was often dug out: such caves, a testimony to the significance of the connection between cave and settlement, have been found at various Maya sites, as well as in central Mexico. For example, there is an artificial cave under the famous Sun Pyramid in Teotihuacan, the largest Mesoamerican city, which flourished in the Classic period and whose remains are northeast of the present-day Mexican capital. At the Late Classic site of Xochicalco, south of the capital, a human-made or artificially modified cave is part of the main architectural complex. Since many Maya archaeological sites are associated with caves, it is no coincidence that in southeastern Campeche as well, almost all the caves we found that contained archaeological remains were in or near ancient settlements.

17

Balakbal and Altamira

In 2002 we focused on the southern portion of the Calakmul Biosphere, and Pepe Orta was with me again. After the locals had shown us some smaller archaeological sites, the surveying of the settled area south of Xpujil was pretty much completed. One more major site needed to be mapped, but we were going to save that for the end of the season.

The year before, I had heard about a man called Mundo from La Victoria, who was said to know the biosphere very well. Pepe and I therefore headed to his village: south on the road leading out of Xpujil, then east to the village of El Manantial and on to La Victoria.

As always when our truck arrived in a remote village, we were greeted on all sides by curious glances, and children encircled our vehicle.

"Is there a gentleman living here who goes by the name Mundo?"

"Yes, Raymundo Sandoval. Head down this street and then take the second left."

The streets were just unbuilt land between the houses without any paving or improvement. We had no trouble finding the house, which appeared very pleasant: a fenced-in yard, flowers, and a modest but neat wooden shack. We disembarked from the vehicle and shouted across the fence, "Buenas tardes!"

The greeting, which literally means "good afternoon," was appropriate given that it was already past midday. The faces of several children first appeared at the door of the house, followed by a slender yet muscular man about forty-five years old, with a bushy mustache and bony face; his wavy hair and penetrating eyes gave him an unusual look.

"Muy buenas," he greeted back and approached us briskly. "How may I help you?"

"We're looking for Mr. Raymundo Sandoval."

"That would be me. Please, come in."

We told him the endlessly repeated story of our intentions and elicited an exceptionally good response. Raymundo became excited while telling us about the various ruins he said he knew of.

"I know a few ruins in a nearby village. We can check those out tomorrow if you'd like. But I also know a bigger *reinado* in the biosphere, close to a village we used to live in. We cannot get there in a day, we'd have to set up camp on the way."

The following day he organized a few helpers and we visited two minor sites not far from La Victoria. For our journey into the biosphere, however, we had to buy food, water, and basic pots and pans.

This time we entered the biosphere on a dirt trail heading west from the village of Once de Mayo (May 11). About fifteen kilometers west of it there used to be a settlement with a similar name where Mundo had lived with his family: Veintidós de Abril (April 22). I do not recall ever being told why these dates were significant or what connection they had with the settlements, but it certainly seemed that the founders did not have much imagination.

The trail was passable for the first few kilometers out of Once de Mayo because the villagers used it to get to their fields. But then it started becoming increasingly overgrown, the vegetation had to be cleared, and progress was very sluggish. Around noon, as the vehicle gently bounced along, we were startled by a thud: the front right side of the vehicle sank and we ground to a halt. The right wheel had become wedged in a crack between rocks sticking out of the ground. This was not going to be easy. The crack was so wide that pushing the truck did not help.

We started to pour stones into the crack to fill it up, but this soon proved futile: just below the surface the crack widened into a veritable cavern into which the stones disappeared without a trace. We had to saw off a few long, strong logs and drag them to the truck; we used some as levers to lift the vehicle out of the crack, while jamming others into the crack to give the wheel some traction.

We were in fact very lucky: just a meter away there was an even bigger crack!

It was dark before we reached the old site of Veintidós de Abril, and we set up camp right on the trail. Mundo proved to be a capable organizer indeed, in setting up camp as well as in preparing the food. He made dough and baked tortillas as everyone else buzzed around doing what had to be done.

The next morning we continued along the trail for a few more kilometers before heading out on foot northwest through the forest. The low, thick vegetation slowed our progress, and Mundo had to occasionally climb a tree to look around. He had not been in the area for years, and it was difficult to navigate in such a monotonous landscape. We encountered small ruins along the way, and around noon we finally found the hill we were looking for. But when we arrived at the top, the disappointment was palpable. The remains of the ancient settlement were modest, scattered around a few courtyards, and the tallest structures were barely seven or eight meters tall.

That evening at camp I told Mundo that I greatly appreciated his efforts, but we were looking mostly for bigger sites. He was visibly disheartened but assured me he would do his best.

"There is supposed to be a huge *reinado* in the biosphere at Aguada Jerusalem."

I had heard about large sites supposedly located in the biosphere many times before. People would use different names, but one was always pronounced with the same gravitas: *Jerusalén*.

The name sounded familiar. Karl Ruppert mentions in his book that his third expedition set up camp on March 25, 1934, at Aguada Jerusalem and visited a large archaeological site nearby. Ruppert called it Balakbal—Mayan for "that which is hidden"—because the most important stela was almost completely covered in ruins. Was *reinado de Jerusalén* in fact Balakbal? It would certainly be interesting to find out. No other archaeologist had visited that site since Ruppert's expedition, which is why no one knew exactly where it was.

"But how do we get there? The roads must be overgrown now."

"Do you remember driving past a crossroads yesterday, a few kilometers from Once de Mayo? A dirt track splits south from there. It runs via Altamira toward Blengio Creek and then on to Aguada Jerusalem."

I knew that trail: we were on it last year when traveling a few kilometers to the abandoned village of Las Delicias; we surveyed and mapped a larger archaeological site nearby. I also remembered the commander in Xpujil mentioning that his soldiers occasionally made rounds on the trail through Altamira, the abandoned chiclero camp where somebody supposedly still lived. That meant we could hope that the trail was not too badly overgrown. In the morning we headed back to Once de Mayo and took a right at the crossroads.

"Not far from here there is an isolated ranch where Don Raúl lives with his family," Mundo said.

In about an hour the forest intersected by the trail thinned and gradually turned into low, dense brush—an indication that there used to be fields here. We soon left behind the remains of the wooden houses in the abandoned village of Las Delicias and drove on as the road once again cut through a forest before a broad grassland opened up to reveal a house, in front of which there were several children frolicking. When we stopped, a slender, tanned bald man stepped out of the house, the lack of hair on his head compensated for by a long salt-and-pepper beard.

"Don Raúl!" Mundo greeted him, and the rest of us did the same. I explained our intentions and asked him about the path onward.

"The dirt trail is pretty good," Don Raúl said. In this remote area he lived alone with his wife and twelve kids. They did not go to school, but their father educated them as best he could. They would go to Once de Mayo or another village only occasionally, by horse or bicycle.

"If you continue in that direction, you'll get to La Unión Veinte de Junio. There used to be a village there but it was abandoned about eight years ago. Then you'll come to Altamira, cross Blengio Creek, and head on to Aguada Jerusalem."

"I heard there was someone still living in Altamira," I remarked.

"Not any more. There used to be a *central chiclera* there, and after it was abandoned Maudaleno Milán lived there with a Guatemalan friend of his for many years. But it must be less than a month ago that he was killed. Some illegal Guatemalan immigrants, when they got there, found him dead in his hammock. His body was already decomposing, and they also found his horses, which had died of thirst. They notified some peo-

Figure 17.1. Pepe Orta and Raymundo Sandoval (*first and third from left*) with two more associates in front of an abandoned house in Altamira.

ple in Once de Mayo, who came and buried the man. His Guatemalan friend disappeared without a trace. Some suspect that they got into a fight, others say it was revenge for betraying a marijuana grower. Still others say that he was involved in shady business himself. Yes, we know he was digging around in the ruins. Maybe he had problems with antiquities traffickers or competitors."

We reached Altamira around midday: two dilapidated houses made of wooden planks, still surrounded by the skeletons of dead animals. We arrived at Blengio Creek early enough in the afternoon to set up camp in daylight.

Blengio is one of the rare surface waterways that do not dry up in the dry season. However, it is not continuous; it vanishes at several points only to reappear on the surface a few kilometers away. The trail we took crossed the creek at a point where the water was pretty deep. This made it the ideal location for a campsite. The water had a high mineral content and was not exactly potable, but it was more than clean enough for personal hygiene.

The following day one of the workers remained at camp to cook and look after our stuff—the trail was reasonably passable, and there was a chance that someone might wander around and be tempted by a piece of our equipment. The rest of us headed south at dawn. In a few hours we reached an intersection with a westbound trail: on a tree next to the crossroads we could make out an inscription carved many years ago and now barely visible: "Aguada Jerusalén."

The trail was badly overgrown; clearly it had not been used for a long time, but luckily the aguada was not far. It was dried out, vindicating our decision to set up camp on the banks of the Blengio. To the south of the aguada was an expansive flat area bereft of large trees: on the ground were the remains of iron kettles, glasses, and cans, indicating that a chiclero camp had once been there.

None of our companions knew exactly where the ruins were supposed to be, but they were convinced it would not be difficult to find them. They must be in the area, and these guys were experts in forest exploration (or so they thought). We agreed to split up and reconvene at the aguada in an hour or two. But when we met again, I realized the veracity of Karl Ruppert's words concerning his search for another site: "The futility of

Figure 17.2. A water cistern (*chultun*) dug into bedrock.

scouring the bush for ruins heard of but not definitely known to any members of the party was soon apparent."[1]

The faces of our companions revealed exhaustion and disappointment —as did mine. But there was another solution: I would enter Ruppert's Balakbal coordinates into my GPS, and perhaps they would lead us in the right direction.

The device led us west of the aguada. We came across a few small mounds. Here and there we found a *chultun*, a water cistern carved into rock, but such remains of ancient life are abundant everywhere and are not necessarily a sign of a major city nearby. The surprise was sudden: in the dark of the tall forest, the ruins of a long building about twenty meters tall suddenly appeared before our eyes. I took off my backpack and pulled out a copy of Ruppert's plan of Balakbal: there was a long structure drawn on the eastern side—and we were coming in from the east—which bordered a plaza with a large pyramid to the west. We burst forward, hurried around the northern side of the long structure, and entered a completely flat space that might once have been a plaza. The vegetation was so thick we could see barely a few meters ahead of us, but after just a few steps west we gazed on a massive pyramidal ruin over twenty meters tall and completely overgrown. We quickly checked the surroundings; a comparison of the layout of the buildings with Ruppert's plan confirmed that we were indeed in Balakbal.

The GPS reading showed that the main pyramid was no more than four hundred meters east of Ruppert's coordinates. Luckily, we were coming from the east and therefore ran into the ruins before reaching Ruppert's point. If we had approached from the other side, I am not sure our quest would have been successful. As we also learned on several subsequent occasions, in the jungle a small mistake can lead to a big problem.

Ruppert's coordinates were remarkably accurate considering the circumstances and the instruments available at the time. Karl Ruppert had a cartographer on his expeditions, who determined the geographical coordinates of major archaeological sites by means of astronomical observations, typically by measuring the position of the North Star or the sun. Not only was this a time-consuming endeavor; an error of only one arc

---

1. Karl Ruppert and John H. Denison Jr., *Archaeological Reconnaissance in Campeche, Quintana Roo, and Peten,* Carnegie Institution of Washington Publication 543 (Washington, DC: Carnegie Institution, 1943), 29.

Figure 17.3. Ruins of a building with a corbel vault in Balakbal.

minute, which was easy to make when reading angles on the theodolites of the time, meant an error of one nautical mile, or almost two kilometers, when determining latitude! It is therefore no surprise that the errors in the coordinates of Ruppert's other sites are larger.

The precision with which Ruppert's expeditions did their job is nevertheless admirable and is also evidenced by their site maps, including that of Balakbal. Unfortunately, this site had also been visited by looters. Of the five stelae Ruppert described, we saw only four, with the remains of carved images and hieroglyphs still visible. There was one in the main plaza and two in a smaller building west of the tallest pyramid: one had been moved by the looters, but the other was still leaning against a wall in exactly the same position as Karl Ruppert had photographed it. In the plaza south of the large pyramid there was another similar albeit smaller structure in whose northern slope looters had dug a deep trench; they had shoved Stela 5, the best-preserved monument in Balakbal, from the top of the building—where Ruppert's expedition had seen it—down the southern slope, letting it slide almost all the way down. The enormous quantities of stones they dug out of the trench were piled up in the plaza, precisely where Ruppert's plans indicated another stela should be. They must have left it there and covered it: stelae were obviously of no interest to them if they left behind even the best specimen. Lucky for us! Stela 5 contains a well-preserved inscription from the early fifth century that mentions a ruler who died in AD 406, just twenty-nine days before the twentieth anniversary of his rule.

The successful search for Balakbal with the help of Ruppert's coordinates encouraged us to try to find Altamira, another equally important site that his expedition discovered in 1933. Nobody knew anything about its location or state, and as it turned out, Ruppert's information was not so accurate this time.

From the camp along the Blengio we followed the trail back to the abandoned houses in Altamira. Karl Ruppert mentioned that the ruins were most easily reached from the Altamira camp by proceeding north along the trail for about an hour, then to the left through the bush for fifteen or twenty minutes. Furthermore, his map marks the Altamira camp as being 1,500 meters from the site at a bearing of S32°20'E, meaning southeast. This information clearly shows that Ruppert's expedition found the ruins northwest of the Altamira camp, but it does not coincide with the coordinates, which correspond to a spot approximately 1,100 meters southwest of the camp. The most likely explanation was an error in the coordinates, so we headed north along the trail. After about two kilometers we arrived at a ruin with multiple exposed walls; we had already seen it on arrival, but it was only now that we realized that Ruppert's expedition had already recorded it. Its features corresponded to the description, ground plan, and frontal view in his book. Its location on the western side of the trail from Altamira to the abandoned settlement of Las Delicias also corresponded to Ruppert's description: it was obvious that the present-day dirt track coincides exactly with the old mule trail that Ruppert's expedition took. We veered off the trail by the building and inspected the area to the west, but all we found were smaller mounds here and there. Mundo would occasionally climb a tree to look around, but he did not notice anything conspicuous in the surrounding landscape.

That was when I recalled a local in Once de Mayo mentioning larger ruins near the abandoned village of La Unión Veinte de Junio. He even said there were stelae as well. We certainly intended to find this site, but it had not occurred to me before that it might be Altamira: La Unión Veinte de Junio, abandoned for about eight years, was only two kilometers to the north.

We headed out there, and Mundo and I tried to reconstruct what the man in Once de Mayo had told us: you have to go through the abandoned settlement past the aguada, cross a meadow, and turn left into the forest.

Leaving the truck on the trail, we walked past the dilapidated houses of the abandoned village toward the aguada, which was almost completely dry, and crossed through a patch of brush before arriving at an area covered in tall grass. The ruins were supposed to be in the forest to the left, which was exactly where we headed. But "left into the forest" was a rather vague instruction. That man may have come to the meadow from another direction, meaning that his "left" may have been very different from ours. In any case, we did not find anything in that forest. In many places, the forest we were crisscrossing turned into *acahual*, secondary vegetation that grows in a few years on abandoned fields. Because this vegetation is low, the sun scorches mercilessly through it, and since it is also dense, it does not allow one to see much beyond the tip of the machete cutting through it, making progress excruciatingly slow. Whenever Mundo found a tall enough tree, he climbed it to look around for any elevation that might have something suspicious sticking out of it: as we know, Maya cities were typically built on higher ground.

Although exhausted, we persevered until late afternoon before we finally decided to cease our fruitless wandering and return. Fortunately I had taken the coordinates of our vehicle: we had covered so much ground in various directions that we could only guess which way to return. Without technical assistance, the most reliable solution would have been to navigate by means of the setting sun and head east, which would surely have led us to the trail we had arrived on. However, this would have required a huge detour. With GPS we were able to return in pretty much a straight line.

As we were heading back, a clearing shimmered in the sun to the left of us—the pasture we had crossed earlier in who knows which direction. But just moments later I saw a fairly large and long ruin to the right, bigger than any other we had seen that day. Even though we were tired, we approached it, walked around, and . . .

This is where the *reinado* started! Beyond the ruin were densely scattered buildings of increasing size, and soon we also gazed on the first stela. A cursory comparison with Ruppert's plan of Altamira sufficed to confirm that we were on the western edge of the ancient city, but we did not have time to do anything more that day. The sun was just setting and night would fall—as it does everywhere at these tropical latitudes—within just half an hour. Finding a way through the forest by flashlight is as slow as it is disagreeable.

The following day we surveyed the entire architectural complex. Looters' trenches were agape in many buildings, but luckily all sixteen stelae that Ruppert's expedition had located were still there, probably because their reliefs were barely discernible. The entire main plaza was overgrown with *acahual*: the flat square space, measuring almost a hectare, was an ideal location for the field that had been there some years ago. As we looked around we realized that with a bit of bad luck we could have entered from one corner of the plaza, crossed it diagonally, and then exited the opposite corner without even noticing that we were right in the middle of the ancient city: some buildings were far enough apart that they could not be discerned through the dense vegetation.

Our rediscovery of Altamira was more about good fortune than smarts. The site was more than four kilometers north of the coordinates provided by Ruppert and around three and a half kilometers northwest of the old Altamira camp.

18

Altar of the Kings

It had come to our attention back in 1996 that there was a gigantic complex of ruins close to Ley de Fomento Agropecuario and that there was also a stela there, but Avelino Díaz López, the owner of the land, had absolutely refused to take us there. Like many of his fellow villagers, Don Avelino had moved here from the Chiapas highlands. He was a Chol and spoke only broken Spanish. But this was not the sole reason it was difficult to communicate with him: the indigenous Chol are known for being reticent and distrustful, no doubt at least in part because of the repression and injustice they have suffered over the last few centuries, although their reserved demeanor may also be attributed to the autarkic nature of their communities, which live isolated in the remote highlands. The locals in the northern Yucatán Peninsula, where indigenous people also make up a significant share of the population, are very different. They are more gregarious and amiable, even though they have shared the fate of all indigenous peoples in the Americas.

We have often encountered such unwillingness to cooperate, sometimes because the ruins were being looted and the locals disliked having "competition," but more often because farmers feared that the state might confiscate land containing archaeological remains. I have always tried to explain that Mexican legislation is not so arbitrary and that our work would not have such negative consequences. But actions speak louder than words. In 1998, when we brought the stelae from the nearby site to Los Alacranes, the venture was sufficiently complex and impressive for word about it to spread far and wide. The people realized that our discovery of the stelae two years earlier had not caused them any harm. On the contrary, instead of the state taking something away, it had even organized the display of both monuments in their village! Naturally, they were proud of that, and many saw the tourism potential of the results of this project.

As a consequence, Don Avelino, whom I visited again in 1998, had changed his attitude as well, and he took us to his ruins. The site was indeed large. The stela in the main plaza was in two pieces and there was a cut in the lower part, the result of sawing, but fortunately the looters had not finished the job. On the front side of both fragments was a well-preserved relief of a sitting ruler, while the back contained a hieroglyphic inscription. That year my colleague Vicente and I were so busy with the Los Alacranes salvaging operation that we took only a cursory tour of the

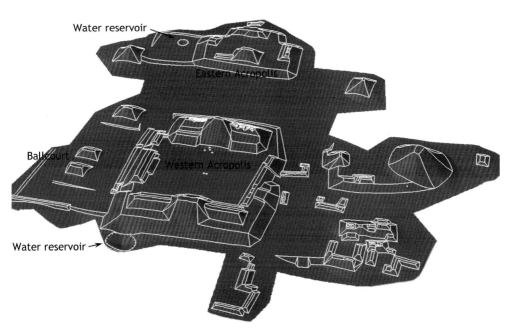

Figure 18.1. The main complex of Altar de los Reyes (3-D rendering by Tomaž Podobnikar).

site. It was not until 2002 that Pepe Orta and I decided to take a closer look and map it.

Site mapping invariably brings surprises. The complex of ruins is always larger and takes more time to survey than we initially think it will, and we always find things we missed on our first inspection. This turned out to be just such a case.

The most important buildings of the ancient urban center are on two acropolises, which are surrounded by multiple smaller structures. The stela we saw in 1998 lies on the western acropolis, at the foot of a large building on the eastern side of a large plaza. There are also two cylindrical altars in the immediate vicinity. North of the western acropolis we found the remains of a ball court, which, like the stela, revealed that the ancient city enjoyed a high status in the regional hierarchy. A large sunken area adjacent to the northwestern corner of the western acropolis must have been a water reservoir of the kind often found in Maya cities. A smaller basin gaping in the plaza of the eastern acropolis must have had the same function. Don Avelino, who naturally knew his property well, told us that none of these depressions held water for long, but he said there was a similar one among the smaller buildings southwest of the urban core that held water until March, deep into the dry season.

At the foot of the largest pyramid, which was about twenty meters tall and located on the southern end of the central part of the ancient city, we found a fragment of a stela with a well-preserved relief decoration. Later, as we were clearing the undergrowth on the western acropolis, I noticed a relatively large stone sticking out of the ground in the middle of the plaza. The plazas of Maya cities were smooth surfaces leveled with finely crushed rocks and finished with a layer of stucco, which made the presence of a large stone suspicious. I asked some workers to remove the leaves and topsoil covering it. While they were cleaning up the rock, I was near where Pepe was just setting up the total station; suddenly, elated screams pierced the bush from the center of the plaza. I ran there and found that the men had uncovered a significant portion of a fragment of a round altar. There were several well-preserved hieroglyphic blocks on the side, and upon closer examination I was stunned.

"Emblem glyphs! And excellently preserved! Here's Tikal, Palenque, and here's Calakmul."

So-called emblem glyphs are composed of a distinct prefix, which is always the same and reads *k'ujul ajaw* (holy lord), representing the con-

Figure 18.2. Transporting a large piece of the altar with emblem glyphs was not a walk in the park.

ventional royal title, followed by a variable element that designates the name of the state or the dynasty that ruled it. The pronunciation of some of these names remains a mystery, but for the majority we know which states or cities they refer to.

Next to this fragment was another big piece of altar, and when we uncovered more of it two more emblem glyphs appeared. This was obviously a very important find. The altar was in pieces and there were probably other, smaller fragments nearby. Perhaps it would be possible to reassemble the altar and its inscription. I decided to find all the fragments and transfer them to Ley de Fomento Agropecuario. This meant performing a small-scale excavation and precisely documenting the position of all the pieces.

At the time, Daniel Juárez Cossío, an INAH archaeologist and an old friend, and Adrián Baker Pedroza, a final-year archaeology student, were working not far from us. In our project they had taken on the task of cleaning up some fresh looters' trenches at the Mucaancah site, which we had discovered in 1996, recording any significant archaeological data and restoring the stability of the damaged buildings with emergency repairs. When I notified them of our find, they interrupted their work at

Mucaancah and relocated to our site to excavate the altar area. All the fragments they found were transferred to Ley de Fomento Agropecuario. The villagers emptied a shack in which we placed the piece of the stela we had found at the foot of the largest pyramid and all the fragments of the altar with the hieroglyphs. We made a frame with wooden boards and filled it with sand to create a surface on which Daniel and Adrián

Figure 18.3. The side of the altar from Altar de los Reyes contains impeccably preserved emblem glyphs that refer to Tikal, Palenque, Edzná, and Motul de San José.

could complete the toilsome work of piecing the fragments together. Even though they had no clue what the final picture should look like, they still managed to assemble most of the altar, which was eighty-five centimeters in diameter, from the available pieces.

On the top surface the outlines of a sitting person were discernible, but what really kindled our interest was the inscription on the side. Although it was impossible to put all the pieces together, it was clear from the preserved fragments that the altar had at least nine emblem glyphs, of which five were perfectly legible. They corresponded to the ancient seats of power that we presently know as the archaeological sites of Calakmul, Palenque, Tikal, Edzná, and Motul de San José.

This was an unprecedented find! Emblem glyphs appear in Maya inscriptions frequently, but they are typically isolated. Only two monuments with multiple glyphs like this had previously been discovered, Stela A from Copán in Honduras and Stela 10 from Ceibal in Guatemala, but they contained only four glyphs each, whereas this one had nine, perhaps even thirteen, as our epigrapher Nikolai Grube surmised. The inscription was not perfectly preserved, which is why we do not know its exact meaning. But since the emblem glyphs were accompanied by mention of "royal thrones," they are a clear reference to the seats of rulers that were partic-

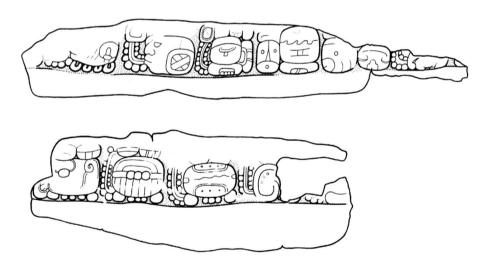

Figure 18.4. Emblem glyphs of Edzná, Motul de San José (*above*), Calakmul, Tikal, and Palenque (*below*) on the altar from Altar de los Reyes (drawing by Nikolai Grube).

ularly important for the city we were exploring. In addition to Calakmul, which is about forty kilometers west, and Tikal, about ninety kilometers away in neighboring Guatemala, it lists several other important centers of the Classic period. The mention of cities such as Palenque (about three hundred kilometers southwest) and Edzná (about two hundred kilometers northwest) are particularly intriguing in that they indicate the geographical range of actual connections, or at least the extent to which our city was aware of other Maya states. Considering that emblem glyphs designate the rulers of states or dynasties, and because there were so many on this altar, I named the archaeological site Altar de los Reyes (Altar of the Kings).

Don Avelino and his son Felipe wanted to show us some other ruins nearby. They had seen them in the forest years before, but this time they simply could not find their way. As we were scouring the area, Avelino suddenly took the gun from his shoulder and, in consternation, started scanning in all directions.

"Look, the robbers who are hiding camped here."

He pointed to a freshly cleared area with some trash. He was referring to some road bandits that had recently been making attacks around El Sacrificio, a village south of Ley de Fomento. Avelino's vigilance was not exaggerated: the bandits were armed. We moved on carefully, but our anxiety evaporated when a large pyramid appeared before our eyes. It rose over a small plaza surrounded by several more buildings built on a platform that occupied a leveled space on the slope of a natural elevation. At the top of the hill we found another group of buildings. This must have been part of Altar de los Reyes, whose urban center was less than a kilometer northwest.

When I dropped by the commander of the Xpujil barracks at the end of the season, he seemed very satisfied.

"We caught the bandits attacking people on the road at El Sacrificio."

"But you had to hand them over to the civilian authorities?"

"Yes, yes," Lieutenant Colonel García Melgar retorted. "But they aren't going to get off easy, they shot at my troops. Attacking the federal army is a serious matter."

I was relieved as well. We would be taking that road quite a few times in the future.

19

Forgotten

In 2004 I wanted to continue fieldwork in the southern part of the Cal-akmul Biosphere. Previous experience suggested that one vehicle was not enough in that remote area if the work was to be done efficiently and effectively. We had to transport all the equipment as well as food, water, gasoline, and of course workers. The one truck we had used in the past could carry only such a small load that we often had to interrupt our work in order to buy provisions. The INAH loaned me a vehicle again, the trusty gray Dodge pickup we had used the previous season, which was in pretty bad shape now. Using project funds—this survey was financed by the National Geographic Society—and with the help of a friend in the United States, I bought a second-hand GMC pickup with all-wheel drive and imported it to Mexico. *La gris* (gray) and *la blanca* (white) would become the standard sobriquets we came to use for the two vehicles. The INAH also loaned me a portable generator, which was essential for en-suring uninterrupted use of cameras, satellite phones, and the electronic theodolite.

Almost none of my previous collaborators were able to join me, be-cause they had other engagements; the only one to respond to my invi-tation was Adrián Baker Pedroza, who had turned out to be an excellent field worker in 2002 and was capable of any kind of work, especially photo documentation, which he was now in charge of again. Despite his nickname of Vaquero (Cowboy), which people around him used much more often than his real name, he did not bring a cow or horse; he came with his jeep, which, truth be told, was much handier than a beast of burden. On advice from a friend in Mexico City, we were also joined by Atasta Flores Esquivel, a final-year archaeology student who had good knowledge of the Maya and of fieldwork, especially mapping. In Campeche I found Raymundo González Heredia, who worked at the university there and had been involved in surveying around Calakmul for several years.

Raymundo suggested we first stop in Centenario, a village about fifty kilometers east of the city of Escárcega on the road to Chetumal, where he knew a few people. We managed to hire some locals who had been engaged in logging in the biosphere and knew their way around the forest, although they did not know of any archaeological sites. They proposed that we drive to Constitución, a village twenty-five kilometers to the east, and find a man named Ciriaco, who they said was a chiclero and knew the forest well—and must also know about some ruins.

Thus we headed to Constitución, where the locals showed us to a house on the northern edge of the village. In response to our greeting, a bare-chested, black-haired, tanned man of around fifty emerged from the house with a stern expression on his face. Raymundo and I explained our intentions. Ciriaco Requena Sandoval said he had indeed done a lot of work in the biosphere and knew about ruins not far from Villahermosa, an old chiclero center in the south of the biosphere. He talked slowly, judiciously, and cautiously. Actually, he looked distrustful and exhibited no interest in working with us. When we started talking about pay, he simply said he had enough work in the village for that kind of money, as he was in demand for building wooden houses and other jobs. But something in his words and the questions he asked made it clear that he really knew the jungle well, was aware of the potential problems, and was adept at solving them. I sensed I had to win him over. When I offered him higher pay and added that a bonus based on individual performance was also possible, he gave in. We agreed to get all the equipment ready and head out in two days.

Later I would realize that this moment was the beginning of a close and genuine friendship that has persisted to this day. Of all the locals I have come to know, Ciriaco Requena is undoubtedly the greatest expert on trees,

Figure 19.1. The southern facade of one of the two major buildings in Olvidado, overlooking the trail from Buenfil to Villahermosa.

animals, jungle conditions, and the skills required to survive and work in a tropical rainforest. He is reliable, shrewd, resourceful, and efficient.

Taking the main road, we drove from Constitución east to Conhuás, before turning south on the only paved road leading to the heart of the biosphere. The road had been built years before for the sole purpose of providing visitors access to the archaeological site of Calakmul, about sixty kilometers away. Close to kilometer 50, where there are two half-demolished shacks east of the road, the remains of an abandoned camp named Central Buenfil, we turned left onto the dirt trail going south.

I knew the way to Villahermosa. We had arrived there in 2002 and found two not particularly large sites east of the abandoned camp. The army had an outpost there, years after the chicleros had left. In the 1990s the administration of the biosphere had started to build a research center of sorts there; they built a few houses but never completed the work. The dirt trail was occasionally used by the biosphere rangers and the army, which meant there were no major obstacles on it, but progress was still excruciatingly slow. The trucks delivering construction material to Villahermosa years before had made huge potholes, and in many places there were large rocks protruding from the ground, which had to be carefully surmounted. On one of them I had crushed the differential housing two years before, draining out the oil, and even the soldiers who chanced to drive by could not help us. Fortunately, it was not the differential on the main drive that was broken, but rather the one on the front axle, used when four-wheel drive was activated; since the terrain was dry, we could continue without it.

Figure 19.2. The remains of stucco decorations on the roof comb on the northern side of the second major building in Olvidado.

After two hours of driving, the trail turned east, and in a few kilometers, a building about ten meters tall appeared on the left, pretty badly damaged but still impressive, with a tall roof comb—a decorative wall punctured with narrow rectangular portholes. We had stopped here back in 2002 because I wanted to verify a report by a group of Mexican archaeologists from several years before that had identified the ruins as Pared de los Reyes, a site that Cyrus Lundell and Karl Ruppert had visited in the 1930s. I had thought it strange that both Lundell and Ruppert said they had headed west and northwest from Villahermosa, whereas the ruins by the trail were about ten kilometers north of Villahermosa, and no less than thirteen kilometers east of the coordinates provided by Ruppert for Pared de los Reyes. After inspecting the surroundings, we realized that this was a significant complex of ruins. Just a few dozen meters from the one adjacent to the trail, we found another, very similar building; its roof comb boasted the remains of human figures and grotesque masks made in stucco, similar to those mentioned by Lundell and Ruppert. Nevertheless, we could tell that neither the position nor the look of the buildings corresponded to Ruppert's photographs and map of Pared de los Reyes.

This, therefore, was clearly another site. I remembered that *Archaeological Sites in the Maya Area*, a map made by the Middle American Research Institute of Tulane University in New Orleans in 1940, recorded a site called Olvidado (Forgotten); the file card for the site states that Lundell had reported it without naming it in a paper published in 1933.[1] Lundell says that after discovering Calakmul at the end of 1931, his expedition headed to Central Buenfil, resupplied, and on the morning of January 3, headed south. He continues:

> All that morning we struggled in deep mud, and early in the afternoon, after again encountering extensive mounds, we turned east, following a very torturous trail along what had been the shore of the extinct Calakmul lake. The most interesting ruined structure beside this trail is a massive wall standing three stories on top of a long low-terraced mound. The upper two stories have narrow window-like openings similar to those in the "Paloma" structure at Uxmal.

---

1. Cyrus Lundell, "Archaeological Discoveries in the Maya Area," *Proceedings of the American Philosophical Society* 72, no. 3 (1933): 158.

It seems that the present-day dirt trail to Villahermosa still follows the old mule trail that Lundell took: starting at the Buenfil camp, it goes south, and when it reaches Bajo El Laberinto, it veers east along the northeastern edge of this expansive basin, which stretches from Villahermosa all the way northwest to Calakmul, and which Lundell thought was the remains of an ancient lake (perhaps he was right; studies have shown at least some bajo wetlands used to be lakes). Moreover, the features of the building next to the trail correspond very well to Lundell's description: the eaves completing the bottom of the southern facade and the two rows of openings in the roof comb give the impression of three floors and are reminiscent of the El Palomar structure in Uxmal, an important Late Classic site in the state of Yucatán in the northern peninsula.

So this was Olvidado, but the mystery of where Pared de los Reyes was remained unresolved in 2002. This was what we wanted to ascertain this season.

20

Where Is Pared de los Reyes?

The dirt trail once again turned south soon after we left Olvidado behind us. The terrain descended into Bajo El Laberinto, which was dry and did not contain any obstacles. After a few kilometers of dense brush and low trees, we passed over the final modest elevation before driving into a wide-open grassy space late in the afternoon—the old landing strip of the Villahermosa camp.

The ride from Buenfil to Villahermosa lasted just over four hours. My record for this forty-kilometer route, which I have taken many times, is three hours and ten minutes, a time achieved only under ideal conditions —when the vehicle was not overloaded and there were no impediments on the road, circumstances that were very rare indeed.

Villahermosa used to be an important *central chiclera*, a collection center for chicle and a place where the chicleros could resupply. Traders would airlift the precious raw material using not just one but two landing strips, cut into the jungle like a cross. The present-day condition of Villahermosa hardly does justice to its name, which literally means "nice little town." The landing strips are overgrown with tall grass and brush. Only one old house remains standing, probably because it is partially built of stone, but even that structure is severely dilapidated. The unfinished buildings of the ill-fated research center conceived years ago still rise from the brush, painful reminders of a misguided investment. Scattered around them are metal and plastic barrels, petrified cement bags, wooden boards, and similar materials, witnesses to a sudden cessation of activity.

Despite that, Villahermosa was a propitious place for us. There is an aguada nearby that rarely dries out. We made ourselves comfortable in the buildings, which saved us the time it would otherwise have taken to set up camp. We also found the lid of a metal barrel that was perfect for baking tortillas.

The following morning I instructed Ciriaco to take two workers and check the condition of the dirt trail that used to connect Villahermosa with La Esperanza, another camp about seventy kilometers northwest. It was along this trail that major ruins Ciriaco knew of were supposed to be, not far from Villahermosa. I reminded him that we were going to drive there, so he should be careful not to cut the brush too low since the stubs could puncture the tires. He interrupted me before I could finish.

"No, no, we're going to cut high enough, twenty or thirty centimeters, so that the wheels bend the stubble."

I immediately got the feeling that Ciriaco was an expert, although at that time I was yet to comprehend just how good he really was.

The rest of us arranged the camp. We grabbed one of the large plastic barrels found in Villahermosa, put it on the truck, drove to the aguada, and filled it up with water. On our way west we would now be better provisioned: our water supply had previously been limited to two fifty-liter canisters. Our oldest worker, Don Germán, was in charge of keeping the camp in good order and preparing the food.

Ciriaco and his team returned in the evening. Everyone was visibly exhausted—no wonder, the day had been very hot—but Ciriaco walked up to me immediately to report on the work they had done. He managed to utter only a few words before I interrupted him.

"Later. Have a drink first and eat up, we'll talk later."

He nodded and stopped talking, his look utterly impassive, and it was not until later that I came to surmise that this was the exact moment his attitude toward me changed and became less reserved. This was probably when he realized for the first time that in our team, every individual's basic needs came first: the work we were there to perform was important, but not more important than the people doing it. There were many things we lacked on our expeditions, but everything we did have was available to everyone: coffee, rum, sweets, or whatever else. The principle I tried to apply was to be rational in consumption, but as long as we had supplies, everyone shared them, just as everyone shared all efforts, nuisances, and deprivations.

After dinner we sat around the campfire and Ciriaco said there would be no problems the first few kilometers, but after that the trail was pretty badly overgrown. At the junction where a smaller dirt trail forked southwest off the main road, which ran northwest, they took the left fork and arrived at Aguada La Fama. I had told Ciriaco that this aguada was an important reference point for us: Karl Ruppert mentions that Pared de los Reyes, which I was trying to find, was northwest of the La Fama camp.

The following day we set off northwest on the trail from Villahermosa with all our vehicles and equipment. After clearing five kilometers, we found a good place to camp among some tall trees in the late afternoon. From that point on the terrain started to descend into a densely overgrown bajo, where low and thorny bushes made it an inhospitable place to camp, and anyway we were less than a kilometer from the ruins that Ciriaco knew of.

When we crossed the bajo the following morning the terrain gradually changed, as the low brush gave way on higher ground to a *ramonal*, a forest with tall trees dominated by the species *ramón*.[1] The tree has tasty fruit and, interestingly, the ruins of Maya cities are typically on ground now covered in a *ramonal*. There must be a connection between the properties of the soil suitable for these trees and the higher ground that the Maya preferred for their settlements.

Ruppert's expeditions had used only the narrow mule trails created by the chicleros. In the second half of the twentieth century, when logging became more important than the collection of chicle, logging trails were bulldozed through the forest to accommodate trucks, and the trail we were on used to serve that very purpose. The machine that created it bulldozed right through the center of an ancient Maya city. After noting some ruins on the left and right, we walked up a steep incline, with the trail deepening into a half-pipe of sorts, and on both sides we saw the cross section of the pavement of an ancient plaza: layers of small stones covered in a thick layer of stucco.

---

1. *Brosimum alicastrum.*

Figure 20.1. The trail cut through the ancient city we named Yaxnohcah exposed a cross section of the stuccoed floor of a plaza and of a ruined building on top of it.

When the ground became flat again, Ciriaco gestured to the right: "Here it is." We stopped. Only a few meters away we could see the foot and a portion of the slope of a giant mound among the trees. It was so densely overgrown that even from quite close we could not estimate the extent or height of the building. We ascended the southern slope and reached a large platform featuring the protruding ruins of three smaller buildings: a larger one on the northern edge and two smaller ones on the eastern and western sides. We realized that we were standing atop a mighty truncated pyramid, a slight bulge along the southern slope of the ruin suggesting that this used to be the staircase leading to the top platform, where there were three temples. A triadic group! Buildings with such configurations were fashionable mostly in the Late Preclassic period, between the third century BC and third century AD. They are common in the north of neighboring Guatemala, in Petén Department, which is quite well researched archaeologically. It was there that the first great Maya cities were built, foremost among them Tintal, Nakbé, and El Mirador.

A quick survey of the area around the pyramid revealed that buildings of significant size continued in all directions. The pyramid with the triadic group suggested that we were in the middle of an important Preclassic center whose size and characteristics would have to be studied. I entrusted the job to Atasta and Vaquero, while Ciriaco, Raymundo, and I continued on the trail northwest. Our aim was to find Pared de los Reyes, the site that Lundell's and Ruppert's information indicated had to be just a few kilometers away.

Cyrus Lundell reports that his expedition left Villahermosa at dawn on January 9, 1932, and took the route leading west along the southwestern edge of what used to be the Calakmul lake (Bajo El Laberinto). After passing the abandoned camp of La Fama, where chicleros from Campeche and Guatemala had engaged in a knife and gun fight in 1929, they arrived at what Lundell described as one of the most interesting Maya ruins,

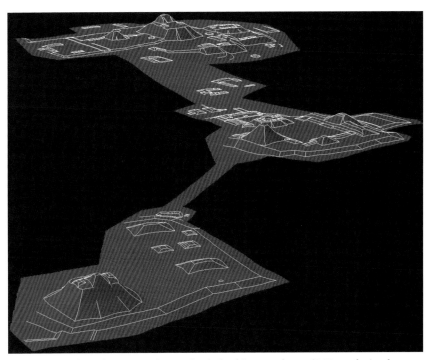

Figure 20.2. The urban core of Yaxnohcah, looking northeast (3-D rendering by Tomaž Podobnikar).

adorned in human figures made in stucco with crown-like turbans, thus earning the site the name Pared de los Reyes (Wall of the Kings).

Subsequently, in 1934, Karl Ruppert's expedition visited Pared de los Reyes. His information on the location of the site coincides with Lundell's but is more complete. Ruppert says that they rode their mules northwest from La Fama and arrived at Aguada Unión after two hours, with Pared de los Reyes a ten- to fifteen-minute walk northwest from the aguada.

Ciriaco and others we had already talked to knew the old camp and aguada of La Fama, but nobody had heard of a camp or aguada called Unión. This time we had a laptop with us with maps we had downloaded from the website of the National Commission for the Knowledge and Use of Biodiversity (Comisión Nacional para el Conocimiento y Uso de la Biodiversidad), a public institute that mapped the roads, aguadas, vegetation, and other natural elements in the Calakmul Biosphere using aerial photographs. On this map we located Aguada La Fama, where Ciriaco and his two helpers had arrived two days before, as well as an aguada 6.5 kilometers northwest of La Fama as the crow flies, a distance that—considering the meandering mule trails—corresponded pretty well to the two-hour trip mentioned by Ruppert. We were also able to determine that the aguada was 2.3 kilometers east of Ruppert's coordinates for Pared de los Reyes, within the margin of error typical of the coordinates Ruppert provided for various sites. It was therefore very likely that this was Aguada Unión.

To get there, we entered the coordinates into the GPS device and first followed the abandoned dirt trail northwest before turning right at an intersection where a second, even more overgrown trail led north. Along the way, a small quarry caught our attention: on a few square meters rocks were protruding from the ground with several smoothly cut vertical surfaces. Such quarries are very common near Maya settlements, and this one lifted our hopes that we were on the right track: Ruppert reports that his expedition encountered a quarry while walking to Aguada Unión.

Clearing the path was so exhausting that we did not get to the aguada before late afternoon; it was dry and overgrown with tall grass. We had to turn around immediately because we had to walk eight kilometers back to camp. By the time we returned, it was pitch black and we were completely exhausted. Coming at the start of the season, when we still lacked the necessary physical conditioning, this march had been exacting. A few sips of whiskey helped us recover, but Atasta and Vaquero also lifted our spirits: in their survey of the terrain south of the pyramid next to the trail

Figure 20.3. The Maya sourced the material for their buildings from limestone bedrock, which is often close to the surface. Quarries of various sizes are found within or near many archaeological sites. The quarry in this photo offered a ray of hope during our first quest to find Pared de los Reyes.

they had encountered groups of large buildings scattered over quite an extensive area. Even though they could not yet determine how large the site was, it was clear that this was a significant center. This was the first major find of the season, and we came up with the name Yaxnohcah (First Big City). We decided to inspect it more closely while mapping during the second part of the season; for now we would focus on finding Pared de los Reyes.

After dinner we lingered around the fire. There were no mosquitoes, the evening was practically romantic, and Ciriaco opened up for the first time. He said he was from Guatemala and had arrived in Mexico as a young chiclero. Even today the border cutting across these uninhabited forests is no hurdle, but in the past chicleros would cross it regularly; there was forest on both sides, people spoke the same language, and they were also after the same precious substance. One day Ciriaco came to Villahermosa to buy some basic provisions. Even though the law of the jungle applied everywhere and there were fights and murders, he found this side of the border more peaceful, so he stayed. Chicle buyers were not interested in where people came from; they just wanted good workers. We listened intently to Ciriaco's story as the conversation inevitably touched on looting, a practice few chicleros shied away from. He said he had never done any on the Mexican side, but back in Guatemala he had quite often. He spoke of different sites he had "worked" on, about how he dug the trenches, the objects he found, the buyers, and the money, which was not bad but was gone as soon as he made it. Aside from the illegality of what he had been doing, he was an admirable professional. Of all the locals I got to know, Ciriaco was the only one to not mince words when talking about such matters. He knew he could not be prosecuted; no one had anything on him. Nevertheless, it seemed that he was starting to trust us—and as he would later show on numerous occasions, he was a trustworthy person himself.

In the middle of the night we were awoken by a heavy storm. Since we had nothing to protect our hammocks, we were soaking wet by morning. We tried to warm up around the fire and dry our things. Ciriaco reminded us that we had to get a plastic tarp for the next trip. The chicleros spent several days or even weeks in each camp and made shelters with thatched palm roofs, but for us that did not make sense given how often we moved camp.

We did not want to expend too much energy trying to find Pared de los Reyes, so Raymundo, Atasta, Vaquero, Ciriaco, and I took the basic equipment and camped out at the aguada we had found the day before. Because it was dried out, it was agreed that the other workers would remain at the original camp and bring us water every day.

Over the next three days we traversed the area northwest of the aguada. We found a bunch of smaller ruins, a few quarries, and even the remains of a two-meter-wide paved causeway raised up to a meter and a half above the surrounding terrain. Such roads, known by their Mayan name sacbé (white way), connected settlements as well as individual architectural groups within cities. Although the Maya did not use the wheel—not even for making pottery—and did not have carriages, such paths or roads, some of which were impressive structures, made it much easier to navigate over the bajos, the low-lying, densely overgrown basins that turned to marsh in the wet season. Our sacbé, which was around eight hundred meters long, connected a larger group of collapsed buildings with two quarries to the south.

Ciriaco had the opportunity to show off the whole range of his abilities. One afternoon, when we ran out of water far from camp, he diligently studied the trees and eventually found what he was looking for: *álamo*, a kind of poplar with a wide root base. He selected a root that was almost entirely exposed on the surface, removed some of the soil, and cut it off with two quick swings of his machete: the two-meter section of root produced about a glassful of whitish but life-saving liquid. This time there were enough roots for everyone to quench their thirst, but overall there

Figure 20.4. The roots of some tree species contain sufficient water in an emergency.

Figure 20.5. Oropendola nests.

are few tree species—just two more come to mind, *amapola* and *matapalo*[2] —that retain water in their roots.

On another occasion, as Vaquero and Atasta were making drawings of a smaller group of ruins, Ciriaco and I were examining terrain west of our makeshift camp when we heard the chirping of oropendolas,[3] birds best known for building characteristic hanging nests high up in the trees. They are never far from water, Ciriaco remarked, which got him thinking that near our dry aguada was another one that contained water. We wanted to find it, not just because it would allow us to secure some water, but also because it was possible that the dry aguada next to our camp was not Aguada Unión, which would mean we were looking in the wrong place. After a while Ciriaco pointed his machete between the trees: there used to be a mule trail there, a *camino de arria*. I did not see any path, so he showed me the roots of a *ramón* on which evidence of gnawing by mules

---

2. *Ficus* sp.
3. *Psarocolius montezuma*.

was still visible. These trails always connected aguadas, so we followed it, but it brought us to a bajo where we could no longer tell where it was heading.

Our working conditions increasingly weighed on us. We were eating mainly canned food, rusk, and crackers, while the water delivered to us each day barely sufficed for drinking and morning coffee. We could use only tiny amounts of water to wash our hands and faces, and even that had a rapidly waning effect: because of our heavy sweating, the water simply slid off our greasy skin. It was not that we lacked the will, but after four days of combing through the jungle, we had to admit defeat. There was no shortage of archaeological remains, but the famous building with stucco figures was nowhere to be seen. We had surveyed a large area and had definitely walked more than fifteen minutes from the aguada, the distance mentioned by Ruppert, all the way to the coordinates he cited, 2.5 kilometers northwest of the aguada. Alas, all our efforts were in vain. Was this place jinxed? Was it possible we had overlooked something? And was the aguada at which we had camped actually Ruppert's Aguada Unión?

We would not obtain answers to these questions until the following year.

21

A Mistake

Having run out of provisions, we had to return to civilization. The vehicles were screaming for a mechanic, not to mention tire repairs. Ciriaco mentioned that there was a man in Xpujil by the name of Guadalupe Lozano, a friend of his and a former associate, who—as a good chiclero—could be of use to us. Don Guadalupe recalled having seen some ruins near El Tintal camp, southwest of Aguada La Fama, and agreed to take us there. He also took his son, Raúl, while Ciriaco found three other workers to replace the previous crew, who were not too keen on heading out again.

Raymundo told me that several years before, he and his colleagues from the university had reached Oxpemul, a major site that Karl Ruppert had discovered in 1934. Like many others, this site had been considered lost until the rediscovery mentioned by Raymundo, which was recorded in a single, very brief report. Naturally, I was interested in the location and state of Oxpemul. I found it odd that Raymundo said he had seen no stone monuments, given that Ruppert mentions nineteen stelae and eighteen altars; even if looters had found it, it was very unlikely they had taken all of them; they would usually just saw off the relief surfaces. Raymundo stressed that they had visited the site only briefly and had not seen everything. It therefore made sense to go there and take a closer look.

We split into two groups. I took Raymundo, Ciriaco, and two other young men, Andrés and Gonzalo, to the aguada at kilometer 27 of the road from Conhuás to Calakmul, where we set up camp and from where we were planning to head to Oxpemul. Atasta and Vaquero took the other workers and continued to Villahermosa, whence Guadalupe was to lead them to El Tintal and the ruins he knew. Not only did we have three vehicles this time, which allowed us to work in two groups, but we had also rented two satellite phones. The idea was not to call each other and talk directly; even if the phones were turned on all the time, which would have quickly drained the batteries, we would not have been able to contact each other much because the satellite signal did not penetrate the forest canopy. Rather, the phones allowed us to send and receive voice messages: at least once a day each team would try to find a space open enough to send a message and check whether the other group had left a message.

Our camp was just a stone's throw from the road, in a pleasantly fresh, high forest adjacent to an aguada with quite a lot of water. This was undoubtedly one of the nicest camps we ever had; it was practically romantic. But make no mistake, this was no picnic by a lake with a sandy beach—far from it. Aguadas are essentially puddles, be they large or small, with muddy banks overgrown with reeds, brush, and tall grass. In order to scoop up water, you typically had to lay down logs to get to a deeper area. When you finally scooped it up, the water got muddied and you had to wait for the muck to settle. And because there was water, there were more creatures, and not just mosquitoes. The campsite needed to be carefully cleared so that it was easier to spot any snakes. Peccaries like to frequent aguadas; they are not prone to unprovoked attacks, but once they are irritated, anyone in the vicinity had better skedaddle up a tree. Tapirs are major consumers of water as well, and although they are meek in general, they are strong enough to trample anything in their path. Jaguars? They are the mightiest cats in the Central American tropical rainforest, but luckily they shun encounters with humans. Although we have come across jaguar tracks many times, I was fortunate enough to see the local king of the animals eye to eye on only two occasions: both times the cat was standing on a dirt trail and moments later turned around in a dignified fashion and disappeared into the brush.

Regardless of the inherent inconveniences, every aguada that is not dry is a cause for celebration on our expeditions. In the rainy season, when the chicleros are working, the aguadas are full and water supply is not even an issue. But because our work can be done only in the dry season, when it is impossible to know whether an aguada will have water, we always have to bring supplies, which naturally are limited. Even though the water in the aguadas has a distinct smell and color because of decomposing plant matter, it is perfectly potable: while the chicleros drink it straight from the source, we boil it or use other methods of purification just as a precaution. Most importantly, if there is an aguada nearby it is not necessary to ration water for washing and doing laundry. Oh, the glorious feeling when, after a sizzling and excruciating day, you can wash the sticky sweat off your body from head to toe! However, it is not recommended to swim in an aguada, not only because a crocodile that might not have had a decent meal lately could be lurking, but also because the mud that is kicked up will immediately negate any purifying effect the water would otherwise have on the body. Fairly clean water can be scooped up with a bucket, which can then be sieved through a cloth if necessary.

Figure 21.1. A crocodile in the roadside aguada en route to Calakmul.

We carefully inspected the site for our camp next to the road, swept away the leaves using some branches, and cleared the undergrowth. There were no snakes or signs of larger animals. There was a crocodile basking in the middle of the aguada, a reminder that we needed to be vigilant, but it ignored us. Ciriaco had to hurl a branch toward it to demonstrate that it was very much alive.

There was a metal tower nearby occasionally used by the biosphere rangers, and this enabled us to see a telling bulge on the eastern horizon. That was the main pyramid in Oxpemul, Raymundo said, about five kilometers away. One of the workers stayed behind at camp while the rest headed there. We found a footpath that Raymundo and his colleagues had made years before; even though it was pretty badly overgrown, it nevertheless made it easier to cross the bajo we had to navigate. After we had crossed the dry bed of the Río Desempeño and passed a group of smaller ruins, the terrain started to rise. We ascended what were clearly human-made terraces, encountering ever-bigger mounds, and then we finally arrived at the biggest pyramidal building, which was about thirty meters tall. Raymundo showed me a low, oblong addition that he said was drawn on the wrong side on Ruppert's map; he was convinced a mistake had occurred and the map was a mirror image of the true situation. We scaled the ruined pyramid, which had some exposed walls, and found that it was on the southern extreme of a fairly significant prominence, whereas on Ruppert's map the biggest pyramid was at the northern end. So, his layout was not just a mirror image, but it appeared that the north was upside down as well.

We descended to the plaza in front of the pyramid and started to walk north among the ruins, Ruppert's map in hand. Not only were there no stelae anywhere, but the more we looked, the more it became clear that the plan reflected neither the layout nor the look of the buildings among which we were walking.

"Raymundo," I said, somewhat hesitantly, "either Ruppert's surveyor was totally hammered, or this is not Oxpemul."

Raymundo stopped, thrust his machete into the ground, and shook his head. "Well, I guess it's not." He took a deep breath, took off his hat, and scratched his head. "We really were here just briefly that time. It looked like the addition to the large pyramid was exactly like it was on the map, just on the wrong side. That was enough. We thought we were in Oxpemul."

Raymundo must have felt queasy admitting the mistake, but he was too honest to make up excuses. "We screwed up. This is definitely not Oxpemul."

The site was indeed large, and we agreed that we would have to return to survey and map it in detail. But when Raymundo left for Campeche a few days later, he found that the site had already been recorded: the archaeologist Agustín Peña included a description and map of the site, which he called Dos Aguadas, in his master's thesis in 1986. The thesis was not published, but it was available, so it did not make sense to map the site again.

Naturally an important question remained: Where was Oxpemul?

Ruppert's coordinates corresponded to a point in a bajo some three kilometers southeast. Because such areas turn into marsh in the rainy season, rendering them completely inappropriate for human habitation—there is not a single recorded Maya settlement in a bajo—it was perfectly clear the coordinates were wrong and Oxpemul was probably built on some nearby prominence.

Once again we ascended the pyramid, whose peak was not too badly overgrown, allowing us to survey the area. As far as the eye could see, the landscape was covered in a lush green carpet. We nevertheless tried to make out an indication of larger structures under the canopy on the surrounding hills. A hill around five kilometers to the east seemed particularly suspicious: its prominent protrusions did not seem natural at all. But to check it out we had to get there. There was a completely flat bajo between us and the hill, no doubt one that would be difficult to cross, but curiosity outweighed our aversion to problems.

We returned to camp and devised a plan for the following day. Looking at the map of aguadas on my computer, I noticed one that was very close to the ruins we had just inspected. We would find it and camp there to save having to go all the way back to the road while making our way east.

Gonzalo stayed behind at camp the next day; the road was so close that someone had to keep watch over the trucks and equipment there, and we agreed that he would later bring us water. The rest of us took basic gear and some food, and we easily found the aguada we were looking for by punching the coordinates into the GPS device. We were delighted to find that it was not completely dry. Ciriaco used a stick to make a small pit in the mud in the hope that it would gather some water by evening. Andrés was sent back to the roadside camp and instructed to stay there

Figure 21.2. Ciriaco making a small pit in the half-dry aguada to trap some water.

and explain to Gonzalo how best to find us to bring food and water, while Raymundo, Ciriaco, and I cleared an area adjacent to the aguada to set up camp.

Using the azimuth I had measured with the compass the day before, I was able to locate on the map the hill we had seen from the pyramid, which would be our destination; I determined the coordinates of the highest point of the hill and entered them into the GPS device. We started east around noon. Close to the aguada we ran across an old dirt trail leading in the right direction and followed it. However, it had clearly not been used in years, and after less than two kilometers, when the terrain descended into the bajo, it became so densely overgrown that it no longer facilitated our progress. Therefore, we simply started clearing a path as straight as possible in the direction indicated by the GPS and compass.

At around five in the afternoon we called it a day, and by the time we returned to camp it was already dark. There was a fire there and Gonzalo was waiting for us. We had the basic pots and pans to make a warm, if improvised, supper. Gonzalo had brought a twenty-liter container of potable water, and we were glad to see that the pit Ciriaco had made in the aguada now had enough water to wash up; the mud had settled, the water was clear, and there were even baby turtles swimming in it. We had not brought a bucket, but we did have two large plastic Coca-Cola bottles. That was the first time I was able to see for myself that four liters of water were enough for a perfectly decent shower, soaping up and rinsing included. The bottles made it easy to ration the water efficiently, with minimal loss.

Water! We take for granted that it flows out of faucets and is abundant enough for showering, doing laundry, washing cars, watering gardens, and keeping parks green; it seems like an afterthought in civilization, but it becomes priceless when not available. It is only when I do fieldwork that I truly realize how important it is. Hunger is the best spice, an old saying goes, and only in privation do small things offer such profound satisfaction. If you have never experienced this feeling, it may be difficult to truly wrap your head around how much pleasure four liters of brownish aguada water smelling of decomposing matter can provide!

That water is practically synonymous with life is felt most viscerally in nature, especially in places where the difference between the rainy and dry seasons is so clear-cut, even in a tropical rainforest, which we typically imagine as being a humid habitat of abundance. True, there is abundant water in many plants, and the air is humid, but the Central American tropical forest is not always the same shade of green. At the onset of the rainy season the change is sudden and obvious: the undergrowth practically bursts into the air, canopies fill out, insects proliferate, birds chirp louder, frogs start to perform grand symphonies. And not until the rains start will crops in the fields start growing. If the rainy season is late, many farmers still have the same concerns the ancient Maya used to have. It is no wonder that the most common elements adorning their architecture are grotesque masks of Chaac, the Maya god of rain.

22

Oxpemul

The following morning Gonzalo returned to the roadside camp to replace Andrés, who was going to bring us water in the evening, while Raymundo, Ciriaco, and I headed in the opposite direction. The previous day we had cleared a path across the elevated terrain and then descended and began to push through into the bajo, but the most difficult part was still ahead of us; according to the map, we had another two and a half kilometers to go to cross the bajo and reach the foot of the slope we intended to climb.

Ciriaco was walking ahead, cutting through the toughest brush, while Raymundo and I followed behind, suitably widening the trail. Every bajo is unpleasant for walking, but this one was especially so. The vegetation was abnormally dense and low growing and offered not a speck of shade, with thorns scratching at every step, and most of the woody plants had such hard stems that our machetes needed constant honing. Once in a while Ciriaco would stop and wait for me to double-check our direction on my GPS and compass. I could only admire his skill, which he would prove time and again, since his course hardly ever needed correcting. True, he would turn now left, now right, avoiding trees and densely over-grown areas, but at the same time he managed to maintain our general direction very accurately. Of course, with a compass I can do that too, or if the sun is low enough, so that with the help of my shadow I am able to keep my bearings. Ciriaco also orients himself by means of the sun; whenever I point in the desired direction, he checks it against his own shadow. What is remarkable, however, is that he is able to do this just as well in the midday hours when shadows—because of the height of the sun in the tropics—essentially do not exist, or even in overcast weather. Such skill, even among the locals who have worked for years in the forest, is anything but common.

This time Ciriaco had to zigzag more than usual. In many places the terrain ahead was so overgrown that it was close to impossible to decide where passage would be least difficult and tiring. After about eight hours of relentless effort, in the afternoon, the terrain began to rise and the vegetation became taller, although it was still unusually thick and featured hardly any distinctly tall trees. Ciriaco remarked that now he understood why the dirt road we had initially followed was so overgrown; he estimated that it had not been used for some thirty years, almost certainly because there were very few useful trees in this forest, either for chicle, the natural gum, or for wood.

At around four in the afternoon we managed to climb the hill, reaching what seemed to be the highest point. But disappointment awaited: there were only a few smaller ruins. Ciriaco climbed a tree to look around.

"The terrain descends in all directions!" he cried.

"Even to the east?"

He tried to find a position that would allow him to see through the foliage to the east. "The trees in that direction all seem very high; maybe the terrain also rises there."

If only that were true, I thought. The GPS was telling me it would be another nine hundred meters before we reached the goal, the highest point of the hill, the coordinates of which I had determined from the map. So we continued toward the east, with the terrain gently but constantly descending. Exhausted as we were, this filled us with gloom. After some time, however, the terrain began to rise, although there was no sign anywhere of even the smallest mound. Only natural rock jutted out in places, while the vegetation remained unusually thick; there were no particularly tall trees, and no *ramonal* of the type that usually covers Maya cities. The end point, our goal, was supposedly only three hundred meters away.

We had been climbing for a few long minutes when suddenly a steep slope studded with stones emerged in front of us. As we approached we saw that it was not a building but a kind of scarp, several meters high, that disappeared into the thicket to the left and right. We climbed up it until we reached level terrain, and there before us rose a heap of stones so high that we could not see the top. Raymundo and I stopped, while Ciriaco climbed the mound and shouted out from the top: "Here to the north there's another one, even higher!"

I took off my backpack and pulled out a copy of Ruppert's map of Oxpemul. The highest pyramid was in the northern part; we had come from the west, and if this was Oxpemul and Ruppert's map was accurate, we would now be at the western foot of the southern pyramid, Structure VI. And if this was so, then—according to the map—a stela should be on the other side.

Figure 22.1. Stela 17 was the first evidence that we had rediscovered Oxpemul, which had been lost for seventy years.

Figure 22.2. Numerous details on Stela 17 were more visible at night in suitable illumination.

Our fatigue completely forgotten, Raymundo and I lunged to the right along the base of the pyramid to reach its eastern side. The thicket, which allowed us to see barely a few meters ahead, was falling under our machetes as if we had not already spent the whole day sweating and cutting. As we followed the curving base of the ruin, the afternoon sun glimmered through the forest behind our backs and then moved to our left and hid behind the building; just a few more steps northward and . . .

There was the stela! It was still standing upright; slightly inclined amid the relentless vegetation, however, it seemed somehow wistful, as if it were mourning the dead city whose grandeur it had once witnessed before it was devoured by the jungle centuries ago. I remembered John Lloyd Stephens, one of the first travelers to uncover the mysteries of the Maya; in his book, published in 1841, he wrote the following upon discovering Copán, the famous archaeological site in Honduras:

> The city was desolate. No remnant of this race hangs round the ruins, with traditions handed down from father to son, and from generation to generation. It lay before us like a shattered bark in the midst of the ocean, her masts gone, her name effaced, her crew perished, and none to tell whence she came, to whom she belonged, how long on her voyage, or what caused her destruction. . . . All was mystery, dark, impenetrable mystery, and every circumstance increased it. In Egypt the colossal skeletons of gigantic temples stand in the unwatered sands in all the nakedness of desolation; here an immense forest shrouded the ruins, hiding them from sight.[1]

On the front face of the stela, which overlooked a former plaza to the east, was a well-preserved relief of a standing person with majestic accoutrements, apparently one of the rulers of the city. Wearing a decorated loincloth and a magnificent chest plate, holding a spear in his right hand and a round shield in his left, he had a grotesque mask of a deity and luxuriant plumage on his head; shod in sandals, he was treading on a mostly prone captive with head turned down and hands tied behind his back. Raymundo and I compared the image with Ruppert's photograph of the stela, which according to his description and map stood on that very spot.

There was no doubt: we were standing in front of Stela 17 of Oxpemul!

---

1. John L. Stephens, *Incidents of Travel in Central America, Chiapas and Yucatan*, vol. 1 (New York: Harper & Brothers, 1841), 105.

Meanwhile, Ciriaco came to us and upon seeing the stela he too gasped in awe; there was also a round, though fairly damaged, altar in front of the structure. Immediately we set out to the north, wanting to see the highest pyramid, and as we stumbled across a few more stelae on our way, our sense of victory only increased; all appeared to have well-preserved images and inscriptions. Once we got to the top of the roughly twenty-five-meter-high Structure IV, the highest in Oxpemul, a magnificent view of the green, gently undulating carpet stretching in all directions opened up. To the west, the highest pyramid of the Dos Aguadas site stood out, while somewhere in the background, as if a miniature, protruded the metal tower on the road to Calakmul. With the GPS device we were able to establish that we were approximately two and a half kilometers northeast of Ruppert's coordinates for Oxpemul. Raymundo could no longer restrain

Figure 22.3. Stelae and altars in the plaza in front of the tallest pyramid in Oxpemul.

himself; he took the satellite phone and called the archaeologist William Folan, his boss at the University of Campeche.

"Doctor Folan, we have found Oxpemul, the real Oxpemul!"

Ciriaco could not believe that no one had ever told him about such important ruins in this area. But in a way it was understandable: the forest was hardly attractive for the woodcutters and chicleros, so they must have stopped going there a long time ago; those who would have seen Oxpemul were almost certainly no longer among the living. No one had ever mentioned Oxpemul to any of us, not even to Ciriaco, whose colleagues and acquaintances included many forest experts, although the chicleros in Ruppert's time had already known it by that name (which means "three [artificial] hills" and hints at the three great pyramids).

The satellite phone reception was excellent and I took the opportunity to check for any messages from the other group. Vaquero informed us that they were clearing a path toward the site to which Don Guadalupe was leading them, and that again they had burst two tires and were having problems with the chain saw. Unable to help, I sent him a message with good wishes and news of our discovery.

The sun had already dropped low on the horizon, so a more thorough survey had to be postponed until the next day. Although we needed headlamps a good part of the way, returning to camp was almost easy, less due to the already-cleared path than to our exuberant mood: on that twenty-second day of April 2004, nearly seventy years after it had been found by Karl Ruppert, we rediscovered Oxpemul, one of the most important archaeological sites in the Maya lowlands.

23

The City of Stelae and Altars

The following morning Raymundo left for the roadside camp because he had to return to Campeche, while Ciriaco and I headed back to Oxpemul to make a detailed inspection of the site. While standing on the peak of the tallest pyramid the previous afternoon, we had seen a hill to the southwest that was probably South Oxpemul, as Ruppert had called a smaller architectural complex about a kilometer away. I suggested that Ciriaco cut his way there and survey it. I gave him a compass and the azimuth to the foot of the hill; from there he would easily be able to find his way to the summit.

In the meantime, with Ruppert's map in one hand and a machete in the other, I started to systematically survey the main complex. Exposed architectural elements were not discernible, except a stairway segment here and there, but the buildings were virtually untouched, even if their original shapes were concealed beneath a top layer of debris. I saw only three or four looters' trenches, but they were all very old, with collapsed profiles and thick layers of debris that had piled up over years of erosion

Figure 23.1. Stela 5 in Oxpemul depicts a deity or a ruler with divine attributes.

and had already become severely overgrown with vegetation. It was clear the chicleros and loggers had stopped coming to the area decades ago, before looting really took off, driven by demand on the black market.

The urban core of Oxpemul lies on a fairly prominent hill, on a largely flat plateau that was definitely artificially leveled, with edges that transition into steep slopes all the way around the perimeter, having been reinforced with a masonry retaining wall that surrounds the entire complex, portions of which we had seen the previous day. Both the natural location and the human-made terraces with steep slopes give the city a distinctly defensive feel, with features blocking approach from all but the southern side, where a narrow ramp of less steep terrain descends from the upper plateau: this must have been the entrance to the ancient city. Pyramidal and elongated structures of various sizes—most likely temples, residences, and administrative buildings—are dotted around the two main plazas and some smaller courtyards.

Although the site is not particularly large, its stone monuments testify to its special importance. Karl Ruppert's expedition found as many as seventeen stelae along with sixteen circular and rectangular altars, and two more stelae with altars in South Oxpemul. At the main complex

Figure 23.2. The front of Stela 9 in Oxpemul, whose upper part was damaged by looters, shows a ruler standing on a snake and holding an ax in his right hand, with his face covered by a mask of the rain god Chaac. The sides contain inscriptions with a date corresponding to May 5, AD 751.

I found all the monuments except Stela 15, which was the smallest of the lot and appears to have been spirited away by looters. All the other monuments were at locations Ruppert had marked on the map. Only Stela 9 had been pretty badly damaged by looters when they attempted to remove the carved surfaces, but the frontal relief with the image of a ruler remained intact, except for a horizontal cut over the upper part. The looters, for some unknown reason, had left some stone fragments on the ground that they had sawed off, and from these a large portion of the lateral hieroglyphic inscription could be reconstructed. Most of the stelae, as well as some of the altars, had surprisingly well-preserved relief images and inscriptions. As Ruppert's epigrapher John Denison had

Figure 23.3. Altar 15 in Oxpemul depicts a sitting deity with raised hands.

determined, all the dates corresponded to the years AD 731 to 830, the Late Classic period. The mighty Calakmul, twenty-four kilometers to the south, lost control of an expansive territory following defeats inflicted by its long-standing rival, Tikal, at the end of the seventh and first half of the eighth century AD. Was the rise of Oxpemul associated with the fall of Calakmul and the collapse of its vassal network? The defensive characteristics of Oxpemul, its limited size, and the period of its short-lived rise coincide with the restive Late Classic period, when larger states lost power and territories and multiple smaller states emerged, with the wars between them becoming increasingly frequent and destructive.

Ciriaco returned in the middle of the afternoon, when my work was almost done. He had found the South Complex; he said it was not particularly large and had one major pyramid surrounded by smaller ruins.

"Did you see any stelae?" I asked.

"There are two fronting the tallest building, each with its own altar. Both are well preserved, with a frontal figure and inscriptions on all sides."

So, both stelae and both altars that Ruppert had reported were still in South Oxpemul. And no looters' trenches, as Ciriaco pointed out. Since he had enough time, he also inspected a nearby hill, where he saw several smaller ruins as well.

We had seen everything we wanted to for the time being. We knew that Oxpemul was important; now it was also clear that it was virtually undamaged—nature's destructive forces notwithstanding—and that almost all stone monuments were still there, no doubt containing important historical data. Karl Ruppert had published photographs and drawings of just some of the stelae and altars; the epigrapher Denison had described all of them, but his transcripts of the inscriptions are limited to calendar data because only numerical and calendar glyphs had been deciphered by the time they were there, and even those not completely. Because the stone monuments with images and texts were precious spoils for looters, who might show up at any time, it was paramount that we precisely document them immediately.

Ciriaco and I returned to camp, where Andrés was waiting for us. The following morning we packed up and headed back to the roadside camp, where Gonzalo was keeping watch. I took them to their homes in Constitución and agreed to let Ciriaco know when everything would be ready for work to continue. I had numerous other errands to attend to in Xpujil and Chetumal in addition to the standard visits to the laundry service, mechanic, and bank, and I had to purchase gasoline and provisions as well.

Multiple people and institutions would have to be informed of the discovery. I addressed requests for the additional funding needed to document the Oxpemul altars and stelae to the INAH, the National Geographic Society, and ZRC SAZU in Slovenia, my home research institution. Our epigrapher Nikolai Grube notified me from Bonn that his teaching obligations prevented him from immediately coming over, which was why I asked for help from William Folan, Raymundo's superior and the head of the Archaeology Department at the Autonomous University of Campeche. He promised he would find someone and try to secure support to clear the old dirt trail through to Oxpemul, where guards would be stationed. I was also concerned that our workers might spread news of the discovery to the extent that it could reach looters, so I stopped by to see the commander of the military unit in Xpujil. The post was still occupied by my old friend Lieutenant Colonel García Melgar. I explained the situation and asked him whether he could beef up the patrols along the road to Calakmul. He assured me he would do so and would also notify his general, the commander of the Thirty-Third Military Zone in Campeche. As we will see later, he kept this promise with striking effectiveness.

Figure 23.4. The ruler carved on Stela 12 in Oxpemul has large earrings, a lavish headdress, and an unusual nose ornament.

24

Miscellanea

Getting everything organized took over two weeks. While I was able to do some tasks in Xpujil and Chetumal, I spent most of the time doing fieldwork, far away from civilization. It was possible to communicate via satellite phone, but problems with the signal were often insurmountable. Without finding anything extraordinary over this fortnight, we confronted problems of all sorts, perhaps best illustrated by field diary entries.

April 28. Vaquero sent a message to me in Xpujil stating that they had found El Tintal, that the site is unique—it has a stela and even exposed architectural elements—and that we would later have to survey and map it in detail. Ciriaco came to Xpujil and notified me that he had urgent business to attend to and could not immediately join me. I drove off alone. On the way to Villahermosa I met a familiar black jeep coming the other way; Vaquero was driving a worker, Teodoro, who had cut his hand with a machete so badly he needed stitches. I found the rest of the group in Villahermosa, where they had already returned from Tintal. Don Guadalupe was edgy because they had been without tortilla flour for two days; I brought some and he calmed down.

April 29. Guadalupe mentioned he knew of another pyramid close to Yax-nohcah. We headed there and found it just a few hundred meters from a complex that Atasta and Vaquero had already checked out. It is almost 30 meters tall, has a triadic group, and is part of the same settlement.

April 30. We cleared a dirt trail south of Villahermosa. A branch smashed into the windshield of the gray pickup truck while Atasta was driving. The glass cracked along the whole left side and bulged inward; we used packing tape to secure it. We arrived at Aguada Dos Caobas, a kilometer north of the border with Guatemala; nearby there were supposed to be ruins mentioned by Ruppert and in border commission archive documents. [Surveyors found these ruins when they were delineating the borderline in the 1930s.] *We determined there was enough water in the aguada so we will move to Dos Caobas tomorrow. I sent Vaquero the coordinates and instructed him to find a worker to replace the injured Teodoro. I advised him to enlist Baltazar Gutiérrez, better known as Bacho; the easiest way to find him would be to check inside Rosita, a cantina in Xpujil.*

May 1. We moved the camp to Dos Caobas and combed through the surroundings, finding only a few smaller mounds with looters' trenches and ceramic sherds. In the evening Vaquero and Bacho arrived with fresh supplies of food. [Bacho had worked with us back in 2002. I met him in Xpujil,

Figure 24.1. Guadalupe and Bacho at the Dos Caobas camp.

where I was told he was a chiclero and knew the ruins in the biosphere well. Whenever I met him he was so totally inebriated that we could not come to any agreement, but because a friend of his told me that he was always like that in the village but sobered up in the forest, I just loaded him onto a truck one day and took him to Villahermosa, as he supposedly knew of a large *reinado* in that area. He really did sober up and found the ruins, and it turned out that he was an excellent worker and a really good man. Just as before, Vaquero picked him up at the cantina, he accepted the invitation without hesitation, and dried out on the long journey.]

May 2. We are continuing the surveys, nothing special. There are only smaller mounds in the area of the coordinates where archive documents suggest Ruina Alta is located. A downpour surprised us in the afternoon; we returned to camp. Everything is soaking wet because we did not protect our hammocks with plastic tarps. It's a good thing the commander lent me a tent. We couldn't start a fire. We finally found a bunch of dry grass: the workers who clear the border every year had recently made a pile when making camp. Under the soaking top layer we found enough dry grass to start a fire; we split wet logs and made kindling out of the dry core wood and placed it on the fire. It has cooled down significantly, but we finished the last bottle of whiskey yesterday evening.

May 3. Vaquero stayed at the camp, started the generator, charged the batteries, and dried the equipment. The rest of us continued to investigate the area. Ruppert mentioned Maabal and provided the approximate coordinates, but there is nothing there.

May 4. We decamped and headed east on the dirt trail recently cleared by the border workers. At the first crossroads we took a left heading north, past the fork for Aguada Jerusalem. The trail is good, as it is occasionally used by the army. We got stuck in the mud crossing the Blengio. The 4WD on the gray truck is not working; we knew that already, but now the white truck's 4WD has broken down as well. It is a good thing Don Martín repaired the winch a few days ago. We dragged ourselves out of the mud and camped on the trail, at a place close to the hill with a conical peak that I had seen from the pyramid in Balakbal in 2002. It rained again during the night, but the hammocks were protected by tarps this time.

May 5. We made it to the hill and surveyed it. What looked like a large pyramid from Balakbal turned out to be just a pointy gypsum peak. There is only a group of small mounds at the top. We continued the journey in the afternoon. The gray truck had coolant problems the entire way and finally overheated just before Altamira and got stuck in the mud; the cooler fan belt slipped off. We put on the spare belt, but it was too loose. Towing is out of the question because the white truck is stuck in the mud too and its 4WD is not working. We transferred the most important equipment from the gray truck to the white truck and the jeep and arrived in Xpujil by evening, encrusted in muck from tip to toe.

May 6. I sought out the commander at the barracks and asked him to help us. He always surprises me: he said the mechanic is on leave but quickly added that he would return tomorrow and that he could send him and a few soldiers out to repair and tow the gray truck. "Would that be OK?" he asked. I was speechless: How could that not be OK?! I did not know how to thank him enough: the army would drag us out of the mud! I took the white truck to the mechanic Martín in Zoh Laguna in order to have the 4WD repaired. Vaquero took the jeep to the tire repair service and helped Atasta sort out the equipment and do the shopping. I went online to try and see what the deal was with the money the INAH was supposed to send me for Oxpemul. The national coordinator for archaeology informed me that I should get in touch with the director of the regional center in Campeche, but he was not available.

May 7. Vaquero and some soldiers drove off in a Hummer to get the gray truck. I called National Geographic and the INAH in Campeche about the money for Oxpemul but did not get through to the people in charge. Folan in Campeche said that the university would provide some money. Atasta and I went to Chetumal to do the shopping; I ordered the spare part that Don Martín needed to fix the 4WD. Vaquero and the soldiers returned with the gray truck; the army mechanic did the most urgent repairs, but they still had to tow it along the muddy dirt trail.

But enough of these field notes. We had to remain in Xpujil a few more days to repair the white truck, sort out finances, and prepare everything for documenting the stone monuments in Oxpemul. Willy Folan notified us that he had found a man who was willing to come and draw them, and all those who had been asked to contribute funding finally delivered: the INAH, the National Geographic Society, the Autonomous University of Campeche, and the Research Center of the Slovenian Academy of Sciences and Arts.

Figure 24.2. Hugh copying the hieroglyphs on Stela 10 in Oxpemul.

Raymundo arrived in Xpujil with a university vehicle on the evening of May 12. He brought along Hubert Robichaux, an American archaeologist who had worked in many places, including the large Río Azul site in Guatemala with Richard Adams. Although he was getting on in years, he was so excited about the rediscovery of Oxpemul that he did not hesitate to accept Folan's invitation. The next day we picked up Ciriaco and the rest of the crew and headed to kilometer 27 on the road to Calakmul. Raymundo and one worker remained at the aguada camp, while the rest of us took all the equipment and headed to the camp at Dos Aguadas, spent the night there, and arrived in Oxpemul the following morning.

Documenting the Oxpemul monuments was a major organizational undertaking. One satellite phone was with Raymundo, who was in charge of the logistical aspects of the project from the roadside camp, and we had the second one at Oxpemul. Ciriaco and Moisés were the only workers who stayed with us, and the other eight were in charge of delivering provisions the next few days. In addition to food, they had to bring us two twenty-liter canisters of water every day. The narrow, winding path from the road to Oxpemul was over ten kilometers long, dotted with the stubble of cut vegetation and beset by low-hanging trees and trunks that had to be avoided or passed under. Even for the most hardened locals, having to walk this distance every day—carrying provisions—was too much. We therefore had to split up the work: one group was with Raymundo and brought food and water to their colleagues camped out near Dos Aguadas; this second group would then carry everything to Oxpemul. We messaged Raymundo every day about what we needed, and Raymundo bought the necessary provisions, organized the transport, and every now and then even seasoned and smoked steaks for us: when they got to us, all we had to do was throw them in a pan.

The organization was good and the satellite phone worked. Raymundo was able to get a signal on the road, and we managed to connect on the tallest pyramid in Oxpemul. We had set up camp in the largest plaza, at the foot of the main pyramid. We had hammocks and a tent tarp that Raymundo had procured, but we realized it leaked when a heavy downpour surprised us in the middle of the first night. Even worse, so much water gathered in a pool on the tarp that the entire structure collapsed. We managed to fix it so that at least the most important equipment was dry, but we did not get any sleep. Hugh and Vaquero had their own tents, but Vaquero's was leaking as well. When the rain subsided in the morning, Vaquero crawled out of the tent and asked Ciriaco, "What kind of creature is this?" He pointed to a bug about three centimeters long crawling in the tent.

"Oh, Vaquero, you can't kill this one."

"Why?"

"This is your blood sister now." Ciriaco grinned.

"How come?"

Ciriaco took it out of the tent and squashed it. There was so much blood that Vaquero leaped in horror and fired off a salvo of not very decent words.

"It's a kind of chinch that sucks blood," Ciriaco explained. "When it bites, you don't feel anything, nor do you feel anything later. That's why they call it the kissing bug,[1] but it may carry Chagas disease. If it is infected,

---

1. *Triatoma* sp.

Figure 24.3. Atasta and Vaquero inspecting a fragment of Stela 3 in Oxpemul that mentions a visit by three noblemen from Tikal.

the disease may take years to appear. It attacks the heart and bowels, and sometimes it is fatal. But don't worry, that's more common in Guatemala. I've never heard of anyone getting sick here."

Vaquero is still alive and well, so we can hope Ciriaco was right.

Over the coming days Hugh drew the monuments by day with others helping as needed, while nights were reserved for photography: the carved relief images and hieroglyphic inscriptions were illuminated with grazing light because the resulting contrast made it possible to uncover details not visible during the day. In addition to mosquitoes, which were unusually abundant that year, these night endeavors were enlivened by huge moths that fluttered violently around all sources of light and, because we used headlamps, often collided with our faces. Annoying pests indeed.

In August 2014, our epigrapher Nikolai Grube visited the site and exhaustively documented all the monuments. The hieroglyphic inscriptions confirmed our thoughts as to the role Oxpemul played in the restive Late Classic period. The texts name individual rulers, major events, and dates, revealing that Oxpemul assumed Calakmul's place in the regional political hierarchy, Calakmul's power having waned right at that time. Aside from usurping Calakmul's original toponym (Uxtetun), Oxpemul also had direct contact with Tikal, which remained the only superpower in the Maya lowlands after defeating Calakmul. Interestingly, on many stelae the rulers are clearly depicted as deities: the grotesque masks and other symbols that make up their lavish gear, as well as their names, reveal that they most frequently personified the sun and rain gods.

25

Tree on a House

After three days I left the team, which continued working in Oxpemul. First I had to go to Chetumal to pick up our surveyor, Tomaž Podobnikar, a colleague from my research center in Slovenia. The gray pickup needed a mechanic again, and we had to go shopping as well. I left Raymundo a message on the satellite phone saying that we would be there on the morning of May 21 and that Atasta, Ciriaco, and three more workers should wait for us at his roadside camp so we could start mapping Yaxnohcah, while Vaquero, Hugh, and the rest of the crew should finish up the work at Oxpemul.

We headed out toward Villahermosa on the agreed day, but just before we reached our destination, the gray pickup started choking and ground to a halt. We left it there, finished the trip to Villahermosa in the white pickup, and somehow got the gray one there the following day, but it was clear that it would have to be repaired. We started mapping Yaxnohcah; meanwhile the crew at Oxpemul finished their job. Raymundo took Hubert to Campeche, and I messaged Vaquero that he should bring along Martín the mechanic. He managed to fix the truck and Vaquero drove him back, but it took him three days to return because his jeep had problems as well.

Figure 25.1. The camp at Yaxnohcah.

In the meantime, we moved camp to Yaxnohcah to save ourselves the daily trip from Villahermosa. Atasta was in charge of the mapping: he drew a sketch map and selected the points at which the workers were to hold up the prisms, while Tomaž manned the total station. Ciriaco and I returned to searching for Pared de los Reyes. We combed all the patches of territory around the aguada that we had not checked at the beginning of the season, and we also looked for the second aguada, which we suspected should be somewhere in the vicinity. Alas, our efforts were in vain. It was a bitter defeat, but continuing the search when it increasingly seemed as if we were groping around in complete darkness made no sense. We had to give up.

The work at Yaxnohcah had been going on for ten days. There was enough water at the aguada near Villahermosa, but we started to run out of food. Vaquero and I therefore left for Xpujil; the shopping took some time and it was already evening before we started the return leg. We arrived in Villahermosa at around three in the morning and discovered that new visitors had arrived while we were in Xpujil: there were tents pitched on the clearing with tall grass that was intersected by the trail leading to the aguada and on to Yaxnohcah. Vaquero turned down the music, which had been blaring out of the jeep as always, and as we got out a few young men and women stumbled out of the tents.

"Good evening," we greeted them. "In fact, good morning."

They greeted us back, said they had come to do some sort of botanical survey in the area, and asked what brought us there.

"We are doing an archaeological reconnaissance of the area. I know this is very awkward timing, but could we ask you to move the tents a bit, so we can pass through?"

"What do you mean, are you continuing onward? Where to?"

"On this dirt trail here, another six kilometers or so west."

It seemed they had not noticed that there was a trail through the forest from the aguada. Surprised, they moved the tents while we thanked them and drove on. Vaquero was quite amused by all this.

"Did you see their faces? Imagine being a biology student sent to do fieldwork in Villahermosa. You come here excited, pitch a tent, and imagine you're at the end of the world. Then you get woken up at three in the morning by music turned up to maximum volume, blinded by headlights, and a jeep bounces in carrying two guys who tell you: 'Could you step aside for a moment? We want to continue our journey.'"

Vaquero's imagination inspired mine as well.

"Yes, you're already thinking how you're going to tell your friends about this godforsaken wilderness, about treading 'where no one has gone

Figure 25.2. Atasta checking the map of Yaxnohcah that Tomaž is updating on his computer with data from the daily measurements.

before,' you fall asleep, and then your pleasant dreams are interrupted by some guy who tells you your tent is in his way because you pitched it on a trail. I guess we really did ruin their party."

The surveying in Yaxnohcah was soon completed; all we had to do now was check out a site close to the old El Tintal camp, where the chiclero Guadalupe had taken Vaquero, Atasta, and others several weeks ago. They had cleared the trail during their first visit but did not document the site in detail.

To get there from Yaxnohcah we had to drive about a kilometer on the dirt trail heading northwest, and another ten kilometers southwest on the fork that led past the old camp at Aguada La Fama. Although there was some water in the aguada, we decided not to move our camp there. Wallowing peccaries and tapirs had dug up Aguada La Fama so badly it had turned into a muddy swamp from which it would be impossible to extract even remotely clear water. Moreover, the masses of animals using the aguada—apparently the only one around that still contained some water—had led to an explosion of ticks. They were an omnipresent nuisance anyway, but it did not make sense to let them make our lives even more miserable. Luckily, in these areas ticks are not infected and do not carry diseases such as Lyme disease or tick-borne meningoencephalitis.

Oddly enough, Don Guadalupe and his crew had cut the vegetation so low when clearing the trail to El Tintal that the stubs had caused two flat tires and now punctured one of ours as well. There was no other choice: we had to cut all the dangerous stubs down to ground level, which took us two days.

The effort paid off. Just as Vaquero and Atasta had described it, the site was truly unique. The main building with exposed walls and reasonably well-preserved interior spaces was wrapped in a tangle of roots of an *álamo* tree growing on top of it, making it quite easy to name the site: Cheyokolnah (Tree on a House).

The frontal facade of the building overlooking a plaza to the west was in ruins, providing a glimpse into the interior of the vaulted rooms. They were laid out on two floors, a rarity at Maya sites: multistory buildings are not uncommon, but the upper floors are usually shifted into the interior of the building and constructed over a solid core, not stacked as these were. The rectangular niches on the interior wall of the central upper-floor space, which still contained stucco plaster, were unique as well. On the slope of a smaller nearby ruin were two fragments of a stela with a preserved hieroglyphic inscription that—as our epigrapher Nikolai later determined—documented the burial of a ruler, most probably in AD 420. The stela had most likely been dragged there by looters, who dug a trench into the building and discovered a room with a vault in the form of a three-leaf clover, such as had hitherto been known only at Palenque in Chiapas. The remains of red pigment were visible on the vault plaster.

Cheyokolnah is fairly large, with many other buildings enclosing courtyards scattered around the plaza in front of the main building.

Figure 25.3. Vaquero and Atasta measuring the main building in Cheyokolnah.

Since the rain had been interrupting the work with increasing frequency over the past few days, we decided to give up on conducting a precise survey of the site. The rainy season was upon us and if the rains were to intensify, the drenched dirt trails would seriously jeopardize our return. We had often heard about vehicles stuck in the mud that could not be towed out until the next dry season.

We made only a sketch map of the site, documented it with photographs, and drew the architectural details of the main building. We were still camping at Yaxnohcah and the rain would not stop. Every day the mosquitoes were so utterly rampant that even dinners by the campfire were miserable. We would put chunks of arboreal termite nests on the fire because the mixture of wood and soil that termites glue together produces a great deal of smoke. This reduced the number of mosquitoes, but our eyes burned badly from the smoke and we did not feel like talking around the fire. Instead, we rushed to get into our tents and hammocks, which were protected by mosquito nets and covered with plastic tarps to keep the rain out.

The last night the downpour was so strong and unending that I was sleepless with worry. I felt the weight of responsibility bearing down on me: I had brought all these people here and had failed to make sure we retreated in time. The biggest danger was the several-kilometer-wide Bajo El Laberinto, which we had to cross just north of Villahermosa. If we were to get stuck in the mud there, even the winch would not be of much use because there were no big trees to which we could attach the cable. Call the commander in Xpujil? Not really an option: the satellite phone was dead because of the dense clouds hanging in the sky. The jungle, meanwhile, was awakening with renewed vigor from the fresh water: plants were sprouting exuberantly, insects were proliferating, and snakes would soon start crawling out of the ground.

Soon after midnight the sky was torn asunder by lightning; the accompanying thunder was ever more deafening, and a violent wind started to blow. A mighty but almost completely dried-out tree close to camp started to creak menacingly. Panicking, we tumbled out of our hammocks and withdrew to a safe distance. The tree swayed, groaned, and screeched until it snapped and crashed to the ground just a few meters from camp.

In the morning—it was already June 13—we broke camp, loaded all our stuff into the vehicles, and headed out. The rain had stopped but the dirt trail was already quite boggy. We drove through Villahermosa and stopped before the elevated terrain descended into Bajo El Laberinto. We exchanged some last pieces of advice, turned on the four-wheel drive, and wished each other luck: this was where the difficult bit started.

I accelerated hard in order to hit the sea of mud with enough speed. I bore down on the gas pedal mercilessly to maintain speed, but the wheels drifted so much I had to constantly adjust the throttle and shift gears. The engine was roaring, the truck was bouncing this way and that, and gobs of mud were flying around on all sides from under the wheels. In my rear-view mirror I occasionally caught sight of Vaquero's jeep, fighting a similar battle. Luckily there were no stones in that wetland. Well, almost none. In several sections there was evidence of the ordeals of those who, God knows when, had become stuck in the mud with their vehicles: rows of large rocks that must have been brought from the nearest elevated terrain to gain at least a bit of traction in the mire. Spinning the steering wheel violently, I tried to avoid these rocks while staying on the correct course. Here and there the truck bounced off a rock, but the mud cushioned the blows to some degree. And anyway, I could not be too concerned about that: blows or no blows, going too slowly could be fateful, and we had to avoid stopping at all costs.

After we sweated it out for many long minutes, the wheels finally gripped firm terrain. We stopped on the first gentle incline, got out of the cars, and started hugging with joy. Now that we had braved Bajo El Laberinto the way forward should be relatively smooth going. We inspected the vehicles. It would have been difficult to guess the color of the otherwise white truck, and Vaquero's jeep no longer looked black, either; even its soft top was weighed down by large clumps of mud. The tires were encrusted with layers of muck so thick they rubbed against the high fenders. We scraped it away, but apart from that it seemed there was no other damage.

Compared to what we had just been through, the rest of the trip was much easier. In one section, my truck made such deep tracks in the mud that Vaquero got stuck behind me. But I was already on firm ground, beyond the mud pit: I turned the truck around, uncoiled the winch, and towed the jeep out without a problem. It was dark before we hit the Calakmul-Conhuás road in Buenfil, but that did not matter. We had succeeded!

We were in for one last surprise a few kilometers later. Driving on a road that is typically abandoned at that hour, with even the rare visitors to Calakmul now gone, we suddenly saw headlights approaching and an

Figure 25.4. "Won't budge an inch," Atasta says.

army Hummer blocking our path. The soldiers jumped out, released the safety on their assault rifles, and surrounded us. One of the workers sitting with me in the cab gave me a worried look.

"What's up with that?"

"Don't worry, we've never had problems with the army."

A lieutenant approached, saluted, and asked where we were coming from and where we were going. I explained everything and showed him the official letter we always had on hand: on National Institute of Anthropology and History letterhead, it contained a brief presentation of our work, addressed to "las autoridades civiles, judiciales y militares del estado de Campeche."

The officer turned on his flashlight, pointed it at the document, and read it carefully. As he returned it he said, "So, you're the ones who discovered some sort of archaeological site nearby?"

"Yes, that would be us."

"We were sent here to patrol the roads in the area and be on the lookout for any looters." The lieutenant did not look familiar. It appeared he was not from Xpujil.

"Where are you coming from, if I may ask?"

"From Escárcega, on orders from the general."

Of course. Lieutenant Colonel Alfonso Cristóbal García Melgar, commander of the infantry unit at Xpujil, had kept his promise: he had informed his superior of the find, namely General Héctor Sánchez Gutiérrez, commander of the Thirty-Third Military Zone in Campeche.

On orders from the lieutenant, the soldiers hopped back in the Hummer and let us pass. We had a similar meeting a bit later when we arrived in Conhuás. The soldiers checking vehicles there were from Xpujil, under the direct command of Lieutenant Colonel García Melgar.

After successfully returning from the jungle, we had been rewarded with some welcome recognition: both the lieutenant colonel and the general were taking our efforts and concerns seriously.

26

A Long Way

In the autumn of 2004 I learned that Lieutenant Colonel García Melgar had suffered severe injuries in a jeep accident and had been transferred from Xpujil to Mexico City. When we met there before the beginning of the 2005 season he recounted how his unit had been notified that a drug smugglers' light airplane had crashed while attempting to land on the grassy airstrip that chicleros had used at Lake Chumpich, on the southwestern edge of the Calakmul Biosphere. The crew had apparently survived and managed to flee, but the airplane debris had to be hauled away by the army piece by piece. While making his rounds in the area some time after that, the lieutenant colonel was driving over rocky outcrops along the Guatemala–Mexico border when the brakes of his jeep failed and the vehicle rolled over. He suffered severe chest injuries, but when I saw him he was already well on the way to recovery and as optimistic as ever. He did not know much about the new commander in Xpujil, but he did advise me to call on the general in Campeche.

Drawing lessons from earlier seasons, we started each season better equipped, even though we had limited financing. In 2005, we had quite a few new things.

In the previous season Ciriaco and Guadalupe had already taken us to the sites they knew of, and we were not able to find any other people with knowledge of ruins. It became clear that those who had worked in the area before the biosphere was established were either already dead or too old to accompany us. We could not rely on their memory, and their hints were not very helpful either. Conversations with them would typically go something like this:

"Outside Villahermosa you drive down a dirt trail and come to a fork."

There are multiple trails out of Villahermosa. "Which one?"

"The one leading to Aguada Jerusalem."

Today there are no trails from Villahermosa to Aguada Jerusalem. One leads to the Dos Caobas camp; perhaps there is a junction somewhere. We will try to find our way.

"And then you get to camp, what's its name again?"

Even if he knew the name, it would not help. The last time there was a camp in that area was ages ago.

"I don't remember, but there is an aguada there. You go around, and on this side [indicates with left hand] there is a tall *zapote*."

Around what? On which side? I know *zapote* trees, but they are plentiful everywhere. And anyway, is that particular tree still standing? And where exactly?

"You continue through the forest, leaving the bajo on this side [another arm gesture], and you come to higher ground. You cross the trail leading to El Tigrito [where is that supposed to be?] and on this side [the hand again!] there is a wall, a tall one, you can't miss it."

Oh yes you can. We have never found anything by means of such directions. Even the people who used to walk around this area years ago can no longer find their way: trails, camps, even trees standing out in a cleared area used to be reference points, but everything is different today, overgrown, and the jungle is pretty much the same wherever you go. Even our trusted guide, Guadalupe, a good chiclero and an experienced woodsman, got lost. When he, Vaquero, and Atasta were looking for El Tintal camp, they took a wrong trail at a crossing south of La Fama. After three days of clearing it, they got to an aguada, and it was only then that Guadalupe realized his mistake; it was Aguada Puerto México, not Aguada El Tintal. They had to return to the intersection; three days of hacking had been in vain.

Since we could no longer hope to find knowledgeable people, we had to use other methods. Krištof Oštir, at that time my collaborator at the Institute of Anthropological and Spatial Studies at ZRC SAZU, is an expert in remote sensing techniques, which have been successfully used in archaeology. He and his colleague Žiga Kokalj reviewed Landsat, Radarsat, and Spot satellite images. We could make out the characteristics of the vegetation to help us plan our rounds, but we failed to identify any suspicious points or areas that would hint at the presence of ruins beneath the tropical vegetation. Just as we had the season before, we had cartographic data from the Mexican Comisión Nacional para el Conocimiento y Uso de la Biodiversidad on a laptop, but in addition we procured aerial photographs at a scale of 1:20,000 that the same national commission had ordered to be taken several years before and that we now checked stereoscopically. This gave us new hope: we could make out prominences that, even though overgrown, appeared to be the remains of pre-Hispanic buildings. I determined their coordinates and made a plan for the season. The first objective was Uxul, a site Karl Ruppert had discovered in 1934. The coordinates he provided were in a bajo, but the aerial photographs showed elevated terrain nearby with conspicuous mounds.

There was another novelty aside from aerial photography, one that was very practical and exceedingly important for our daily needs: we had a cook. It had never occurred to me that a woman would be willing to join us until Ciriaco recalled how they had always had cooks at chiclero camps and said he could easily find one. And he did: he talked his wife, Laura, into joining us. After just a few days we became so accustomed to the regular and surprisingly diverse food that it was difficult to imagine how we had survived without a cook in the past. As if we did not have enough work during the day, before she joined us, one of the workers would have to make the tortilla dough in the evening and prepare whatever he could. No wonder our meals used to be more a necessary evil than something to look forward to. Now, everything was different. Doña Laura could dedicate herself to cooking and maintaining the camp, and all the men had to do at camp was collect kindling, cut the occasional fallen tree, and make firewood.

Our fleet expanded as well. We had the white pickup and Vaquero's jeep, but Ciriaco brought his new acquisition as well: since logging was a major business for him, he had recently bought a three-ton 1964 Ford truck, badly beaten but still powerful and effective, or so Ciriaco made us

Figure 26.1. Ciriaco's "new" Ford.

believe. A section of the windshield and many other details were missing, but that was hardly important.

Thus equipped, our convoy left Constitución for Escárcega. To approach Uxul we had been planning to use the southbound dirt trail from Constitución to the Guatemalan border. However, I learned from the commander of the Thirty-Third Military Zone in Campeche—still General Héctor Sánchez Gutiérrez—that the army had made this trail impassable after the unsuccessful landing of the smugglers' small airplane that Lieutenant Colonel García Melgar had told me about. We therefore decided to make a long detour and get to the border using roads leading south from Escárcega. Once we made it to the border we believed we would have no problems because there was a trail running along the border that workers used for their annual deforesting of the border slash. This was carried out by the CILA, which I had heard of before: the acronym stands for the Comisión Internacional de Límites y Aguas (International Commission for Borders and Waters), responsible for maintaining the border according to an agreement between Mexico and Guatemala. The locals also used this term to refer to the team of workers the commission employed to cut the thicket once a year and, if necessary, repair and paint the obelisk-shaped concrete markers erected every few kilometers along the boundary line; the section of border separating the state of Campeche from Guatemala follows a straight line along the 17°49' north parallel.

We set off on Good Friday, March 25, 2005, and first arrived in Escárcega. The only reason the city was booming—it had risen from nothing in the past few decades—was that it is at an important road crossing: this is where the road to Chetumal forks off the main road from central Mexico to Campeche on the west coast of the Yucatán Peninsula. For the average visitor, this city offers hardly any points of interest. While tourists regularly do pause here, it is only because every bus stops here by default. For us, however, Escárcega had a special significance: there may not have been any tourist attractions, but there was no lack of mechanics, tire repair shops, and stores selling spare parts and tools, not to mention food. This time we treated ourselves to one last lunch in civilization before leaving Escárcega and heading south.

Alas, we did not get far. I was at the head of our caravan, Ciriaco's light blue (if any color could be found on it) Ford was behind me, and Vaquero was last with his jeep. Without paying particular attention to the rearview

Figure 26.2. Such obelisks with signs are erected along the Mexico-Guatemala border.

mirror, I suddenly noticed a puff of smoke coming from Ciriaco's engine as if from a minor explosion, and his truck ground to a halt. Vaquero and I stopped as well. It turned out that the electrical wires in the truck were fried. There must have been a short circuit somewhere. Escárcega was still close by and Ciriaco knew an automotive electrician. Vaquero received instructions, drove to the city, and returned in half an hour with the guy. Mexico is one of the most Catholic countries in the world, but it appeared that Good Friday was no obstacle for our electrician: a rotund man in appropriately dirty overalls stumbled out of the car with a large toolbox, his arms greasy to the elbows, indicating we were by no means his first customers that day. He got down to business, discovered what was causing the short circuit, removed all the burned cables, pulled a bunch of new cables from his box, and connected them one by one. He kept rolling around in the cab and bending under the hood in the relentless heat, but he got the job done in less than an hour. The bill? Three hundred pesos, less than thirty dollars. I gave him four hundred pesos, thanked him kindly, and remarked, "It looked nasty for a while there. Thank you so much. I didn't think such a quick remedy was possible. And on Good Friday afternoon!"

"Todo tiene solución, menos la muerte" was his simple and good-natured reply, as if this whole thing were nothing special. There is a solution to everything, except death. How simple and how true! His words would set the tone for what lay ahead of us. And indeed, I later recalled them many times: plenty of problems seemed insurmountable, but we always managed to pull through. Optimism can work miracles.

This was also a very tangible display of why modern vehicles are not fit for the jungle: repairs are simply too complicated. Under the hood of Ciriaco's Ford there was more empty space than engine, and he was able to fix most of the problems himself. Our vehicle problems were far from over, but we were never left desperately stranded.

As it was getting late, we returned to Escárcega, spent the night there, and set out the following morning. We drove through several villages, first heading southwest and then southeast. In late afternoon we arrived at El Desengaño, near the border with Guatemala. The paved road ended there and we set up camp in the nearby village of Santa Rosa, less than a kilometer north of the border. Nobody imagined just how arduous the journey to Uxul would be.

The following morning a boy from Guatemala came by, carrying a rooster he wanted to sell in the village. Unable to find a buyer, he soon returned with bird in hand, so we bought it off him. That the border here was hardly an obstacle soon became clear when Vaquero and I wanted to determine where to proceed. A dirt trail took us to a shack just across the border—actually it was partially in Mexico. The man of the house told us that the trail east at first traced the boundary line but soon turned right into Guatemala. We took it and soon encountered a truck, whose driver told us that we had to return to El Desengaño and take the gravel road east through Solidaridad and Julubal to the village of San Dimas. That is where the dirt track used by the CILA starts: it passes through the abandoned hamlet of Balamkax before it reaches the border a few kilometers from there and continues east, mostly along the actual border slash.

We returned to El Desengaño, but Ciriaco's truck was having problems again. So much brake fluid had leaked from the rear wheels that the brakes barely functioned. While a mechanic was attempting to fix the leak, Vaquero and I used the opportunity to drive his jeep to San Dimas and check out whether this was indeed the right road. Upon returning we were greeted by the news that the brakes could not be repaired. Did we dare continue? It made no sense to return, Ciriaco argued, because the leaking was exacerbated when the brakes were applied, and they needed to be used more on roads than on dirt trails. The situation was worrying: we had a very long journey ahead through the biosphere, where there would not be a living soul, let alone a mechanic. The decision was not easy, but our undertakings would never have happened without taking risks. We would confirm whether the old Latin adage *fortes fortuna adiuvat* (fortune favors the bold) was still valid. Having procured ten liters of brake fluid, we headed out and when night fell pitched camp adjacent to the aguada between the villages of Solidaridad and Julubal. San Dimas, where we arrived the next day, is practically at the end of the world: to the east there is nothing but uninhabited forest. Well, there is the occasional lost soul, but that was a discovery we would not make until later.

The village was a handful of simple shacks made of poles and covered by palm-thatched roofs, which were home to four families. The inhabitants received us with curiosity and allowed us to camp on the banks of a nearby stream. In these parts, on the eastern edge of the Candelaria watershed, which drains into the Gulf of Mexico, an occasional waterway can still be found, but farther east there are none. Ciriaco did not know the area. He did know that Lake Paixbán, which we were bound to pass because it was right on the Mexico-Guatemala border, never dried up, but we were still twenty-five kilometers from the lake as the crow flies.

After a tasty dinner prepared by Doña Laura—the recently acquired poultry made for a nice addition to the menu—we discussed the plan for the next few days and then fell asleep. We were awoken at the crack of dawn by the roosters in the village vying to outdo each other in a wild crowing match. It was a beautiful morning, with the breakfast and the burbling of the creek by the camp inspiring us with optimism, which was only slightly dented by a small detail: the white pickup had a flat. No big deal; it was neither the first nor the last, plus we had two spare tires—Ciriaco's truck could carry quite a load.

We spent the next few days clearing the trail in the white pickup and jeep, returning every evening to San Dimas, where Doña Laura was in charge of the food and the camp: it made no sense to move until we found the next source of water. But it all lasted much longer than we had anticipated.

Figure 26.3. Typical obstacles on an abandoned dirt trail.

The first part of the journey was easy. The very first day the trail, which wound through the fields of San Dimas and then through the forest, brought us to Balamkax, an abandoned hamlet that was now a few dilapidated shacks on a hill covered in tall grass. From there the trail led through the forest and we had to clear more overgrown sections, but it was not until the following day when we arrived at the border that the real work began. There, the trail followed the border slash separating Mexico from Guatemala, and it was terribly overgrown. Because the ten-meter-wide slash is devoid of trees that would block sunlight from reaching all the way to the ground, the thicket absolutely flourished. The CILA clears the slash every year in April or thereabouts, but it had not yet been there that year. We arrived at a dry aguada with a band of tall, dry grass around it, and then the vegetation turned into dense shrubbery. Whereas tire ruts had been more or less visible before, Ciriaco was now unable to find any, no matter how hard he tried. The path did not continue along the border, he concluded. A few hundred meters back we had noticed a trail leading from the border slash north and decided to check it out. It weaved through an abandoned settlement that had clearly not seen any human presence in years, although there were fairly fresh horse droppings, indicating that someone had used it not long before. The trail continued north, before it encouragingly turned northeast.

Filled with the hope of being on the right track, one that would surely soon turn toward the border again, we followed it the next day and arrived at a fence. There were a few cows in a pen, and a horse with a bearded rider appeared from around a bend. Although he said his name was Mateo, we could not resist giving him a different moniker because of his appearance: for us, he was Osama bin Laden. He wanted to know all the minutiae of our work and we happily obliged him, but he was not very chatty and would not come clean as to whether the CILA was in fact using that trail. However, he did stress several times that the eastbound dirt trail from his ranch to Lake Los Manguitos was navigable because soldiers had cleared it the previous year and that it would be best for us to head to the lake and descend toward the border from there. Ciriaco knew Los Manguitos, which lies about eight kilometers north of the border, but he did not know whether it was possible to get to the border from there, and in any case we were still over seventeen kilometers from the lake in a direct line.

We went to take a look at the dirt trail and were not encouraged by what we saw. Not only was it overgrown but thick saplings were sprouting up everywhere. When "bin Laden" lagged behind a bit at one point, I turned to Ciriaco and said, "Listen, if there's anything I know it's that no one has driven here for the past five or ten years."

"That's exactly what I wanted to tell you." Ciriaco nodded. "This guy would like us to clear the trail to Los Manguitos for him."

"But where the hell do the CILA trucks drive?"

We had no idea, but we had to return. Before we bid each other farewell, the bearded man showed us a ruin close to his house. A small pyramid, nothing special, and anyway we had bigger things to worry about: Where was the trail leading east?

We returned on a dirt trail that the owner of the ranch used for contact with civilization, which brought us to El Desengaño. The trail was well trodden; if only we had known about it before! In a store where we quenched our thirst we ran into a man who provided some new information: he assured us that the path used by the CILA ran almost entirely along the border; after the aguada we had run into the day before, it veered into Mexican territory but soon returned to the border slash.

Vaquero did not feel well and woke up feverish the next morning; it was clear he had caught the flu from the just-recovered Ciriaco. He remained in camp while the rest of us, instilled with new hope, started our search again on the border, at the point where we thought there was no way forward. We bypassed the section overgrown with thick and impenetrable brush but returned to the border after two to three hundred meters to slightly less overgrown terrain, and—there were the tire tracks! It was easy to spot them in the grass and follow them back. We lost them again in the thicket, but there was no path into the forest left or right. It was thus clear that the trail traced the border but had become so overgrown within a year that it was no longer visible.

We cleared out a corridor for the vehicles and drove on. Just as we had been told the day before, the trail soon turned onto Mexican territory and then returned to the boundary line. I measured the coordinates when it was time to return in late afternoon. We were eight kilometers from Lake Paixbán, and the return to San Dimas took almost three hours. We therefore decided we would all leave San Dimas the next day and attempt to reach Paixbán together.

27

From Paixbán to Uxul

Fortune was on our side. We made good headway, and around four in the afternoon the trail turned right, into Guatemala (we had yet to be asked to show our passports), and eventually led us to a place that the border workers must have used as a camp: there were remains of a fireplace and a simple wooden structure for pots and equipment. To the north a flat surface overgrown with tall grass opened up, and just a few meters farther we saw water glinting: Laguna El Paixbán.

Once we made camp, it started to rain lightly and did not stop until the small hours of the morning. At dawn when the sky cleared we were treated to an almost romantic scene: the expansive clearing to the north was mostly covered in grass and only partially filled with water since it was the middle of the dry season; through the misty haze above the lake we could discern the outlines of trees on the banks. The pale blue of the sky purified by rain melded into a vivid red in the east, which became brighter and brighter until the first rays of the sun rising from behind the dark tree canopies—sharply delineated in the eastern sky—poured over the landscape.

No swimming, no sandy beach, lots of mosquitoes—but for us Paixbán was like manna from heaven. To get to the water we had to cut the brush

Figure 27.1. Morning mist above Lake Paixbán.

and lay down logs over the muddy banks. But there was plenty of water, and until we could find a new source as we made our way east, this would be a more than ideal place to camp.

Besides, Paixbán was almost legendary. Nowadays all you can see is wilderness, but there used to be a settlement somewhere on the banks that shared the lake's name and was encountered by the first Spaniards to penetrate this area in the seventeenth century. Although the population declined drastically after the demise of the Classic Maya civilization, the territory was not completely abandoned. Records of the first attempts by the Spanish to Christianize and subjugate the remote areas of the central Yucatán Peninsula mention several settlements, but these must have been very simple and sparsely populated because their remains are not visible on the surface; we had done fieldwork over an expansive area but found hardly any archaeological remains that could be dated to the Postclassic period. The expeditions coming in the second half of the seventeenth century from Mérida in the northern Yucatán Peninsula, whose main goal was the still-independent kingdom of the Itzá in what is now the Petén Department in northeastern Guatemala, passed through several settlements, among which Chumpich and Paixbán are also mentioned. The descriptions of places and trails that these missionary and conquering expeditions blazed suggest that both settlements were somewhere near the lakes that have retained these names to this day: Lake Chumpich is twelve kilometers north of Paixbán. Considering that the Spanish incursions helped reduce the already sparse population and contributed to the demise of many villages, it is interesting that even after the area was abandoned, both toponyms were preserved among the chicleros and loggers, who would come to the area only occasionally and set up their transient camps along the aguadas and lakes.

Even the route the Spanish expeditions traveled through Chumpich and Paixbán has changed little to this day: it was described by some late nineteenth-century travelers, including the famous Teobert Maler, who went from Yucatán to Petén in 1895 and mentioned some native villages along the way. Maler was one of the first explorers who undertook serious study and documentation of Maya archaeological sites in the second half of the nineteenth century. Born in Italy to German parents, he moved to Vienna as a young man, took Austrian citizenship, and, eager to travel and see faraway lands, joined the army of the Habsburg archduke Maximilian, who let himself be crowned emperor of Mexico in 1864, a victim of the political machinations of his brother, the emperor Franz Joseph, and French Emperor Napoleon III. Because a financial crisis forced the Mexican president Benito Juárez to decree a two-year moratorium on debt payments to France, England, and Spain, an army from the three countries attacked Mexico at the behest of Napoleon III in 1862. The English and Spanish forces soon retreated, but the French continued their conquest and, after their initial success, declared a Catholic empire with the support of Mexican monarchists. At Napoleon's initiative, the crown was offered to Maximilian, who accepted it, but a sad fate awaited him despite his adherence to enlightened ideas regarding governance. With the support of the United States, Juárez's army eventually defeated the French and they withdrew, but Maximilian, refusing to retreat in time, was executed in 1867. I was interested to learn that the Habsburg monarchy's Mexican adventure also featured Slovenian soldiers, because it was in Ljubljana—currently the capital of the Republic of Slovenia, my home country, but then part of the Austrian empire—that the Imperial Mexican Volunteer Corps was formed under the command of General Thun-Hohenstein. And it was in Ljubljana that the young Teobert Maler also joined the recruits. Many returned after the defeat, but Maler took advantage of the general amnesty Juárez granted to those who helped the occupying forces, and he remained in Mexico, where his research endeavors took him into the heart of the Yucatán Peninsula.

The route Maler described was also taken in 1934 by Karl Ruppert's third expedition, and a subsequent logging trail cut out a similar path. Leading south of Constitución on the main Escárcega–Chetumal road, it is more or less passable all the way to the abandoned chiclero camp called La Esperanza—now a watch post of the Calakmul Biosphere, which reaches as far southwest as Lake Paixbán—but then continues farther south past Lake Chumpich. This was the trail we had intended to take to the border before we abandoned our plan and opted for a detour after the general in Campeche mentioned that the army had made it impassable.

Many traces of this turbulent history have long since been covered by jungle. Without excavations, all one can see today are the ruins of grandiose stone buildings constructed during the Classic Maya florescence, but no one knows where the later settlements of small, impoverished

Figure 27.2. The workers who maintain the border slash sometimes use the clearing as a football pitch. Each game thus takes place in Mexico and Guatemala at the same time, but fans from either country are notably absent.

communities mentioned in the historical records were located, or what they looked like. Even the simple chiclero camps left more evidence: the remains of iron kettles, glassware, even the occasional grassy airstrip that drug traffickers attempt to use every now and then. The notion that people used to live and walk here—but left no trace whatsoever—imbued Lake Paixbán with a mystical sheen. Today, it is in the middle of nowhere; the lush tropical rainforest stretches in every direction, truly the sole victor over the course of time. The only regular visitors are the workers who maintain the border, but even they come just once a year, pitch a camp, clear the nearest stretch of the border slash, and move on.

The morning idyll of the lakeside forest was interrupted by the noise of the generator we had to operate to charge the batteries of our satellite phones, cameras, and the computer on which we accessed the maps and satellite photos of the area and approximated our position. We were still fifteen kilometers from our goal—the place Uxul was supposed to be. Following the trail, which circumscribed the south shore of Lake Paixbán and shortly returned to the border slash, we first reached the next camp of the CILA team; as a name cut into a tree revealed, for some reason it was called La Güera (The Blonde). There was a dry aguada nearby, and next to it another trail that forked northwest from the boundary path—was this the trail leading to Lake Chumpich and farther north?

Continuing east, we arrived at the next camp, where the letters "Chumbec" were carved into a tree. We decided to pack up the camp at Lake Paixbán and relocate here. Not only was the setting pleasant, but it was also a good point of departure in the quest for Uxul, which was supposed to be less than five kilometers north, according to the coordinates. If we ran out of water we could always return to Lake Paixbán to fetch some.

So the following day everyone was on the road again. There were a few steep climbs with horribly sharp rocks in this section, and it was about here that the former commander of the Xpujil unit, Lieutenant Colonel García Melgar, got hurt. Equipped with four-wheel drive and reduction gears, the white pickup and Vaquero's jeep steadily climbed the rocks, but Ciriaco's truck worried us. It was overheating and the brakes were not reliable. At the top of the steepest climb I turned the white pickup around, uncoiled the fifty-meter cable from the front winch, hooked it up to Ciriaco's truck, and slowly pulled it up the slope.

At La Güera camp we were pleased to discover that we would be spared having to clear the trail any farther along the border. We had expected to sooner or later encounter the group that clears this segment of the border every year around April, and now they were here: fifty machete-wielding cutters working in the wake of a large, roaring truck. As I stepped out of my pickup and approached, the driver greeted me, no less surprised than I was.

"Don Iván!"

"Don Alfredo!"

It was Alfredo Díaz Torres, who had led us to the sites of Champerico and El Gallinero some years before. For the second time he had secured a job with the commission in charge of border maintenance as the driver of a truck carrying equipment, water, and food. He said the trail northwest indeed led to Lake Chumpich, but he knew only the first six kilometers of it, to the point where there was a small aguada that never ran dry. So, there was another source of water nearby in the event we ran out.

We pitched camp at Chumbec, but there was no trail from there to our destination, which meant we would have to hoof it. In the afternoon we cleared the first kilometers of the footpath north, and the following day we came across the first small ruins before midday. The terrain was gradually rising, and the GPS device soon led us to a tall pyramidal building. This was the prominent point I had seen in the aerial photograph. A few dozen meters farther was a stela with a fairly well-preserved frontal relief, standing in front of a long building. We immediately checked the photocopy of the chapter on Uxul from the book by Karl Ruppert and his epigrapher John Denison; they had published photographs and drawings of only the better-preserved monuments, and the one that we were facing was among them: we were standing before Stela 8 in Uxul!

After surveying the site, we found many looters' trenches, but all fifteen stelae recorded by Ruppert's expedition in 1934 were still exactly where they should have been. We discovered that, as usual, Ruppert's plan of Uxul was precise, but there were some major buildings missing. They must have been in a hurry: Ruppert complains in his field diary that work on this site, during the last leg of the 1934 season (which is precisely why they called it Uxul, "the end"), was conducted under time pressure and was, on top of that, hampered by constant rain.

The results of our previous season, in particular the discovery of Oxpemul, aroused so much interest from the National Geographic Society that it financed this expedition as well and commissioned one of its photographers to document our work. As I reasoned that the photographer

Figure 27.3. After an extended intermission, Stela 8 in Uxul once again had visitors.

would want to come to Uxul and that our epigrapher Nikolai Grube would join us at the same time, we deferred any detailed documentation of the site and continued east from Chumbec the following day. The plan was to return via Villahermosa and check out a few more points along the way that we had noticed in the aerial photographs.

28

Four Stelae

In the pleasant aguada that Don Alfredo had told us about we indeed found fresh water. In the following days we examined two complexes of ruins: we stumbled upon one of them only by coincidence, while the second confirmed our expectations based on aerial photographs; thus we christened it Chicaanticaanal (Seen from Above).

The dirt trail leading east, which partly followed the border and partly ran through the Mexican territory alongside it, brought us on April 7 to an intersection where the chiclero camp Tres Marías used to be. There, we took a left toward Villahermosa and set up camp at a point from which we were able to set off on foot through a forest toward the west. In aerial photographs we could see a slope there with a pointy top: a pyramid perhaps?

We had to clear almost two kilometers of path before reaching the hill. Close to the top the slope gradually transitioned into a pyramidal ruin, onto which we immediately clambered. It was just slightly over ten meters tall, but it had a stela sitting in a looter's trench at the top. Unfortunately, the relief image and inscription on it were in poor condition. Pascual, one of our men, was the first to climb down the other side of the pyramid and announced another surprise.

"There are three more stelae here!" he cried.

Three more?! The aerial photograph did not show any large structures. Could there be four monuments at such a relatively small site?

We all swiftly descended toward Pascual and laid our eyes on three stelae at the northern foot of the pyramid. Although leaning sideways, they were still upright and arranged in a line, with their fronts facing north across a plaza rimmed on the east and west by two smaller structures. To the north a thicket obstructed the view. Naturally, we first went to check out the stelae. Was anything inscribed on them?

They all seemed extremely effaced at first glance, but then our attention was drawn to the western side of the easternmost one, where a date written in the Maya calendrical system was clearly discernible: 8.18.0.0.0 12 Ahau.

Like other Mesoamerican peoples, the Maya, too, used two basic calendrical cycles. The calendar year had 365 days and consisted of eighteen periods of twenty days, or "months," followed by five additional days, which were believed to be inauspicious. This 365-day year, called *haab* (year) in Yucatec Mayan, did not maintain a permanent correlation with the slightly longer tropical year (the year of the seasons), because the Maya and other Mesoamericans did not use any regular intercalation system comparable to the leap year adjustments in our own calendar. The second important cycle, which had 260 days, is often designated with the Yucatec name *tzolkin* (count of days) or referred to as the Sacred Cycle or Divinatory Almanac, since it played an important role in religious life and astrology. Each day had a unique name consisting of a number—one through thirteen—and one of twenty signs, whose Yucatec names at the time of the Conquest were Imix, Ik, Akbal, Kan, Chicchán, Cimí, Manik, Lamat, Muluc, Oc, Chuen, Eb, Ben, Ix, Men, Cib, Cabán, Edznab, Cauac, and Ahau. Since the numbers and signs always followed one another in the same order and without interruption, 260 days had to pass for all possible combinations of the thirteen numbers and twenty signs to appear. These sacred cycles followed one another continuously, independently of the 365-day year—similar to the seven-day week going around without a break in our calendar. Therefore, in different years a certain day of the 260-day cycle would fall on different dates, and it often appeared twice in one 365-day year.

Each day thus had a name from the Sacred Cycle and was also marked as a day in a month of the 365-day year. As a simple calculation shows, the intermeshing of the two cycles was such that the same combination of dates from both cycles occurred every 18,980 days, or every fifty-two 365-day years. Both calendrical cycles were used throughout Mesoamerica beginning as early as the final centuries BC. The fifty-two-year cycle, now referred to as the Calendar Round, was also known throughout the area. Because the same dates were repeated at fifty-two-year intervals and because individual calendrical cycles were not uniquely marked, this system allowed the precise dating of events only within each fifty-two-year cycle.

While most Mesoamerican peoples knew only the cyclical calendar described above, in southeastern Mesoamerica another system was devel-

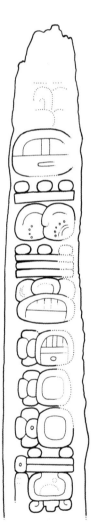

Figure 28.1. On the right side of Stela 2 in Candzibaantún the date 8.18.0.0.0 12 Ahau is inscribed (drawing by Nikolai Grube).

oped slightly before the Common Era, which enabled the unambiguous, absolute dating of events. Today it is known as the Long Count and was introduced by the Olmecs, who in the Preclassic period created the first great Mesoamerican civilization along the southern coast of the Gulf of Mexico. However, in later periods the Long Count was used only by the Maya.

The basis of the Long Count is the positional or place-value notation of numbers. In such a system the value of each digit in a number is determined by its position, thus making it possible to write large numbers with relatively few digits, which simplifies calculations. We are, of course, familiar with such a notation; however, ours is the decimal, or base-10 system, while the Maya—and the Olmecs before them—used the vigesimal, or base-20 system, comprising 20 digits, 0 through 19, and place values, each of which was a power of 20. More accurately, in all their texts a modified vigesimal system was used, with the following place values: 1, 20, 360 (= 20×18), 7,200 (= $20^2 \times 18$), 144,000 (= $20^3 \times 18$), 2,880,000 (= $20^4 \times 18$), and so on. With the value of the third position (360) being close to the number of days in a tropical year, such a modified vigesimal system clearly indicates its use for calendrical purposes.

Similar to our calendar, the Long Count also has a starting point, which in the Gregorian calendar—if reconstructed for the time before its official introduction in 1582—corresponds to August 13, 3114 BC. Obviously, this date does not refer to any true historical event, as it falls some three millennia before the earliest inceptions of calendrics and writing in Mesoamerica. It was undoubtedly calculated retrospectively on the basis of mythological, numerological, and possibly also astronomical criteria. The dates of the Long Count denote, using the modified vigesimal system, the number of days elapsed since the beginning of the count, as well as the number of individual cycles that have passed. Place values correspond to the duration of the individual time units: *kin* (day), *uinal* (the 20-day month), *tun* (18 *uinals*, 360 days), *katun* (20 *tuns*, 7,200 days), and *baktun* (20 *katuns*, 144,000 days). The earliest (Olmec) dates reach back to the first century BC, the time of *baktun* 7, while the latest ones fall in the tenth century, in *baktun* 10. Naturally, only historical dates, referring to events more or less contemporary with the inscriptions recording them, fall within this time span. Besides these, however, other dates can be found that have no real connection to contemporary events, since they reach back into the deep mythological past, or even into the distant future.

For such calculations, which encompass millions of years, numbers with higher place values—that is, longer cycles—were used.

The Maya typically wrote in double columns from top to bottom and from left to right. Many texts on stelae and other monuments begin with a series of calendrical data: the characteristic introductory glyph is followed by the date of the Long Count, the dates of the 260-day and 365-day cycles, and often also by other calendrical and astronomical data referring to the day of the event described thereafter. The numbers could be recorded in two different ways. In one, somewhat esoteric and more difficult to read, the individual digits were represented by the heads of deities depicted in profile. The other, simpler system was the bar-and-dot notation, in which a dot or circle stood for 1 and a bar for 5, while 0 was recorded with a shell cut in half, or a sign similar to a four-petaled flower or clover.

The date on our stela was written in the latter system. The introductory glyph at the top was followed by the numbers 8, 18, and three 0s shaped like a clover. Below was the corresponding date in the 260-day cycle: 12 Ahau. The three 0s indicated the end of a *katun*. The Maya would often celebrate such "round" dates with ceremonies and immortalize these events on monuments. I had a program in my calculator for converting Maya dates to our calendrical system: the date on the stela was July 7, AD 396.

There was no way to know who had celebrated that day or in what manner: everything else on the stela was effaced. However, the date was interesting in itself. On Stela 5 in Balakbal—Ruppert's site that we had rediscovered some years ago—a date is inscribed corresponding to the year 406. Up to that point, it was the earliest of all the Maya dates known in Mexico, but now our stela beat this "record" by ten years. Otherwise, the oldest known date on Maya monuments was the one on Stela 29 of Tikal, Guatemala, corresponding to the year AD 292.

The site was not especially big: a ridge of some kind, probably a ritual path, led north from the plaza with the stelae, and there was another group of buildings to the northwest, most likely residences for the local elite. In the following days we also found several smaller groups of buildings and a few quarries on nearby hills.

The decision as to what to name the newly found site was not too difficult: Candzibaantún (Four Inscribed Stones).

29

Great Effort and
Little Reward

Delaying our return to civilization much longer was not an option. The engine of the white pickup was making strange sounds; the vegetation on the overgrown trails had been coiling around the drive shafts for so long it had started to damage the differential gaskets on the pickup and Vaquero's jeep; Ciriaco's truck was guzzling not only brake fluid but also engine oil; and we were starting to run out of food. We resupplied with water in Villahermosa, continued north, and pitched camp at Central Buenfil, the old chiclero camp by the junction with the road that connects Conhuás with Calakmul. We wanted to check out two more points we had noticed in the aerial photographs.

When we visited Calakmul last year and I stood on the tallest pyramid, I noticed a conical protrusion on a hill about ten kilometers north. I could not see much more than that with binoculars, but it looked as if it could be a pyramid. I measured the azimuth with the compass, identified the hill on the map, and later took a closer look at the aerial photographs: they suggested there might indeed be a pyramidal structure on top of the hill.

We drove to the nearest point we could on the road and, after entering the coordinates of the hill into the GPS device, headed west into the forest.

About a kilometer in I must have pressed something on the GPS device and realized, to my horror, that I had erased all the data, both the waypoints we had already recorded and those that should be checked out. We had already transferred most of the waypoints recorded this season into the computer, but the problem was that the point we intended to find now was gone as well. My cursing did not help; we had to find a solution. We were on an elevation and Pascual had just started to climb a tree to look around, so I handed him the compass and, once he saw the hill with the protrusion, instructed him from below how to read the azimuth. He had never held the device before and the position he was in did not make the job easy: clinging with one hand to a branch high in the canopy, he held the compass in the other hand as he attempted to read a direction toward the hill through the dense leaves.

"The hill is in the direction somewhere between the numbers 220 and 240," he yelled.

We continued in that direction and arrived at a completely overgrown and long-abandoned dirt trail. From my backpack I pulled out the stereoscope and aerial photographs of the area, and I was pleased to notice a dirt trail from the east that turned south before it reached our target hill. If we followed the trail it would take us to the eastern foot of the hill, where we could make our ascent. I also tried to determine again the coordinates of the hill we were searching for, but that was not easy in the middle of the forest surrounded by pesky bugs, without a desk or the proper tools. I entered the resulting numbers into the GPS, but the device kept trying to send me in a completely different direction from the one that Pascual had determined. Considering the trouble I had determining the coordinates, I chose to trust Pascual over the navigation device.

We followed the dirt trail we had just reached. It was turning in a direction that seemed right, but it was badly overgrown, and we made excruciatingly slow progress. After we had walked for what seemed like forever, we came across a fairly extensive area of medium-sized ruins, but then we suddenly descended into a bajo that appeared never ending. As far as we could make out, there were no hills anywhere around, whereas in the aerial photograph the closest bajo was over two kilometers southwest of the hill we were searching for. Apparently we had gotten the direction completely wrong.

After turning around, we arrived at the foot of a hill rising toward the north. Pascual offered to survey it. I checked my GPS once more and discovered that the coordinates I had determined from the aerial photograph but did not trust were indeed toward the north, no more than six hundred meters away. Since it was already late and I was the only one with a flashlight, I told the others to return to the road along the path we had opened, while Pascual and I climbed the hill. Stubbornness and frustration with having spent an entire day wandering around in vain helped me overcome my fatigue, and anyway I simply could not turn down Pascual's offer.

This was the right hill, but the site on it was fairly modest: there was a pyramid about ten meters tall, dominating a leveled area to the west, no doubt a plaza, bounded by a few low mounds. Pascual tried to look around from the pyramid. He recognized the prominence from which he had determined the direction in the morning and showed it to me.

"Are you sure it was that hill?"

"Of course, we came from there," he said, pointing. "Then the terrain rose, and somewhere on that hill I climbed the tree."

There was no reason not to believe him; he had proven many times before that he had a very good sense of direction in the forest. I took the compass, sighted the hill—and the reason we had gone astray suddenly became clear.

"My dear Pascual, now I know why we got lost."

He gave me a perplexed look.

"That hill is at 144 degrees. This means that from there the direction toward the hill we're standing on now is approximately 324 degrees. You told me you saw that hill in the direction roughly between 220 and 240 degrees, but in reality, it was between 320 and 340 degrees!"

This information did not tell him much, but it was not difficult to explain.

"Instead of walking northwest, we were heading southwest," I said as I also illustrated the not-insignificant mistake with my arms.

He took off his hat and scratched his head in embarrassment.

"Well, you know, a poor farmer doesn't know these things."

"Don't worry about it. We are both at fault. I made the first mistake by erasing all the waypoints from the device, and then you read the direction incorrectly. But it doesn't matter; we made mistakes and corrected them too. At least tomorrow we won't have to come here again."

"But when we passed by this morning, I told you we should check out this hill."

He really had said that, but it did not make sense to me because it was in a completely different direction from the one he had read before. Instead of trusting his numbers, I should have trusted his natural sense of orientation and the coordinates I had determined in the aerial photograph.

We were satisfied but exhausted, and it was already pitch black when we returned to the road, where everyone else was waiting for us. The day was not lost; the effort had not been for naught.

It was a different story the next day. I stayed behind at camp to sort out my field notes and make several calls on the satellite phone. I had to call the mechanic to arrange repairs and contact the people who would be joining us in the coming days: the National Geographic photographer, our epigrapher Nikolai, and the surveyor Tomaž. The rest of the crew went to check out another point north of camp. I drove them to the best spot on the road and agreed to wait for them there in the afternoon.

They returned at around six in the afternoon, completely exhausted. First, they had to quench their thirst with the fresh drinks I had brought; Vaquero chugged half a liter of liquid, lay down on the asphalt breathing heavily, and remained there pretty much motionless for some ten minutes, his arms and legs stretched out, his eyes closed, and his mouth shut as the rest gradually spoke up. They had walked more than twelve kilometers over mostly nasty vegetation but found practically nothing. On the way, they stumbled across a few mounds, the remains of simple houses, but what looked like a giant pyramid in an aerial photograph was in fact just a natural gypsum peak. Such features are pretty steep, and because the depth is exaggerated when aerial photographs are viewed stereoscopically, they appear much higher and more pointed than they really are. We had likewise been fooled by a similar hill near the Blengio last year. But that is just the way things are in our line of work: unless we check things out on the ground, we might never dispel that nagging doubt—what if something is there after all?

30

Where Is Ruppert's Diary Leading Us?

As usual, we had plenty of errands to run in civilization. Aside from all manner of vehicle repairs, we had to do the shopping and even take care of some medical issues. We stopped by the clinic in Xpujil, whose director, Dr. Ricardo Silva Alcántara, we had met years before when he was still working at Ley de Fomento Agropecuario. He was always ready to help in any way possible, and we were far from the only ones he was willing to help. I also talked to the photographer who was supposed to join us. It was Kenneth Garrett himself, one of National Geographic's best, and he was to be accompanied by his Mexican assistant Jesús López, likewise a photographer, and Virginia Morell, who was assigned to write a story about our work. But their arrival was still quite a few days away, which allowed us to do a bit more fieldwork in the meantime. The epigrapher Nikolai notified me that he could not come before early May.

I also stopped by the military base. The commander was not around but I did talk to a senior officer, who, to my surprise, told me that the trail south of Constitución, past La Esperanza camp and toward Lake Chumpich, was passable: after the incident with the smugglers' airplane, the army had disabled only the landing strip in Chumpich, not the trail. It seemed that the general in Campeche had not had good information and that our long detour via Escárcega had been unnecessary; we could have avoided the time-consuming effort along the border, not to mention the turn down the dead-end trail where we encountered "bin Laden." On the other hand, we would not have seen Lake Paixbán. It was also true that no one actually knew what the trail was like beyond Chumpich, but it was not so far to the border from there. The next time we visited Uxul we would definitely take that trail.

But this time we went to Villahermosa. We first inspected several points around Candzibaantún. During our first visit to the site we had noticed something that looked like a pyramid to the southwest. In fact, it turned out to be just tall trees: we combed a large area in that direction but found nothing. We did, however, discover a larger group of buildings on a nearby hill, and a quarry with well-preserved cuts into the limestone bedrock.

Before I had to pick up the National Geographic team I took an evening to explain the plan for the next few days to Atasta, Vaquero, and the rest of the crew. We needed to clear the trail to Cheyokolnah, where the photographer Ken Garrett would undoubtedly want to go. We had opened the trail last year, but since then there must have been plenty of new growth and perhaps the occasional fallen tree; once he arrived it would not make sense to waste time clearing. I also told them to check out a few points around Yaxnohcah. I showed them aerial photographs in which I had noticed two potential groups of larger architectural structures northeast and southeast of the urban core, which we had inspected and mapped the previous year: looking through the stereoscope, I could see two conical shapes about a kilometer southeast, and another sticking out from a hill a similar distance to the northeast, almost at the edge of Bajo El Laberinto. If these were pyramids, there must be other buildings in the area as well.

As we talked, Atasta asked with hesitation, in his typical reserved manner, "What about . . . Pared de los Reyes? Aren't we going to look for it anymore?"

The mysterious site, which we had searched for so stubbornly last year, still gnawed at everyone. Ciriaco immediately chimed in as well.

"Yes, Pared de los Reyes. I've asked a few more people who have walked around here and know these places. No one has ever heard of these ruins or an aguada called Unión. But if Ruppert says what you said, Pared de los Reyes must be somewhere around here, from La Fama toward La

Esperanza, where his expedition went. The structure could not have just sunk into the ground. It may have deteriorated further, but there must be something left."

"I think so too," I replied. "If you really want to find Pared de los Reyes, I am delighted, because I haven't given up on it either."

I showed them a satellite image of the area on my computer and summarized the information they already knew. Ruppert said they had ridden mules from Aguada La Fama on a trail northwest and arrived at Aguada Unión two hours later. After a ten- to fifteen-minute walk northwest of the aguada, they encountered a quadrangle whose western building had stuccowork representing human figures with headdresses. The previous year we had found an aguada we thought was Aguada Unión because it was the right distance and direction from La Fama. We combed a vast part of the surrounding area and found many ruins, but the building Ruppert described remained elusive. We did not find any other aguadas either.

"But I have new data this year. You've already seen the aerial photographs. So far, they've helped us quite a lot—well, except for that gypsum peak."

Vaquero rolled his eyes and spewed out a few words not fit to print.

"In the aerial photographs I checked the area around the aguada that we found last year, and southwest of it I found another one. At least it looks like it could be an aguada. If it is, it's very small, but this does not mean it was not important in the past."

"No no," Ciriaco concurred. "Sometimes small aguadas are more reliable than big ones, and they may contain more or better water. Many chiclero camps used to be next to small aguadas."

"Remember, Ciriaco? When we walked close to that dry aguada last year you said there had to be another one nearby—you saw the traces of a mule trail that we followed and then lost."

"Yes, and I told you it definitely contained water—we heard birds, oropendolas, which are never far from water."

"Exactly. But I have one more thing," I continued. "The Peabody Museum at Harvard University keeps Ruppert's field diaries. I have procured copies of them and—this is unbelievable, Ruppert's notes are so precise and exhaustive . . . come to think of it, Atasta, have you ever seen Ruppert's diaries?"

"No, why?"

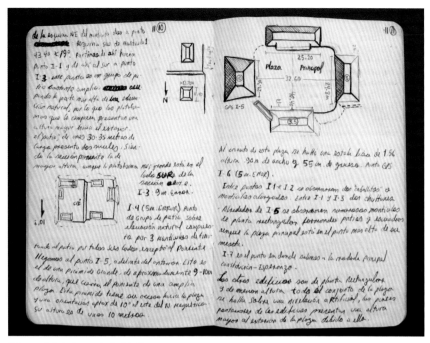

Figure 30.1. Atasta's field diary.

"Your diary is in the same style as Ruppert's—just as precise, neatly written, full of drawings . . . if anyone were to see my diary . . . better not, I'm the only one who can decipher it."

Atasta smiled, embarrassed, and cast his eyes down. He was always reserved and taciturn, sometimes outright uncommunicative; he was quite soft-spoken, and the only time he raised his voice was while mapping in order to tell the workers where to position the prisms. He lived for archaeology and the Maya. His field diary was exemplary: detailed descriptions, whole sentences, legible writing, drawings; he used every opportunity to sketch a building floor plan, no matter how small or uninteresting the building was. He would often spend evenings in the light of the campfire adding information he had not managed to write down during the day.

"So," I continued, "Ruppert's diary is staggeringly precise. He even recorded what time they got up, when they had breakfast, and such things. And, what is particularly important for us, he describes in detail the trails they were traveling on."

I showed them a copy of Ruppert's diary for 1934.

"In this diary entry he describes how they got to Aguada Unión. He says that on April 4, 1934, they left La Fama at 8:20 a.m. heading northwest with the mules. They first passed a small graveyard holding the remains of three Mexicans killed in a fight between Guatemalan and Mexican chicleros several years before. Lundell also mentions this dispute, which was over who could collect chicle on the Guatemalan side and who on the Mexican side."

"I've heard about that," Ciriaco remarked.

"A sad scene, Ruppert says: graves with rickety crosses completely overgrown with brush. And then he continues that they crossed a *tintal* at 9:15 . . ."

"This means they crossed a bajo," Ciriaco interrupted me once again. "That is the only place where the *tinto*[1] grows."

". . . yes, and that the trail turned north there. At 9:20 a.m. they saw a quarry on the right side of the trail, at 9:35 they crossed another *tintal*, at 9:50 they walked over a smaller group of ruins, still going north, and at around 10:10 they arrived at Aguada Unión. So, they walked about an hour northwest and another hour north. I've plotted their path on the satellite image of the area, assuming they walked with an average speed of four and a half kilometers per hour."

"This is more or less how much you can cover in an hour," Ciriaco said, "if you consider that the path is winding and that they probably made a brief stop at the quarry."

"Of course, there's even a small sketch of the cross section of the quarry in the diary. I surmised that they walked at this average speed also from other instances when Ruppert mentions at what time they left a place and when they arrived at another place: we know where many of the camps were—for example Altamira, Villahermosa, Jerusalem—and we can measure the distances on the map."

I showed them the path I had drawn on the computer screen.

"Here you see the line that I drew in: first it leads from La Fama northwest—I simply took the median northwest, 315 degrees azimuth—and before it turns north it does in fact cross a small bajo. This must be the *tintal* that Ruppert mentions. Then the line turns north and crosses another bajo, which again corresponds to Ruppert's notes. So, if his information is accurate and they did in fact walk at an average speed of around

---

1. *Haematoxylum campechianum.*

4.5 kilometers per hour, they walked around 4.1 kilometers northwest and then a similar distance north. And when I plotted this path, it took me to a point less than five hundred meters from the aguada that I discovered in the aerial photograph, whereas the aguada around which we were searching last year is almost 2.5 kilometers to the east."

"Great," Vaquero exclaimed. "We have to find this aguada. It must be Aguada Unión."

"I hope so. If it is—well, if what we see in the photo is an aguada at all—then all we have to do is check the area to the northwest; we did not get that far last year. But first it would make sense to open up a few more kilometers of the dirt trail toward La Esperanza. That way we could approach closer to this point with a vehicle and not have to walk all eight or more kilometers from the turn for La Fama."

I showed them the abandoned dirt trail, which was quite visible in the aerial photograph: maintaining the same direction it followed from Villahermosa to the junction for La Fama, the section we had cleared last year, it continued northwest and came within a kilometer of the place we believed the aguada would be.

"Write down the coordinates of this aguada," I told Atasta and Vaquero, "or just enter them into the GPS, along with the coordinates of those points around Yaxnohcah that it makes sense to check out. Tomorrow evening I'll pick up the National Geographic team from the airport in Chetumal; while I'm with them, we'll keep each other posted over the satellite phone about progress and plans."

31

The Wall of the Kings

Virginia Morell, Ken Garrett, and Jesús López came to Chetumal on the evening of April 23. We settled into the modest cabins of the Hotel El Mirador Maya in Xpujil and talked. Virginia could stay only a week, after which Ken and Jesús were to travel to Palenque to record another archaeological project and then possibly return to us for another few days.

The core theme of the story Virginia was to write turned on our rediscovery of Oxpemul the year before. Soon after our work had finished, the team from the Autonomous University of Campeche reopened the old logging trail leading from the main road all the way to the foot of the hill on which Oxpemul lies, making the site far more easily accessible. They also built a wooden watchman's house there. Our difficulties in reaching Oxpemul the year before and later documenting the stone monuments were now a thing of the past. In two days Ken took hundreds of photographs with the eager assistance of Jesús, while Virginia asked me endless questions about our discovery and about Ruppert, the Maya, and so on while dutifully taking copious notes. Meanwhile, Vaquero informed me they had already cleared the trail toward Cheyokolnah and part of the route leading to La Esperanza; they had also found the much sought-after

Figure 31.1. Aguada Unión in a dry state.

aguada—and it really was an aguada—and started to look for Pared de los Reyes, but without success.

With the National Geographic team we then joined the others in Villahermosa and over the next few days visited Cheyokolnah and Candzibaantún. After finishing our work, I drove them to Chetumal: I took Virginia to the airport, while Ken and Jesús hired a car to drive to Palenque. We returned to Xpujil and spent the evening reviewing the photos on the computer. Ken was very pleased, and I was particularly thrilled by a short and meaningful message Vaquero had sent me via the satellite phone: "Today we checked out the GPS coordinates around Yaxnohcah; there are large pyramids at all the points you marked. Tomorrow we'll again be looking for Pared de los Reyes."

Ken and Jesús left the next day, April 30, but we had already agreed they would come back on May 8, which was when our epigrapher Nikolai Grube was also due to arrive.

I bought the necessary provisions, filled up the tank, and drove to Villahermosa.

I arrived late in the afternoon. After I unloaded the truck, Doña Laura served me dinner. When night fell, the men returned from the field, sweaty and exhausted as always, practically speechless. After exchanging greetings, in response to my question as to how it had all gone, Vaquero shook his head and said, "I think there is no point in searching in this area any more. Well, Atasta found something and it might be a good idea for you to check it out."

He took the camera out of his backpack and showed me a photo: an overgrown wall with a molding that looked familiar.

"Hang on a minute . . . isn't this Pared de los Reyes?"

"*It is*, Pared de los Reyes!" was the slow answer Vaquero gave me, his glowing face emphasizing every syllable.

I shouted for joy, congratulating them, and suddenly we couldn't stop hugging each other. They couldn't have picked a better moment for celebrations: I had just come back from civilization bearing cold beer, rum, and whatnot, and they began to tell me the story.

A few days ago, with the help of the coordinates I had given them, they easily found the aguada, which we had hoped was Aguada Unión; they also covered part of the terrain to the northwest, but to no avail. There wasn't enough time for a thorough exploration of the entire area, and before their next attempt Atasta studied the map carefully. He marked the position of the aguada on the topographic map—at a scale of 1:50,000, as detailed a map as existed for the area—in an attempt to find any clue in the form of the terrain. It became apparent that some slightly elevated terrain extended to the northwest—beyond the area they had already walked, but still within one kilometer, which roughly corresponded to Ruppert's description of a fifteen-minute walk. Given the known Maya architectural practice, Atasta concluded that if Pared de los Reyes were anywhere close by, then it had to be somewhere along the slight elevation, which, judging by its contours, extended roughly in the shape of the letter *L*. He came up with an ingenious plan: along the winding patch of the elevated terrain he marked three points intended to be signposts, determined their coordinates, and entered them into the GPS; he picked the points in such a way that by walking from one to the next the entire ridge of the slope would be covered, so that the site, if it were there, could not be missed.

Up to that point Vaquero and Atasta had done most of the talking. But now everyone else's tongues loosened as well.

"And so today we again went to the aguada," continued Vaquero. "Ciriaco noticed a peccary trail there and decided he would follow . . ."

"Because I wanted to see if it led us to some other aguada," Ciriaco jumped in.

". . . and the rest of us headed for the first reference point. Atasta was leading, and when we got there and looked around we saw there was nothing there. Pascual went his own way . . ."

"Well, it made no sense for all of us to be walking together," Pascual interjected.

". . . and Atasta, Gerardo, and I carried on toward the second point. Gerardo was at the front, clearing the path with a machete, Atasta was following behind, GPS in hand, keeping an eye on the direction. I was lagging behind a bit, and suddenly I heard a cry: 'There's a wall!'"

"I was just checking my GPS and realized that we were less than a hundred meters from the second point," Atasta said, finally rejoining the conversation. "But suddenly I hear Gerardo in front of me: 'There is a wall there!' With his hand he was pointing somewhere to the left."

"How did this happen?" I turned to Gerardo to hear his version of the story.

Gerardo, Ciriaco's twenty-five-year-old son, inherited many virtues from his father the forester: he had an extraordinary talent for orientation; he was hardworking, prudent, reliable, and honest through and through. I once overpaid him by 2,500 pesos; the sum was not negligible and most people would have said nothing and kept it, but Gerardo immediately alerted me to my error. I was so surprised by this that I happily let him have five hundred pesos extra. Usually he was quite reserved, but this time he too was brimming with excitement and enthusiasm. Smiling broadly, he went on to tell me the gist of what had happened.

"Well, I was just opening the way in the direction Atasta had shown me. Even before we got to the second point I saw a ruin before me and cried: 'There's a wall there!' And in that moment Atasta, who was walking behind me, plunged wildly forward, overtook me and, without cutting anything, trampled through the brush like a tapir; in a few seconds he reached the wall and began to shout: 'Encontramos Pared de los Reyes! Encontramos Pared de los Reyes!'"

"As soon as I got closer, I recognized the building with its masks, which Ruppert had published," Atasta added.

"And by then I had caught up with them too," Vaquero continued. "You can't imagine the scene. You know how Atasta is, always calm, cool-headed, but there he was stretching his arms toward the sky and screaming like a

Figure 31.2. Vaquero, Atasta, and Gerardo upon the discovery of the Wall of the Kings.

madman: 'We have found Pared de los Reyes! We have found Pared de los Reyes!' He even started singing. He made such a noise that Ciriaco and Pascual soon came running to us."

After such a long and exhausting search, the event threw even the placid Atasta off track. Of course, I was also thrilled beyond belief. We were all clinking glasses and were even able to please Atasta with his favorite music. Along with all kinds of tools and other equipment that Vaquero hauled in his jeep, he also had a tape recorder, an MP3 player, and other sundries. The available repertoire was well known, and Atasta decided without hesitation: Pink Floyd. It was one of those evenings that are difficult to forget. Far from any artificial lighting, a clear sky studded with stars arched above the clearing in Villahermosa, the chirping of crickets resounded over the landscape, while out of a collapsing house amid the jungle one could hear "Shine on you crazy diamond . . ."; the otherwise always so silent Atasta even sang along. The desolate place, which a long time ago had witnessed brisk trade and the roaring engines of aircraft transporting precious tree sap, once again had visitors; they too, just like the chicleros many years before, were gathered around the evening fire, talking about the experiences of the day. But the reasons for their laughter and joy would have seemed very odd to an observer accidentally passing by: they were celebrating the discovery of long-forgotten ruins, the remains of a comparatively small and unimportant town in which life had come to an end over one thousand years ago.

In the following days, we carefully examined Pared de los Reyes, documenting every detail. In 1934, when Karl Ruppert saw it, he wrote that it consisted of a single quadrangle of buildings enclosing a rectangular courtyard. We too were unable to find any other buildings in the imme-

Figure 31.3. The only remaining part of the stuccowork that once adorned the western facade of the structure that gave Pared de los Reyes its name is a partially preserved deity mask on the northern extreme of the roof comb (*upper left*).

diate vicinity, although it was obvious that many of the ruins we had already chanced upon in the previous year when investigating the extensive terrain to the east pertained to the same settlement, which, judging by the potsherds found on the surface, was active in the Classic period.

The best-preserved building of the quadrangle was the one flanking the courtyard to the west. The botanist Cyrus Lundell, who visited Pared de los Reyes on January 9, 1932, described it as a wall about thirty meters long and decorated on every side with stucco friezes. The lower part of each frieze was composed of five grotesque masks, with a stone protruding from the wall above each of them and supporting a human figure seated in a cross-legged position. On the torso of each of these figures was a chest plate in the form of a human face, and on the head a crown-like turban, the reason for the chicleros naming this monument "Wall of the Kings." Judging by the remains of red pigment, Lundell concluded that the friezes must have originally been painted.

As Karl Ruppert was to correctly conclude after two years, the wall with the stuccowork was merely the decorative roof comb of an elongated building. The western facade, consisting of finely dressed stone blocks and decorative horizontal molding, is still fairly well preserved, while the vaulted rooms with entrances from the courtyard, from the eastern side, are almost completely destroyed. Lundell's description and Ruppert's photos reveal that the stucco figures were already badly damaged in their time—in his fieldwork diary Ruppert wrote of being disappointed—and we, of course, were to see much less. Only the far northern side of the roof comb boasts fragments of two reasonably well-preserved grotesque masks of earth or rain deities on the eastern and western sides, and a feathered headdress that once adorned a human figure is just barely discernible over the mask on the eastern side. In fact, very little is left today of what made Lundell declare Pared de los Reyes to be one of the most impressive of Maya ruins.

Nonetheless, and although in our many years of research we had found a number of large centers with far more magnificent buildings, sculptures, and even hieroglyphic inscriptions, the rediscovery of this particular site was something of a special occasion and triumph for us. After so many days and weeks of unsuccessful searching, Pared de los Reyes had turned into an almost personal quest; not only for those of us "burdened" with archaeology, but also for our loyal workers: they too had caught the bug of excitement and had a stubborn desire to find this elusive place. Now that

Figure 31.4. Fragments of stuccowork are also preserved on the eastern face of the structure.

we had found it, we had the satisfaction of knowing our efforts had not been in vain. When a year ago we were combing the extensive area around the small lake, which we mistakenly thought was Aguada Unión, we also came to the coordinates that Karl Ruppert had provided for Pared de los Reyes; we found nothing special in the vicinity. Little did we imagine that the famous building was barely a kilometer to the west. Well, this was not our first experience of this kind. There had been previous occasions when we had wandered in the jungle, having no idea we were so close to the monumental core of a former city. Since Maya settlements were not compact but consisted of clusters of buildings separated by empty spaces of various sizes, and because the sizes of buildings could also vary greatly and had nothing to do with proximity to an urban center, it is practically impossible to determine in the middle of the jungle whether the remains of houses we find along the way are the outskirts of a big town or just part of a small settlement, of the kind that was commonly present everywhere.

After completing the work at Pared de los Reyes, Atasta, Vaquero, and the others took me to the coordinates they had investigated near Yaxnohcah.

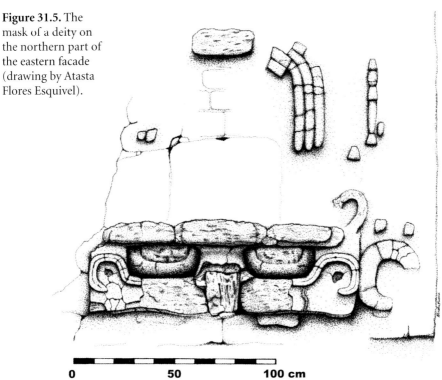

Figure 31.5. The mask of a deity on the northern part of the eastern facade (drawing by Atasta Flores Esquivel).

0   50   100 cm

In this case, reality exceeded all expectations. It turned out that the two pointed protrusions, visible on aerial photographs about a mile southeast of the urban core, were two mighty pyramids looming over two clusters of buildings on large platforms. An even bigger surprise was the point that protruded northeast of the city center. In the aerial photographs it looked as though it was a pyramidal structure built on a hill, whereas in fact what appeared to be a natural elevation was a soaring acropolis with an approximately rectangular ground plan. The massive platform on which the pyramidal shrine and several smaller buildings stood was almost two hundred meters long and about seven meters high.

Judging by the types of sherds found on the surface, we were able to conclude that the first construction phases of this architectural complex had been completed as early as the Middle Preclassic period, around 500 BC. After we took geodetic measurements, it became clear that the entire complex was astronomically oriented, namely toward sunrise at the winter solstice (December 22) or sunset at the summer solstice (June 22). This orientation coincides with the early date indicated by the ceramics: solstitial alignments are particularly common in early periods in Mesoamerica, no doubt because the solstices attract attention in their own right. Anyone observing the sunrise day after day will readily note that the sun's point of ascent moves along the horizon, eventually reaching the extreme northern point, and then it slowly begins to return, reaching the extreme southern point in six months (the same movement can be observed, of course, on the western horizon too). For this very reason, the solstices were the most elementary reference points for temporal orientation in the tropical year, not only in Mesoamerica, but anywhere the emergence of agriculture required the appropriate planning of tasks for each season.

On the agreed day, in Xpujil we met Ken and Jesús, who had returned from Palenque. Our surveyor Tomaž was already there, and we were also joined by Nikolai and his Swiss friend Marco Gross, who had been living for many years in the town of Melchor de Mencos in Guatemala, almost on the border with Belize, and who had brought his off-road vehicle. We set out for Uxul, this time heading south along the dirt road from Constitución. With the other workers, Ciriaco had set out ahead of us early in the morning to clear the path. They had no difficulties in getting to La Esperanza, the former chiclero camp, where today there is a Calakmul Biosphere checkpoint, but the rest of the trail was rather overgrown, so they made it only to Lake Chumpich, where we caught up with everyone and set up a camp for the night. The next day we reached the border at La Güera camp, and after that Chumbec camp, from where we had to walk to Uxul.

Once Ken and Jesús had finished their photography, I drove them to the airport in Chetumal and returned to Uxul, where Nikolai had meanwhile drawn all the stone monuments and already discovered a whole array of interesting facts. Among other things, he had read in some hieroglyphic text that the ceremony performed by the local ruler at the end of the calendar cycle in the year 662 was attended by none other than Yuknoom Ch'een II, a powerful king of the Kaan dynasty, which then reigned in Calakmul. For his vassal, the ruler of Uxul, the visit must have been immensely important, because it is immortalized on two stelae.

After Nikolai had documented the stelae in Candzibaantún, he and Marco drove off, leaving us with a few more days of surveying. With Tomaž and Atasta in charge, we mapped Candzibaantún and the peripheral architectural groups of Yaxnohcah, discovered that year.

32

Far from the Trail

It is always hot, but it has been a long time since it was as hot as today. Besides, we have no reason to be especially pleased. The site is not nearly as big as it seemed in the aerial photographs. It is already late afternoon and we have only just started going back. Although the path is now clear, our camp seems endlessly far away and walking is a huge effort. Thorny plants prick our skin as we stumble along, tripping over vines, tree roots, and the stubble of cleared vegetation. The afternoon is especially muggy, without the slightest breeze to take the edge off the pressing heat. We are drenched in sweat and the little water we have left is too warm to quench our thirst or cool our overheated bodies. In the morning we left some water in a trench dug by looters in a minor ruin about halfway back, which has remained fairly fresh and gives us some new strength. But we still have more than two hours to go. The sun has sunk low, but it is still boiling hot. After sunset, the forest turns black in a mere half hour, yet we have three more kilometers ahead of us. Struggling along the path in torchlight is the ultimate nightmare. Our eyes glued to the ground, we navigate around obstacles, hoping to not overlook a poisonous snake somewhere. No one utters a word; the only noise is the crackling of dry branches and the rustling of leaves under our feet. Numbed with exhaustion after trotting for who knows how long, we suddenly feel a flush of relief: between the trees we spot the flickering of our campfire. Doña Laura awaits us there.

Before we manage to finish dinner and recuperate a little, piercing flashes of lightning and deafening thunder announce an imminent tropical storm. We quickly put away all our equipment to protect it from the rain and again gather underneath the awning spread above the area we use for cooking and meals. In spite of the heavy downpour with no end in sight, everyone is slowly cheering up. We are back safe and sound, our stomachs are now full, and there is a stock of beer and rum to look forward to. Our tiredness subsiding, we are gradually able to talk once again. Ciriaco raises his glass, saying sternly, "Well, Saša—hats off to you!"

Saša smiles, visibly relieved, and lifts her glass as well. "Oh, thank you very much. Cheers!"

It was April 14, 2007, and our seventh field season had just begun. We had Saša Čaval on our team, my colleague from the Research Center of the Slovenian Academy of Sciences and Arts. She had obtained her degree in archaeology some years before and had expressed a desire to come with us on at least two occasions. However, I had not dared take her as I had been worried about how a woman would cope with all that hardship. Besides, I already had an experienced team. But then Vaquero's mother got sick and he bailed at the last moment. So, I decided to bring Saša along to take over Vaquero's tasks—especially photographic documentation. Over the past two weeks that we had already been in the jungle doing fieldwork, Ciriaco had expressed his concerns regarding Saša a few times, asking me whether I thought she would be able to push through until the end. "I sure hope so; I know she has plenty of experience doing fieldwork," I said, trying to conceal my own concern. Today Saša had passed her baptism of fire, convincing everyone, including Ciriaco.

"I told you. I know whom to bring along," I said, attempting a touch of smugness, although I was greatly relieved myself.

"Yes, yes," Ciriaco responded. "But you could see it yourself: even Elías didn't make it, and he's a man, from our village, used to working hard."

That was true—Elías, one of our local workers whom Ciriaco had brought, had told us three days ago that he couldn't take it any longer. And so yesterday I took him back to Constitución, where I needed to buy some provisions. As his replacement, Ciriaco's son Eric came back with me.

"I know Elías," Ciriaco continued, "and I know he won't shy away from any work. But he's clearly inexperienced at working in the forest. He didn't know how to conserve his energy. You could see how he would clear away much more than needed."

Again, Ciriaco was spot on. In the tropics one has to adjust the intensity and rhythm of work to the specific conditions. The heat around midday is so severe that the chance of exhaustion rises steeply while efficiency plummets. Our work does not follow a set schedule: we will work throughout the day, taking a break every now and then when needed. Therefore, performance can vary quite a bit. For farmers, the situation is completely different: they wake up very early and are out in the fields at the break of dawn in order to finish the hardest work in the morning when the heat is still somewhat bearable, with afternoons being reserved for lighter tasks and rest. Although visitors from places with moderate climates tend to categorize slow movement, lounging in the shade, and similar tendencies typical of people in tropical areas as laziness, such behavior is primarily a consequence of the climate. In a tropical environment work wears you out much faster than elsewhere; in order to not "burn out" it is necessary to rest more, as well as to conserve energy while working. Ciriaco was a true master of this: he was very efficient but carefully deliberated everything he did, never making an unnecessary move. For example, we often used him when mapping—even though he found it boring and would always happily volunteer to do any other task instead—because he was capable of removing only and exactly that which interfered with measurements. A less skilled person would cut away a large amount of brush, yet the sighted point would still not be visible. But not Ciriaco: he would first examine the situation, following the visual line from the theodolite to the prism, and would then move forward and cut off only the branch obstructing the line of sight. He undoubtedly acquired such skills mostly from experience, but it is fair to say that Gerardo, his son, and Pascual did not lag far behind.

Elías was simply too impetuous and would clear out trails unnecessarily wide, which left him much more exhausted than the rest of us. During the previous few days Atasta and Saša had examined, together with two other men, several smaller ruins in the vicinity while Ciriaco, Elías, and I cleared a path to a site that I deemed sizable based on the aerial photographs. It was a great distance from the dirt trail where our camp was set up. Two days of work later, when we had reached a point only eight hundred meters from our destination, Elías, now also suffering from a stomachache, announced that he would like to return home.

"El monte es difícil," Ciriaco said seriously. *El monte* is an expression locals commonly use to refer to a thicket of any kind, even a real tropical forest, which is called *selva* in more refined Spanish. "And today we are all worn out, despite being used to this kind of work. You have the map: How far have we walked today?"

In my palm computer with integrated GPS I had saved cartographic data and was thus able to keep track of our movements.

"The path we have cleared to the site is about twelve kilometers long. On top of that, we walked another kilometer to get to the farthest group, and then we returned . . . altogether we covered a distance of at least twenty-five kilometers."

"Just imagine! Walking twenty-five kilometers on a road or a well-trodden path is not a big deal. Here, though, we constantly trip over stuff and have to stoop under the branches we have not cut off. I often stumble but don't fall; however, today you saw even me fall. Saša didn't, though, not even once."

"Actually I did, twice," Saša admitted.

"So what! You bumped the ground three times or so," Ciriaco said, casting a somewhat teasing look at me.

"At least." I nodded peevishly.

As our trails were not intended for prolonged use, there was no point in clearing them thoroughly—that would be too exhausting and time consuming. As we did not cut the brush all the way down to the ground or remove thicker branches, we had to take care while walking. Such a provisional forest trail enabled us to travel about three kilometers an hour. Thus, the distance we covered was relatively enormous—the longest to date actually—which made naming the site a no-brainer: Unachililbé (Farthest from the Trail).

Based on the aerial photograph, we had expected more from the site. Also, the strenuous access was not quite proportionate to the "reward" gained. However, looking at it again now, when we were somewhat rested and our ability to think clearly had returned, we concluded that the site was actually not insignificant. True, it had no stelae or major buildings, but two of its architectural complexes were rather extensive, and its tallest pyramidal temple was fifteen meters high, which was not negligible. Here and there a wall built of roughly cut stones was exposed. While the rest of

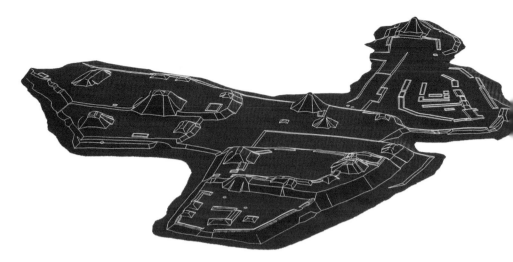

Figure 32.1. Uitzilná, looking southwest (3-D rendering by Aleš Marsetič).

us inspected the area, Atasta managed to sketch the main complex and Saša found a few ceramic fragments, which made it clear that the settlement was active predominantly in the Classic period.

Before getting to this site, which was about fifteen kilometers northeast of La Esperanza, in the first two weeks of the field season we had discovered some other sites, all with the help of aerial photographs. The most sizable one was approximately thirty kilometers south of Constitución, five kilometers east of the trail leading south from the village. The city core features pyramidal temples up to twenty meters tall, as well as elongated, most likely residential and administrative structures placed around plazas and on top of massive platforms built of rough-hewn stone blocks. A *sacbé* almost two hundred meters long and fifteen meters wide, which in places is raised up to one meter above the surrounding ground, connects the main complex with a large temple to the west. To the north of this avenue a stretch of smaller residential buildings can be seen, while the area on the south side is slightly sunken and collects water in the rainy season, as indicated by the characteristic vegetation there. It had most likely been a water reservoir, such as are common in Maya cities. The plentiful potsherds found on the surface testify to the settlement being inhabited from the final centuries BC until the end of the Classic period. The dense urban core is on a hill encircled on all sides but the east by an expansive bajo. Although bajos turn swampy in the rainy season and are themselves not suitable for settlement, the Maya in the lowlands of the

Figure 32.2. At the top of one of the buildings in Uitzilná we came across a relatively well-preserved vaulted space.

Yucatán Peninsula established most of their cities near these low-lying basins filled with sediment, most likely because they also retain moisture in the dry season, which makes them suitable for intensive agriculture. In some of them canals for draining excess water are preserved; since these lowered the groundwater level, the plots in between, which may have been elevated with the material dug up, became more suitable for cultivation. While in southeastern Campeche we did not notice such terrain modifications, commonly called "raised fields," almost all major urban centers are a short distance from bajo wetlands. As recent studies have shown, the alluvial soil deposits that accumulated along their edges, having washed down from the surrounding slopes, were particularly fertile.

Because we were aware of all this, the position of the site did not come as a surprise; what is interesting, though, is that the "peninsula" of higher terrain on which the city core is located has extremely steep sides going down into the bajo, and a torrential streambed separates it from the elevated terrain continuing eastward, where ruins of smaller temples and houses are scattered. Furthermore, along the eastern and northern fringes of the urban core the remains of a defensive wall have been preserved, and this was once palisaded, as can be concluded from other similar examples. Such features, inspiring us to name the site Uitzilná, meaning "fortress" or "castle," show that defensive concerns were a significant factor in planning the position and architectural configuration of the city. No wonder, if we recall that the Maya lived in more or less independent states that were often at war with one another. Although not long ago researchers thought otherwise, today we know that defensive walls were not uncommon in Maya cities, while it is also true that many were not fortified. Certainly, the importance attached to defense varied in each case, depending on whether the settlement was in the center or on the periphery of a particular state.

33

Fruitless Search

The second half of the 2007 field season again found us deep in the southern part of the biosphere with two more sites fueling our hopes. Our camp was at an aguada, which—as far as Ciriaco could remember—was called Los Hornos. It was a little more than twenty-five kilometers northwest of Villahermosa, along the trail to La Esperanza. We had been clearing the trail for more than a week, starting from the point where we had stopped in 2005 when we found Pared de los Reyes. After having first discovered several groups of ruins along the road connecting Conhuás and Calakmul, in the past few days we had come across some smaller complexes while clearing the dirt trail toward Aguada Los Hornos. Not every site would meet our expectations—one of them we simply named Desilusión (Disillusionment), but we could nonetheless be satisfied with the results thus far. Uitzilná was undeniably a remarkable center; Atasta drew many sketches of architectural groups and Saša took umpteen photos. Also, thanks to her expert eye, we ended up with many more bags of potsherds than ever before. Up to that point in the season we had recorded and documented as many as thirteen previously unknown sites, thus increasing the total number of sites discovered throughout our seven field seasons to about eighty, which was a significant contribution to achieving a more complete archaeological picture of the central Maya lowlands.

Despite this success, in those May days weariness would occasionally take hold of us as we approached Aguada Los Hornos. By that point we had been in the forest for two months, almost without a break. While we were clearing the trail the blaring of our chain saw upset a swarm of wild bees, which then came at us. While everyone else immediately took to their heels, Saša stood petrified on the spot—despite our cries for her to run. Who knows how it all would have ended had the ever cool-headed Ciriaco not turned back, grabbed Saša by the hand, and dashed into the nearest bush with her. This was only a few days after she had been an unlucky target of an enormous hornet, which luckily chose a less sensitive spot than the one that had stung Gerardo under his eye. The swelling had been enormous; it had completely disfigured his face and left him temporarily unable to see out of that eye, so I granted him two sick days. Atasta was handling the situation stoically for the most part, with occasional stretches of surliness. The trail had already crossed a number of bajos, the preferred biotope of the *chechén*[1] tree, whose sap causes skin burns. This made Ciriaco's son Eric increasingly anxious: while this sap is harmful to any skin that comes into contact with it, for Eric it was much worse because he had a specific allergy and thus could not safely go anywhere near these trees. Eventually he was in such distress that he wanted to walk back to his village. He also complained that his pay was lower than that of the others, even lower than the cook's. That was true, but when I had hired him to replace Elías he had agreed to the amount, which was the same as for anyone else who was with us for the first time. I had to work hard to convince him that he was a valued member of the team, and that he could not possibly walk seventy kilometers through the forest alone. As expected, I finally won him over with the promise of increasing his pay because he had proven himself to us. Anyhow, it was quite clear that we were in a bit of a rut; even the cheerful Pascual, who would always sing while working, was much quieter than usual.

This time the site mapping was going to be done by Aleš Marsetič, a surveyor and my colleague from ZRC SAZU in Slovenia. We had already decided to map Uitzilná, but this had to be postponed until the end of the season, because while I was on my way to get Aleš from the airport in

---

1. *Metopium brownei.*

Chetumal, the rest of the team had already begun clearing the dirt trail toward La Esperanza, all in an attempt to reach two sites we hoped were of decent size and thus worthy of mapping with a total station. Aleš had been with us for almost ten days now, yet we could see no end to struggling and hacking our way through the thick and thorny vegetation, tirelessly wielding our machetes. Aleš did not in the least lag behind, which made my fellow workers quickly take to him as one of their own. We could only hope that days and days of cutting and slashing—which he increasingly mastered—would not erase his memory of what he had originally come there for, or how to operate the theodolite and the tripod.

Upon finally reaching Aguada Los Hornos, we unanimously agreed that we had had enough trail clearing and would make it through to both designated sites on foot. In the aerial photograph I had noticed that one of them was approximately three kilometers west of the aguada, as the crow flies. Ciriaco had information on the second one: according to a colleague of his, along the dirt trail near Aguada Clarín we would encounter a large complex of ruins with exposed walls and stelae.

There was no water in Aguada Los Hornos. For the entire time it took us to get there we would periodically have to go back to Villahermosa to get water. The relatively low-growing forest, without much shade in which to set up camp, had a few surprises in store for us: every day at dusk we would inevitably hear a dull hum, just like the sound of a plane circling somewhere high in the sky. The sound, though, was coming from millions upon millions of green insects—a type of a chinch bug—which would settle on the ground right at dinnertime, attracted by the light from our improvised oil lamps—glass jars economically filled with diesel fuel. They would circle around the lamps like mad, with some occasionally burning up in the flames and many more landing in our dishes. Other visitors included swarms of ants, which would march right through our camp, undeterred even by gasoline being poured on them. Were a human foot to block their path they would immediately besiege it in huge numbers, biting here and there, which often made some unlucky team member perform an odd dance featuring some wild foot stomping. And then there were ticks, which forced us to regularly carry out an evening ceremony, a training of sorts, which included shedding light onto and examining any spot where the uninvited guests were likely to have settled. This ritual, which we each performed in the intimate environment of our hammock or tent, was accompanied by extremely interesting, often downright acrobatic poses.

But despite all the trouble, we had not quite run out of optimism and humor. One evening, when Aleš was just about to grab a second serving of custard pudding, Doña Laura called out to him, "No, Aleš, esto es para todos!" (No, Aleš, that's for everyone!).

To that Aleš responded in all seriousness: "Pues sí, yo me llamo 'todos'" (But my name is 'everyone'), which provoked a great deal of laughter and comments, noticeably brightening up the otherwise dull evening.

From Aguada Los Hornos we followed the trail toward La Esperanza, which kept going northwest. After nearly two kilometers we arrived at a spot where it veered north, and another trail forked off to the southwest. We took the latter trail and soon spotted a relatively large pyramid on a hill not far from the intersection, as well as a few smaller buildings scattered nearby. After two more days of wading along the trail, we branched off at the most appropriate spot, took a northwest turn through the forest, and finally reached the long-sought ruins.

The site consisted of two groups of buildings and was big and significant enough for Aleš to finally start his work. The South Complex was entirely encircled by a defensive wall, and the ruins of buildings, mostly elite residences, were laid out around smaller plazas and courtyards. A seven-meter-high pyramidal structure on the north side had a trench dug by looters, which revealed fine masonry walls; a smaller building nearby had a stela leaning on it, unfortunately without any relief carvings. In the ruins of another building we found stone slabs featuring reliefs with geometric ornaments, clearly fragments of a former facade. The North Complex, which was less than half a kilometer from the southern one, was larger and clearly more important. Buildings of various heights and shapes, some over ten meters tall, were laid out around several plazas, and here and there we could catch a glimpse of the remains of vaulted rooms. Between the two complexes we discovered two small aguadas, probably artificial, and around the hill on which the site—simply referred to as Los Hornos—was located, an extensive bajo stretched in all directions except southwest.

First, we carefully examined the area where the ruins were, collected ceramic fragments, and recorded the architectural details. Afterward, Atasta, Aleš, and three other men began to map the site while the rest of us went looking for the site Ciriaco had heard about. According to him, Aguada Clarín should have been the first to follow Aguada Los Hornos along the trail to La Esperanza. The aerial photograph did indeed show another aguada some four kilometers northwest of Aguada Los Hornos. To get to it we separated from the mapping group at the intersection west of Aguada Los Hornos—they turned left while we followed the trail north, mostly through a beautiful high forest, which was therefore less overgrown than was typical. We reached the aguada and an intersection of two trails: one continuing north, the other going west. The site we were looking for was supposed to be along the trail to La Esperanza—but which way was that? After so many years, even Ciriaco could no longer remember.

Later that day we walked back to camp. It was almost dark when we stopped to rest a bit at the intersection west of Aguada Los Hornos. Ciriaco remarked, "Aleš, Atasta, and the rest of them have not returned from work."

"How can you tell?" I asked.

"They haven't been through here yet. Take a look at these long blades of grass, which hang into the trail. Had they gone back, the grass would be bent the other way, in the direction of the camp. But it is all turned in this direction, just the way they left it when going to work this morning."

In itself this piece of information was not exceptionally meaningful right then; however, it did again prove Ciriaco's mastery of track reading. Indeed, we did not find our colleagues upon returning to camp.

Expert trackers who know how to read the ground, especially well enough to find a lost person, are quite rare. In 2005, when Ken Garrett was taking photos at Cheyokolnah, his assistant Jesús got lost, having gone too far into the forest when taking care of a most natural physiological need. Once we noticed he had gone missing, someone luckily remembered which direction he had walked, thus enabling Ciriaco to look for his tracks and find him. Upon realizing he was lost, Jesús was clever enough to stay right where he was and wait. His calling and shouting had no effect until Ciriaco finally approached close enough. Walking through a high forest such as the one surrounding Cheyokolnah is very pleasant, but it is also extremely easy to get lost. Because of its scarce undergrowth, which barely needs to be cleared out, one can quickly take a completely wrong turn upon coming back. In order to avoid this, those who know the forest well will cut, at appropriate intervals, some shoots of young trees, even if they do not obstruct the path, thus marking the way they should return. Naturally, following such trails, called *picados*, also requires attention and experience.

In the days to follow we inspected the area around the aguada we had found the day before. First we headed west, following the old dirt trail for a few kilometers and scanning the terrain to the left and right. We found nothing but a few small mounds. Besides, the trail was heavily overgrown, leaving the ruts barely noticeable, from which Ciriaco concluded that it could not be the main route to La Esperanza, which two decades ago would still have been very much alive with traffic. The trail along which the ruins were supposed to be must therefore have been the one going north from the aguada. That one, too, was quite densely covered with vegetation because it crossed a sizable bajo, meaning that we could not expect an archaeological site anywhere near it.

Ciriaco was not so certain anymore that the aguada we had found was Aguada Clarín. "How far is it to the next aguada?"

"I don't know. In the aerial photographs the trail leading north is visible only until the end of the bajo; after that it gets lost in the high forest and I can't tell which of the trails appearing farther north and northwest is the one to La Esperanza."

"And is there no sign of ruins anywhere?"

"I've examined everything, but I can see nothing major anywhere in the area. Naturally, that doesn't mean that there is nothing there. As you know, sometimes even fairly large ruins cannot be seen. Remember Olvidado? Both main buildings are about ten meters tall and we know exactly where they are located in the aerial photographs, but there you can't see anything but trees; nothing stands out."

"We should follow the trail leading north," Ciriaco said.

"If we want to do that, we would first have to move our camp here. We're more than five kilometers from Aguada Los Hornos as it is, and if we continue on foot, we'll waste a lot of time walking back every day. However, were we to relocate the camp, we'd first have to clear the trail up to here and make it passable for vehicles. And since this aguada has no water either, we'd have to drive all the way back to Villahermosa to get some. The thing is, you see, we're running out of time—that is, money is getting low. I truly hope Atasta and Aleš will finish soon."

Despite being aware of all this, Ciriaco would still not give in. "You know what, tomorrow I'll continue walking on this trail alone, until I find the next aguada. If this one is not Aguada Clarín, it must be the next one."

Ciriaco was dead serious. His pride was hurt since he was rarely wrong about anything. We were in a challenging situation similar to when we

Figure 33.1. Saša and Aleš surveying.

were trying to find Pared de los Reyes. Still, I could not consent to his proposal.

"No way, you can't just go alone. Who knows how far the next aguada is, and you simply cannot carry enough food and water, and a hammock on top of that. Anything could happen to you."

Convincing him was not easy. He felt guilty for claiming that there was no other aguada between Los Hornos and Clarín, when now he had to question his memory.

"That guy said that the ruins would be near Aguada Clarín right next to the trail. We've inspected the area south of this aguada, finding nothing, and going north one runs into a big bajo. Either this isn't Aguada Clarín, or . . ."

". . . or the site isn't as close to the aguada as the guy claimed. What if he never saw it at all, but only heard about it?"

"Well, that's not impossible." Ciriaco tried to find some solace in this thought.

Which one, then, was Aguada Clarín? Where were the ruins that Ciriaco's acquaintance had spoken of? Were there really well-preserved buildings and stelae, perhaps even with legible inscriptions that could tell us something completely new? We could not get questions like these out of our heads; this time, however, they had to remain unresolved.

34

Terra Incognita

Ciriaco was kneeling in the mud, tying thick ropes around the back wheels of his three-ton truck. We were stopped before a fifty-meter-wide watercourse with a lazy stream slowly rolling along, turning the shallow bottom into a thick layer of ooze. Ciriaco had just managed to get his smaller pickup across by means of a hand winch. It was four-wheel drive, but the big truck was not, which made it unlikely that it would easily make it across the muddy water. It soon turned out that the ropes did not help either. The truck was stuck in the middle of the current, sunken so deep that its wheels could no longer be seen. To top it all off, darkness had fallen.

"What now?" I asked Ciriaco.

"We'll get it out tomorrow," he said, unperturbed, and then turned around and crossed the stream. It was not clear how he was going to accomplish that, but he was clearly not in the mood to elaborate.

I did not follow him since my truck was still on this side of the water. I hung my hammock and drifted off to sleep, albeit not exactly restfully. To me, the whole situation seemed fairly hopeless.

I would see the solution only the following day when a loud, optimistic-sounding hubbub woke me up at the crack of dawn. Ciriaco and his men were delving around in the mud, digging the wheels of the truck out of the sludge.

"We'll use the yo-yo method," Ciriaco cried out to me.

He had mentioned this technique to me before, but I had never witnessed its actual application. The back wheels of the truck had double tires on double rims, and the men tied one end of a long, thick rope between the two tires of each wheel, fastening the other end around two trees on the near side of the creek. The most time-consuming part was digging the wheels out of the mire; everything else took less than a minute. The driver put the vehicle in reverse and stepped on the gas. The ropes coiled around the spinning rear wheels between both pairs of tires and, with the other ends tied around trees, pulled the vehicle out of the mud in the blink of an eye. Unfortunately, this method could not be used to get the truck to the other side. In any case, even if we had managed to get it across, we would not have made it much farther—that much was now clear. Thus, we would continue with only the two pickup trucks—mine and Ciriaco's. With his already on the other side, we only needed to get mine across, so I courageously drove into the creek. I got stuck in the mud a bit before the opposite bank, but Ciriaco's truck had no trouble pulling me onto dry land. Good ropes are an indispensable part of our equipment.

It was the beginning of July 2012. We had concluded work in the southern part of the Calakmul Biosphere back in 2008, when we recorded a few more sites while shooting a documentary. Judging from the aerial photographs, we could not expect to find much more there. However, the northern part of the biosphere was still a big blank area on the archaeological map of the Maya territory. Unfortunately, it was years before we finally managed to resume this task, as other matters had to be taken care of first. We had to publish the results of all our previous work, after which I embarked, together with my friend Pedro Francisco Sánchez Nava—my former boss at the INAH—upon extensive archaeo-astronomical research, measuring the orientation of buildings at many sites in Mesoamerica. Meanwhile, a German team from the University of Bonn, headed by Nikolai Grube, began intensive research in Uxul; a Mexican team from the Autonomous University of Campeche conducted work in Oxpemul; and the Canadian archaeologist Kathryn Reese-Taylor from the University of Calgary began excavations in Yaxnohcah. Naturally, I recommended that they hire Ciriaco, who—being increasingly engaged in archaeological work—had gradually managed to upgrade his fleet. He replaced his previous three-ton Ford truck with a newer model and bought a Chevrolet pickup. Unfortunately, during that time he also suffered a tragic loss: his wife, Laura, who used to cook for us, died from injuries in a traffic accident.

The northern and southern parts of the Calakmul Biosphere stretch north and south from the Escárcega-Chetumal road. The narrow strip of land connecting the two parts crosses the road some ten kilometers west of Xpujil. Becán, Chicanná, and numerous other archaeological sites in the broader vicinity of Xpujil boast a refined architectural style characteristic of the Late Classic period (from the seventh to the tenth centuries); this style was named after the Río Bec site, which is fifteen kilometers southeast of Xpujil. The area where this style was deployed has been fairly well explored, as has the area approximately one hundred kilometers to the north, where a similar architectural style called Chenes developed at approximately the same time. Between the two zones, however, is an archaeologically completely unexplored stretch of land, extending across some three thousand square kilometers largely within the northern Calakmul Biosphere.

A distinguishing feature of the Río Bec and Chenes architectural styles is buildings with fine stone facings. Artistically shaped stone slabs were assembled like a mosaic to form geometric ornamentation and stylized depictions of deities. In both areas one will frequently come across temples featuring imposing fronts with entrances shaped like the wide-open maw of an earth deity. Another special characteristic of the Río Bec style is buildings with two lateral towers, which are replicas of pyramidal temples but do not serve any specific function; the sanctuary on top of each tower is only hinted at, without any internal space, and a steep stairway leading up to it was not usable because the stairs were too narrow. While numerous differences can be spotted between the sites of Río Bec and Chenes, there are also many architectural similarities. What is the significance of these affinities? Both styles were used simultaneously, suggesting rather close connections, perhaps even political ties, between the two zones. If so, could we expect similar architecture and transitional forms in the intermediate territory?

This is what various researchers wondered about. With no known archaeological sites in the area in between, there were no answers, but the questions were not irrelevant. Our lack of understanding of what went on in the heart of the Yucatán Peninsula in the Late Classic period makes for a very incomplete image of the Maya and their development.

For all these reasons, continuing our exploration in this territory was quite a challenge. In examining the aerial photographs, I noticed a number of archaeological sites in this area, one of which looked especially large. Thus, in 2012, after Pedro and I had concluded our fieldwork and saved some funds, I wanted to take a quick look at it.

I consulted with Ciriaco. It was already the rainy season but the heavy rain had not yet kicked in, which is why he thought we could give it a shot. He gathered a few men, and we bought provisions and headed off, our fleet consisting of Ciriaco's Chevrolet, his three-ton Ford, and our Toyota pickup. The Toyota, an all-wheel drive, had served us well since 2007, when it replaced the old and weary GMC truck. From Xpujil we first headed north on a road past the village of Zoh Laguna. From that we veered onto an abandoned dirt trail leading west, which the aerial photographs indicated would bring us closer to the site.

After just one kilometer we encountered the first serious obstacle: although the area does not have any perennial waterways, in the rainy season many otherwise dry riverbeds fill up. Although it had not rained much by that point, we still ran into a lazy stream slowly rolling down a barely noticeable muddy riverbed.

The only thing we could do was leave the big truck and most of the equipment on the near side of the stream and carry our essentials over to the other side on foot, where we set up camp. In the following days we managed to clear about eight kilometers of the long-abandoned and heavily overgrown trail, which led almost due west for that distance but then started turning south. Since our destination was about five kilometers to the northwest, we continued on foot through the forest straight in that direction.

In late afternoon, as we were approaching the site, the terrain began to rise. We had just caught a glimpse of two monumental pyramidal masses through the vegetation when Ciriaco, walking ahead, suddenly leaped to the side: he had come very close to stepping on a rattlesnake. The reptile had to be taken care of before we could pass between the two pyramids and enter the leveled surface, clearly a former plaza. Turning left, we came across a stela partially protruding from the ground, with some hieroglyphs visible on it. Apart from the two pyramidal structures on the eastern side of the plaza, two others rose loftily on its southern flank. A

Figure 34.1. While walking among the ruins we came across a caterpillar of the moth *Automeris metzli*, whose poisonous stinging hairs cause a burning rash if they come into contact with skin.

massive elongated building was on its western side, with others nearby; there were also several altars, one with relief carvings.

It was getting late and we had to head back to camp, though we were nowhere near having seen the entire site. Heavy rain throughout the night and the entire next day postponed our return by two days. Getting back to the first complex of ruins was relatively easy, as the trail had already been cleared. From there we continued northwest until we reached the second, even larger complex with more voluminous buildings. There we made our way from one plaza to another, with cylindrical altars and stelae only increasing our excitement and curiosity, which made us spread out without order in all directions. Suddenly, one of our men came running over to me, saying "Víctor has found something."

We rushed across one plaza, then another, then a third, until we finally spotted Víctor, standing victoriously next to his find. In front of a pyramidal building stood a stela, leaning sideways. Not much was discernible on its front, but the back revealed several large, well-preserved hieroglyphs. It appeared from the space available that the original inscription had only two columns. Best preserved were four lines of the left column with a clearly visible number 9 on top, a 0 below it, and another 0 underneath, attached to a well-preserved *kin* glyph, the symbol for "day." "A date!" I cried. Farther down was the date 2 Ahau of the 260-day cycle. In the right column only the number 13 was visible in the third line, following the *kin* glyph and clearly referring to the day of a twenty-day month.

As described in chapter 28 of this book, Long Count dates are written in the Maya vigesimal system, and the place values (1, 20, 360, 7,200, 144,000) correspond to the duration of individual time units: the day (*kin*), the 20-day "month" (*uinal*), the 360-day "year" (*tun*), the 20-*tun* period (*katun*), and the 20-*katun* period (*baktun*). In the third line on the stela a 0 associated with the day sign was clearly visible, and the distribution of glyphs led us to conclude that the digit 9 in the upper left-hand corner indicated the number of *baktuns*, while the 0 below, in the second line, referred to *tuns*. The *katuns* and *uinals*, which must have been recorded in the right column, were missing. Was a reconstruction of the date possible despite the missing parts?

Given that the Maya would very often immortalize the ends of *katuns*, the most likely conclusion was that the number of *uinals* in our date was zero. A *katun* ends on the same date of the 260-day cycle only once every 13 *katuns*—that is, once every 93,600 days. Using a calculator, I managed to quickly solve the problem: in *baktun* 9 it happened only once that a *katun* ending fell on day 2 Ahau and on the thirteenth day of a month. That date was 9.16.0.0.0, 2 Ahau 13 Zec, or in our calendar May 5, AD 751.

As excited as we might have been about the date, which informed us of the city's importance in the Late Classic period, a closer examination of the hieroglyphs simply astounded us—they were not carved in stone but rather molded from a thick layer of stucco, on which patches of red color were preserved. The Maya decorated numerous buildings with stuccowork—a mixture of lime, sand, and other ingredients—and even some stelae were covered with thin layers of stucco, but I was not aware of any stone monuments covered with glyphs or other motifs made of stucco.

We examined the site only briefly, having no idea how far it stretched, although it was clearly huge. Most surprising was that we were less than thirty kilometers north of Becán, the largest city featuring Río Bec architecture, and thus also from the Late Classic period, but our site was different: instead of facades with delicate ornamentation or twin towers, we saw several monumental pyramids approximately twenty meters tall, and stelae with inscriptions on them. In the Río Bec area stelae with inscriptions

Figure 34.2. Stela 1 in Chactún, with hieroglyphs modeled in stucco.

are rare, and pyramids are virtually nonexistent—the only true pyramidal temple is the imposing Structure 9 in Becán. Our site exhibited a much greater resemblance to the ones we had encountered during our previous explorations far to the south. So what were the implications of these peculiarities for understanding the trade networks and political geography of the Late Classic central lowlands?

There were sufficient reasons warranting a more detailed investigation. Once again, the National Geographic Society's Committee for Research and Exploration found my research proposal convincing enough to finance an expedition. Some additional funding was provided by Martin Hobel, a Carinthian Slovenian, whom I had first met not too long before. At the end of 2012 he asked me to prepare a lecture on the Maya for his Slovenian association in Klagenfurt, Austria, in which I was to address a very trendy topic at the time, namely the prophecies allegedly made by the Maya regarding December 21, 2012. Because nothing happened on that date, the story has now faded into oblivion, but back then the Maya were the center of attention: Had they truly predicted catastrophic events, even the end of the world, as some proclaimed, or a period of spiritual awakening, as others preached? Even if we were willing to believe in Maya clairvoyants, the problem—which most devotees refused to see—was that they had predicted absolutely nothing for our era, neither disasters nor positive changes. Everything that innumerable modern prophets ascribed to the Maya was simply a figment of their imagination, and very lucrative for some: more than a thousand books have been published on this topic, but only a handful of them serious—not to mention countless articles, web publications, and films. In Klagenfurt, as I had many times before, I was therefore able to calm those who might truly have been concerned, while I had no other choice but to disappoint those who may have hoped that the world was finally going to become a better place.

One important consequence of this lecture was my newfound friendship with Martin Hobel, who for a long time had been something of a Maya buff, even though his job had nothing to do with this topic—he was in charge of the Slovenian market for the Austrian company Villas. I told him about the goals of our next expedition, and he convinced his company to provide some funding, while he also contributed some money personally. Another financial supporter was the Slovenian entrepreneur Metod Zavodnik.

For this expedition I managed to recruit—besides Atasta and Aleš—Octavio Esparza Olguín, a young Mexican archaeologist specializing in epigraphy. He was a very lucky find, as became apparent when Nikolai Grube, who had agreed to do epigraphic work for us, was so busy with his own project in Uxul that he did not manage even to visit us.

We had everything ready for the new expedition by the end of March 2013. Well, almost everything. Upon my arrival in Chetumal, where my friend Bibiano Gómez took care of our institute's pickup, I learned that not long before, the engine had seized up, apparently because something had gone wrong with a previous repair. A new engine was needed or the old one had to be fixed. Either way, the repair was going to take a while.

We could not wait. Ciriaco had the team of workers ready, and we decided to head off in his pickup and the three-tonner, even though this was not an ideal solution. Before making this agreement with me, Ciriaco had already promised to help the German team in Uxul. Since Nikolai had made him a foreman, he would have to be there as required. So he would be able to spend only a few weeks with us before moving to Uxul, and naturally he would also take his pickup. Would ours be repaired by then?

35

Río Bec Dreams

A little more than ten kilometers west of Xpujil, en route to Escárcega, lies Río Bec Dreams Hotel. Richard Bertram and Diane Lalonde, the owners of the tidy bungalows and a restaurant with excellent food, snatched this spot from the grip of the wilderness and turned it into a dream destination. It is no coincidence they named their hotel after the Río Bec archaeological site: Rick, a Canadian, and Diane, from England, are Maya archaeology enthusiasts and guide organized tours to nearby sites. Therefore, it is hardly a surprise that we have known each other for years. Not only have they always given us a good price when we stay at their hotel, but during long conversations we have become very close friends and share a mutual trust. We would often leave some equipment with them that we would not be needing in the field, thereby turning their hotel into our base camp.

On the evening of April 3, 2013, Ciriaco took us there from Chetumal. We entered the open-air restaurant, and after the initial hugs and greetings Diane asked, "So where's your truck? Who brought you here?"

In the darkness, Rick and Diane had not noticed Ciriaco, who had let us off at the parking lot and headed on to his village of Constitución.

"Bad news," I said, serious now. "My pickup's broken." I explained the situation regarding my truck. "Ciriaco brought us. Tomorrow he's coming with the workers and we'll head off. I simply can't wait for the truck to get fixed, so for now we'll have Ciriaco's pickup and his large three-ton truck. But he is going to Uxul soon, and I truly have no idea how we'll manage with just one vehicle, and the three-tonner at that, which is not so easy to maneuver."

Noticing my worried face, Rick said, seriously and without a moment's hesitation, something so simple and artless that it became deeply ingrained in my memory: "Well, take the Rodeo!"

He was referring to his Isuzu Rodeo all-terrain vehicle, but he spoke with a straight face and in a tone that sounded more as if he were talking about a lighter, a screwdriver, or some similar inconsequential object.

"What?" I gazed at him in surprise. "But you must need it yourselves?"

"Not at all, we have two other vehicles," Diane added immediately.

Such a selfless offer truly exceeded all my expectations. And it proved to be our salvation.

"If you're serious . . . I don't know how to even begin to thank you . . ."

"The Rodeo has just been repaired and you can have it for as long as necessary," Rick said with a note of determination in his voice.

I cannot recall what else I might have said in thanking them, but such friends are a rare find. Rick dismissed my concerns with a wave of his hand, saying, "Don't worry."

At that point, a man came over and introduced himself. A surprise! It was Ken Jones, an American I had met a few years before. He and Dan Griffin, who was tending bar, were taking a break from fieldwork in the Puuc region and visiting their old friends Rick and Diane.

"Ivan, how are you doing? Last time I saw you was at my birthday party. Pedro really brought down the house!"

"How could I forget!"

It happened one evening in March 2011. It was during our archaeoastronomical project, when Pedro and I were taking measurements in the famous Uxmal in the northwestern Yucatán Peninsula. We were staying at a rather small hotel in the nearby village of Santa Elena. As we arrived for dinner we were invited to join a party of several Maya researchers. We were all introduced, and I ended up sitting next to Ken Jones and his wife, Julie. Ken—a retired businessman from the United States—had long been interested in the Maya. At that time their group was researching some lesser-known sites nearby and the prior day had located a previously unreported site. Ken told us he was familiar with our work in Campeche and had heard about me in Los Alacranes when exploring the site years prior. Throughout dinner we discussed our respective projects and determined we had a common set of interests. I mentioned to Ken that we were planning to begin research north of the highway within the Calakmul Biosphere, which greatly piqued his interest. Julie then chimed in and stated that they would be interested in providing resources if and when the project became a reality.

That night he was celebrating his fiftieth birthday, and his friend Manuel's trio of local musicians was playing for the occasion. With the atmosphere already quite relaxed, Pedro, who plays the guitar and is a great singer as well, understood my cue, turned to the head of the ensemble, and said, pointing to his guitar, "Maestro, may I?"

Manuel, clearly delighted to have a short break, immediately handed Pedro his instrument. Pedro was received so enthusiastically that he went on to play and sing all evening.

Now that we were going through the events of that evening, Ken reminded me of his interest in the project. We grabbed a couple of drinks from Dan and went over to a *palapa* for a further discussion. I showed Ken the stereoscopic aerial photographs of several of the sites, and he was duly impressed. As a result, we arranged for Ken and Dan to come into camp once we were reasonably close to our destination. In the meantime, they would work on a cartography project in southeastern Campeche. However, over the following few days our work did not go as planned and I could not keep my promise. What a shame, I thought to myself; funding for our explorations is never easy to come by, and had Ken seen the site he might have been inspired to donate some money. Naturally, I later sent him a letter of apology, to which he responded with understanding, suggesting that I keep him posted on our work, as he might be able to come toward the end of the field season. I had a feeling that ship had sailed, though. It was not until some weeks later that it became clear how significant that accidental meeting was for our further work.

The following morning Ciriaco and his team arrived in his Chevrolet and the three-ton Ford, while Rick graciously handed over the Rodeo. We headed off and set up camp on the dirt trail not far from the road. We did not have to do much to reach the end of the trail clearing from the previous year—only here and there did we need to remove a fallen tree or bush that had grown back—and the following day we were already able to move our camp there. The site we were after was five kilometers to the northwest, but the trail, which up to that point had led almost straight west, now turned south. Still, we had to continue on it: in the aerial photographs I saw that another trail—forking off after a few kilometers and going north—was the only one that would bring us close to the site. A few days later we reached the point where the fork should have been—but we could not locate it anywhere.

"Are you sure that this is where the road forks off?" Ciriaco asked in disbelief.

I rechecked the coordinates on the aerial photographs.

"It should be somewhere here, a hundred meters this way or that, at the most."

I carried my pocket stereoscope, so Ciriaco was able to check for himself the two photographs on which the fork was visible.

"True, the trail going north is clearly discernible but it is a minor one. The main way is the one going south and that one, too, is heavily overgrown. It has been abandoned for at least twenty years. Sometimes it happens that from the trail an intersection is not noticeable because vegetation grows most densely on trail edges. We'll have to look for it in the forest."

In order to not miss it, we continued far enough south and then took a right into the forest. After about fifty meters or so we changed direction again and started walking north, parallel to the trail we had come on. This search was not easy. Old trails can be recognized from their vegetation: in old ruts the growth is lower, with thinner stems. However, in a lot of places fallen trees and the shrubbery they knock down make it impossible to even suspect that an old trail might be underneath. We noticed possible indications in several places and even followed one such lead, but a few dozen meters later it became obvious that the vegetation pattern was a mere coincidence. It took us several hours to discover the actual trail, which we then cleared all the way to the fork and continued going north from there.

In the meantime, Atasta and Octavio examined several groups of ruins scattered along the trail and sketched them. Once we finally made it across a heavily overgrown bajo, we reached an aguada, which had been our big hope, as it seemed fairly large in the aerial photographs. We relocated our camp, only to come to the unfortunate realization soon thereafter that the conditions were anything but favorable. The place was swarming with mosquitoes, the low vegetation provided barely any shade, and the aguada was full of mire, the prints in it revealing that it must have been a favorite meeting place for peccaries and tapirs, which would use it not only as a source of drinking water but also as a pool and toilet. The water was in fact very scarce, and what could be found was outrageously dirty and smelly—so much so that even our workers, used to anything, deemed it unsuitable for washing, let alone anything else. That meant occasionally having to go get water from Xpujil, but at least we were lucky enough to have a thousand-liter tank and two barrels that could each hold two hundred liters on our three-tonner.

From the aguada a barely discernible track led toward the site, crossing a heavily creased bajo: lumps of compact soil and roots are common in wetlands, but these were so enormous that we had to use a pickax to remove them to some degree. As we finally reached higher terrain the track ended, and according to the GPS, our destination was only about one kilometer away. We found a spot in the abundant shade of tall trees and decided to move our camp there. It was already April 20, meaning that clearing the sixteen-kilometer trail, half of which we had done the previous year, had taken us more than two weeks. But even with it cleared, driving that distance would still take more than two hours.

Rick's Rodeo was a huge help in transporting equipment and people. Nevertheless, some trouble was inevitable: the truck's very worn tires did not handle the difficult terrain very well—a nuisance for us, but not so much for the tire repair services in Xpujil.

As we reached the site it soon became apparent that it was even larger than we had thought the year before. Aleš and Atasta began mapping it and Octavio set about documenting stone monuments.

36

Red Stone

Ciriaco had put together an excellent team comprising colleagues from his village of Constitución. They were very efficient, masters of their "craft," and functioned together like a well-oiled machine. Despite working from dawn until dusk every day, and even at night sometimes, the men were never reluctant to embark on any task. Ciriaco left after the first month to go help the German team in Uxul. Luckily, my pickup had been repaired by then. The driver of the three-tonner was Enrique, otherwise a farmer and beekeeper but skilled at a variety of tasks; among other matters, he effectively dealt with several minor problems with my pickup. Like many Mexicans, he, too, had spent some time working in the United States. Later he returned to take care of his wife and daughter. Obviously, everyone was very good with the machete, most noticeably Mario, or Terminator, as we called him because of the great vigor with which he would hack away at anything that stood in his path. Ciriaco's son Miguel took on the task of moving the total station each time and was also responsible for the electric generator. Every night, while Aleš transferred data from the station to a computer, processed it, and then went through the results with Atasta, Miguel took care of the generator: he would turn it on, ensure that it did not run out of gas, and stay on duty—sometimes nodding off in a chair—until Aleš was done with his work. Our team also included José and his father, Lencho—during the last few weeks he was replaced by Moisés, or Moi, as we called him, who had been with us at Oxpemul. And last but not least, our good-natured cook Magda had truly mastered in-field improvisation, and the food she prepared for us could almost be described as decadent. In order to eliminate the need to bend down, thus making her work easier, the men constructed a wooden frame and covered it with dirt to create a surface for a fireplace—the locals use similar "stoves" made of wooden boards in their homes—and put together shelves for storing kitchenware and supplies. We had brought along plastic tables and chairs, all borrowed from our friend Bibiano, the owner of a restaurant in Chetumal. We could afford such luxury only thanks to the three-tonner, onto which we could load a lot of stuff, including water barrels and the electric generator borrowed from the INAH.

Figure 36.1. Octavio and Aleš at work at the camp near Chactún.

The inspection of the site disclosed an urban core consisting of three complexes of monumental architecture. We came across many more groups of buildings nearby, some bigger than others, but we were not able to assess the true extent of the former settlement: we were simply too busy dealing with the central area.

The largest, the West Complex, which stretches across some twelve hectares, includes buildings laid around seven plazas on different levels; the largest, the northwestern plaza, is over one hundred meters long and more than sixty meters wide. Besides some massive, elongated buildings that once served residential or administrative purposes, there are several pyramidal temples, the tallest one rising twenty-three meters high. An important city like that naturally could not go without a ball court, which we located toward the southeast, outside the elevated area with most of the buildings. Next to the ball court we spotted stones arranged in two parallel lines some ten meters apart, leading toward the southeast. This must have been the remains of a causeway connecting the West and Southeast Complexes, the latter less than three hundred meters from the ball court.

Aerial photographs revealed an aguada a few hundred meters to the west, in the southeastern part of a square of land with vegetation very different from that in the surrounding area. In the photographs the plot looked like an *acahual*, a recently abandoned farming field overgrown by secondary vegetation. However, upon inspecting the terrain we realized that the squarish, somewhat sunken area was not an *acahual* but rather a *tintal*; *tinto* trees typically grow in wetlands—that is, in areas of lower terrain that are periodically flooded. We could see that the aguada, which was dry and covered with tall grass when we arrived, was the lowest part of the sunken rectangle, which is why it would get filled with water most frequently. The *tintal*, however, suggested that the rest of this area would occasionally be flooded or turn swampy as well. Its regular shape—and even its orientation, conforming to the urban layout of the entire West Complex—indicated that the sunken rectangle must have been artificially created, most likely to serve as a water reservoir. Rectangular reservoirs, probably former natural aguadas, which were subsequently artificially broadened and reshaped, are also known from other Maya cities, such as Calakmul, Uxul, and Becán. Because of their size, making them must have been a huge endeavor. According to Aleš's calculation, the volume of all the materials used to construct the buildings of the West Complex

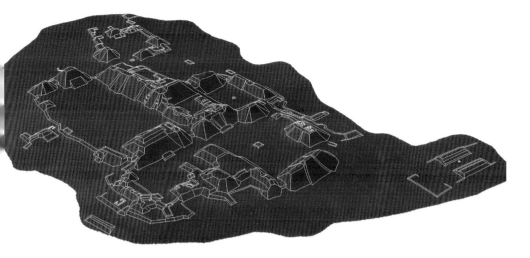

Figure 36.2. Chactún, West Complex, looking northeast (3-D rendering by Aleš Marsetič).

exceeded 100,000 cubic meters; in digging a rectangle measuring approximately 220 meters from north to south, 170 meters from east to west, and 3 meters deep, the Maya had to move a comparable amount of material, which they piled around the reservoir's edges.

The Southeast Complex is smaller than the western one, but it also boasts four nearly twenty-meter-high pyramids, soaring toward the sky on the eastern and southern sides of the main plaza. A ball court abuts one of the two pyramids on the southern flank of the plaza, and a number of somewhat smaller buildings are laid out around courtyards and smaller plazas in the surrounding area. The Northeast Complex, less than two hundred meters from the western one, is much smaller, but even here, two pyramidal temples more than fifteen meters high rise above the central plaza. The three groups of monumental architecture stretch across an area of more than twenty hectares.

We had more than enough reason to be excited: the volume and size of the buildings put this site on par with Becán, El Palmar, Nadzcaan, and some other Maya cities in the central lowlands. While Aleš and Atasta performed measurements and would check the results every evening, Octavio kept busy analyzing stone monuments, which would soon reveal no less exciting information. The ceramic fragments collected on the surface were mostly Late Classic, and the inscriptions on the stelae confirmed that the city had reached its apogee in that period.

Octavio's first project was the stela covered in stucco decorations; he ascribed it number 1. In removing the debris of a nearby building, which over the centuries had piled up enough to cover the foot of the stela, he found not only potsherds but also fairly large pieces of stucco that had fallen off the stela. At that point there was no longer any doubt as to the date being 9.16.0.0.0: he found a glyph for the *uinals* with the number 0, as well as a fragment of number 16 pertaining to the *katuns*. The sherds were largely from the Late Classic period but included several fragments of effigy censers of the so-called Chen Mul type. This finding was especially interesting since such censers were used in the Late Post-classic period, in the final centuries before the arrival of the Spanish. By that point powerful states had long since vanished from the area and the construction of magnificent architecture and the erection of stelae with extravagant imagery and inscriptions had ceased. However, the remains of a censer found in front of our stela indicated that the area was not completely uninhabited. People still lived here, probably in smallish, im-poverished groups and modest villages. Archaeological data from certain sites bear witness that they occupied some of the still usable buildings constructed by their ancestors and would occasionally honor their works by making offerings, just like the Lacandon Maya in the state of Chiapas, who performed such rituals as late as the midtwentieth century in the ruins of Yaxchilán.

The front face of Stela 1 was severely damaged, with only the bottom part of a human figure made in stucco—most probably a ruler—pre-served. The side surfaces featured an unusual mix of glyphs, first carved in stone and subsequently also made in stucco, preserved only in places. In daylight not much was discernible, but when one night after dinner we returned to the site equipped with cameras and strong flashlights, which we pointed at the decorated surfaces from different angles, glyphs were revealed that we had not been able to identify before. On the right side the Calendar Round date 2 Ahau 13 Zec was repeated—this date was not entirely preserved on the back side, but we had managed to reconstruct it correctly. It was followed by two more blocks of hieroglyphs. As Octavio explained, the inscription meant that a red stone was erected on that day.

"A red stone?" I asked.

"Yes. Here you can see the expression *tz'apah*, which means 'it was erected.'"

Figure 36.3. Stela 1 of Chactún: Octavio is showing where the glyph for the *uinals* with the zero pertaining to it used to be.

We had Magda with us, our cook. After dinner she had time, and we had brought her along for the first time so she could see why we were there and what we were actually doing. As a child, Magda had come from Chiapas and could speak Chol.

"How do you say 'to pound something into the ground' or 'to erect something'?" Octavio asked her.

"*Tz'pê*," Magda answered.

"Well, back then they would say *tz'apah*," Octavio added. "And that's what's written here."

"Is that so?" she said, her interest stirred.

"Yes, yes, they wrote in your language. Well, it's changed a little, which is no wonder; it's been more than a thousand years since this stela was erected!"

"What else does it say?" Magda was curious.

"On the bottom it says that the red stone was placed or erected at that time." He pointed at a symbol: "This sign means *tun* or stone."

"Yes, yes, stone; some say *šahlel*, others *tun*," Magda said with increasing eagerness.

"And before it is a glyph, which is read as *chac*, meaning 'red' or 'big,'" Octavio continued. "A very suitable name for the stela, which was not only large but clearly also red: its back side has red patches preserved on stuccowork."

"So, a *chactún*?" I interjected. "Does it say here that a red stone, *chactún*, was erected?"

"The *tun* part is clearly visible; the prefix is quite eroded, but I have no better explanation for the part that is visible. Yes, a *chactún*," Octavio confirmed. "Should we just name this site Chactún?"

For several days we had been mulling over the most suitable name for this splendid city.

"Excellent idea!" I was immediately on board. "This stela is clearly one of the most prominent characteristics of this site. It's unique, with hieroglyphs made in stucco. Have you seen anything like it anywhere else?"

"As far as I can remember, there are no such monuments anywhere else," Octavio said.

"Besides, here we can see the remains of red paint, the inscription states that this was a red stone, and to the best of my knowledge, there is no other site called Chactún."

Figure 36.4. The right side of Stela 1 in Chactún.

"No." Octavio nodded in agreement after short deliberation. Atasta agreed as well, and thus the decision was clear: the site would be named Chactún.

The glyphs on the left side provided another interesting piece of information: they spelled the name Aj K'inich B'alam. Thus we also learned the name of the ruler who had erected the stela in order to celebrate the end of a *katun*.

Stela 1 was so unique that I notified the INAH of the find, recommending that it be restored in order to prevent any further decay of the stuccowork. The institute responded promptly and sent a team of conservators from the INAH center in Campeche; after they had carried out the most urgent tasks, my team set up an improvised roof to protect the monument.

While mapping and surveying the site and its surroundings, we counted twenty stelae and fifteen cylindrical or oval altars. The actual number must have been higher, because we were not able to establish how many original monuments the many scattered fragments belonged to. Only two of the altars were decorated with reliefs. Several stelae were either severely weathered or had never been carved. We numbered and documented all the monuments. Octavio paid some of them special attention, not only because of the reliefs but also because of the positions we found them in.

In the West Complex, the northwestern corner of the ball court had a stone with relief decorations jutting from the ground. Octavio and his two colleagues began removing the earth and rubble that covered it, carefully documenting all layers and profiles along the way. When they got to the bottom edge of the stone, which was upright, it became clear that it was a fragment of a stela. Numbers were visible on its sides, but they could not figure out what the well-preserved relief image on the broad side facing the ball court depicted.

Once again, night came to our aid. We shed light on this stela, assigned number 12, from all possible angles. For a long while we did so without success, with Octavio muttering to himself and shaking his head in annoyance, until suddenly it dawned on him.

"I see!" he exclaimed, sounding like Archimedes must have when announcing his famous "Eureka!" "The stela is upside down! In fact, this is only its upper part."

Now we all started tilting our heads and could gradually recognize the motif: the relief depicted the profile of a face with a luxurious headdress consisting of three god masks on top of one another and a tuft of feathers. The person, certainly a ruler, was looking to the left, toward the stylized gaping maw of a snake. Similar imagery can be found on other stelae, though researchers disagree as to the meaning of the gaping snake maw. One of the sides had the numbers 9 and 16 preserved, and the other featured glyphs with astronomical data on the moon—such as would commonly accompany dates on stelae. The date was not complete, as the bottom part of the stela was missing.

"If here, too, a *katun* ending was recorded, which seems most probable, the date is 9.16.0.0.0—the same as on Stela 1," Octavio said, think-

Figure 36.5. The upper fragment of Stela 12 standing upside down in the corner of the ball court in the West Complex of Chactún. The relief depicts the face of a ruler wearing a headdress, and the gaping maw of a snake (drawing by Octavio Esparza).

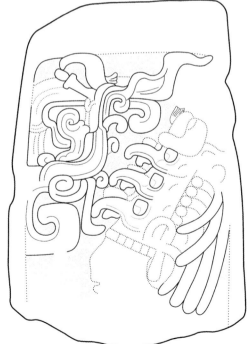

ing aloud. "And if so, the guy depicted on this piece is Aj K'inich B'alam, whose name is written on Stela 1."

Naturally, it was not Aj K'inich B'alam who had the stela placed in the corner of the ball court. Only its upper part was here and even that was upside down, and we were unable to locate the lower piece. Where had the stela originally stood at the time of its consecration in the middle of the eighth century by a ruler wanting to celebrate the end of a calendrical cycle? When and why was it broken into two pieces, with the top part being used as a cornerstone for the ball court? The rubble that Octavio dug up and removed revealed pottery originating from the Early Classic and Late Classic periods; so the ball court had probably been built before the consecration of the stela, and its upper part must have been placed in the corner during a subsequent reconstruction. How did those who placed it there perceive the ruler depicted on the monument? Was he still alive in their memories? Were their feelings toward him hostile, which then made them turn him upside down? Or did they simply not care? Perhaps they could no longer read hieroglyphs?

Figure 36.6. Enrique and José excavating fragments of Stela 18 in a corner of the ball court in the Southeast Complex of Chactún.

These and similar questions remain unanswered, but numerous other monuments in Chactún also reveal that after a period of flourishing, as reflected in the inscriptions on the stelae, the city must have experienced major changes, possibly even population shifts.

The ball court in the Southeast Complex, too, features fragments of stelae in three corners. The northwestern cornerstone is actually the bottom piece of a stela, on which the remains of a relief can be seen; the upper part has not been found. During the excavation, Octavio and his colleagues came across nearly three hundred pieces of chipped chert, which had most likely been placed there as an offering. The northeastern cornerstone is also a fragment—the upper part—of a stela. On it a Long Count date is discernible but cannot be fully reconstructed. The greatest surprise awaited

Figure 36.7. The reassembled fragments of Stela 18 of Chactún.

us in the southeast corner: two pieces of the same stela—Stela 18—were used as cornerstones, with the upper one again turned upside down. Once our workers had put the two parts together, on the front and back of the stela we could see two well-preserved reliefs, each depicting a figure in ostentatious attire. It is not possible to say whether they are one and the same person, as the inscription on the sides contains merely a date and astronomical data on the moon. Once again, a *katun* ending is recorded, only this time the date is 9.15.0.0.0, 4 Ahau 13 Yax (August 18, AD 731), two decades earlier than the date on Stelae 1 and 12.

The same date is carved on Stela 14, also in the Southeast Complex. It rose barely seventy centimeters out of a massive platform in front of a smaller pyramidal building, with hieroglyphs clearly visible on its sides. When Octavio began digging it up, he expected that there, too, he would find only a fragment. But he was wrong. He found the entire stela, and a wall abutting it partially covering its front, which had parts of modeled stucco preserved—fragments of the depiction of a ruler. The stela was so deep in the ground that Octavio could not get to the bottom of it—more extensive excavation was required, for which we lacked the necessary time and permission. He was nonetheless able to read the date on it, but questions remained: Why was the stela—who knows how long after having been erected—obstructed by a wall, which was probably part of a room in some building? And why was everything subsequently almost entirely covered up and only a minor part of the monument left protruding from the newly formed platform?

The site featured more examples of altered and reused monuments. On one of the plazas of the West Complex, Stela 3 was found in several pieces: three fragments of its lower part were found approximately fifteen meters from its upper part, which was upright, barely lodged in the ground of the plaza. On the main plaza of the Southeast Complex a fragment of Stela 15, with a few illegible glyphs, jutted from the ground. It had been placed there purposefully, as it was supported by a small but finely dressed stone block. In the same plaza and in a similar position we found a fragment of Stela 16 and several pieces of a cylindrical altar, with depictions of captives in a prone position and some severely damaged glyphs on its sides. When Octavio reassembled it, he realized that its upper part was missing. Although the reuse of monuments has been documented at several other lowland sites, we still do not have a convincing explanation for such practices.

Figure 36.8. Stela 14 of Chactún, as we found it; only its upper part was protruding from the ground.

Figure 36.9. The excavation of Stela 14 in Chactún revealed a wall attached to its front.

Once the conservators had finished their work on Stela 1, news of the site spread across the INAH. I was notified that they wanted to send over a team of journalists to prepare a press release on the find—the INAH has a special Public Relations Office. The team arrived toward the end of the field season. In the meantime, our generator broke down, meaning that Aleš could no longer transfer data. And so, we all left the site together with the journalists. A heavy rain began on the way to Xpujil. Two days later the generator was repaired, but the rain just would not cease. We wanted to venture back on June 4; however, the slippery terrain caused our three-ton truck to give up at the first—and most prominent—slope on the trail. After trying for several hours, we finally admitted defeat; it was clear that the upcoming muddy sections would be even harder to surmount.

Late that evening we returned to Río Bec Dreams Hotel, while our workers went back to their village. We could not go back into the forest until the rain stopped. We had not finished our work, and most of our equipment had been left at camp, meaning that we would have to return. But what if the rain did not subside? The three-tonner would not get us far, and my pickup simply could not take it all.

The situation was becoming critical. This season the cost of vehicle repairs had been unusually high, on top of which we were now behind schedule and wasting money without making any progress. A while ago I had applied to the National Geographic Society for additional funding but received no answer. The financial situation of my home institution was quite miserable because of general economic circumstances, and thus I could expect no help from it either. Could the Austrian company Villas, which had cofinanced the expedition, provide some additional funding? Could Martin Hobel put in a word for us? And how about Ken Jones? We had a productive conversation weeks ago, but I was not able to follow through. Might he be willing to save us from this predicament?

I wrote to both men, explaining the situation and summarizing how significant the site was. Naturally, I did not forget to enclose the most representative photos.

Again, luck was on our side: they both responded with a financial injection sufficient for us to conclude our work in an appropriate manner. We also received a new vehicle, a replacement for the three-tonner, thanks to Lirio Suárez Améndola, director of the INAH center in Campeche, who knew of our work. She had urgently sent the team of conservators to work on Stela 1, and now she arranged for us to be lent a pickup with four-wheel drive.

We had to wait until June 10 to return to camp. We had Ken Jones with us, who had announced his visit and arrived just in time to be shown around the site and presented with a much better account of the results of our work than would have been possible had he come at the beginning of the season. I was happy to be able to give him something in return for his generosity, and even more so because of his excitement, which was no less than our own. After another visit, from Rick and Diane, we finished our work on June 15.

37

Deep Well

The INAH press release concerning the discovery of Chactún circled the world in only a few days. It was recapitulated in both the Mexican and all major media worldwide. The news was sensational: it is incomprehensible to many that humankind has already landed on the moon and is making ever further advances into space and yet still does not know every corner of the earth. That such a sizable Maya city had remained undiscovered for so long made the broader public realize that the jungle still holds many surprises, and that further surveying of this vast, hitherto unexplored territory could result in discoveries of similar significance. Our previous sponsors, as well as some new ones (Ken Jones, Martin Hobel, Aleš Obreza, the Austrian company Villas, and the Slovenian companies Ars longa and Adria kombi), warmed up to the idea of financing the next field season, and Rick and Diane offered us free accommodation and food at their hotel each time we found ourselves back in civilization to buy supplies or run other errands.

Our plan for the 2014 season was to examine two sites south of Chactún. We took the dirt trail we had cleared the year before to get to the intersection where we had taken the turn toward Chactún and followed the path southwest. As the forest was tall and the trail not too overgrown, we quickly made it within approximately seven hundred meters of our first destination, as determined from the coordinates I had calculated by means of the aerial photographs.

We set up camp there. Once again, Octavio, Atasta, and Aleš were on my team. Ciriaco was not with us, as he had become indispensable to the German team in Uxul. However, he had put together a good team for me again, which included some of our old colleagues—Enrique, Miguel, and our cook Magda—as well as some new faces—Cristóbal, Gaspar, and Crescencio, who soon proved their worth as well. Like Magda, both Gaspar and Cristóbal spoke Chol, having ancestors from Chiapas. In fact, Cristóbal spoke three languages: while working in the United States he had also learned English. His younger brother Gaspar stood out in his own way: on one occasion when Enrique and I were heading off to Xpu-jil to buy some necessities, Gaspar noticed Magda's shopping list on the table, and while reading it out he would occasionally murmur to himself that this or that word was actually spelled differently or that a letter was missing. I overheard him and half jokingly put him in charge of checking the list from then on. While Gaspar was embarrassed, the ever-cheerful Magda laughingly accepted my suggestion; she always carefully prepared a list so that we were never missing anything—but she was not very good at spelling. Our expedition thus had some educational enrichment.

As the most prominent feature of the first site was its *chultuns*, some of them very deep, we named the site Tamchén. This means "deep well" in Yucatec Mayan. We found more than thirty of them just in the large leveled area in the urban core of the ancient city. As already mentioned, such underground chambers—hollowed out of bedrock and reachable through a cylindrical vertical shaft—are very common in Maya settlements, where they served as water cisterns or underground food repositories; some may have been used for other purposes as well. However, it is not typical to find so many *chultuns* in the civic and ceremonial center of an ancient settlement. At Tamchén some appear in pairs and are connected by tunnels at the bottom. Over their cylindrical necks are squarish covers made of cut stone. Many of the *chultuns* here extend five or six meters into the ground, a typical depth, while some go as deep as thirteen meters, which is most unusual. Were these *chultuns* used to collect rainwater? Any other use is hard to imagine: while gathering water with a bucket on a rope and pulling it up seems quite feasible, it would have been very difficult to descend those narrow shafts had the *chultuns* been used to store food. Did they perhaps serve not only a practical function but also, or even primarily, a religious one? Their concentration in the very core of the city, as well as the cylindrical stones we found beside the openings of some of them, which looked more like altars than covers, could certainly lead to such a conclusion.

The largest buildings at the site, as massive as those in Chactún, are laid around two sizable quadrangular plazas. While time has turned most buildings into mounds of debris, the northern part of the eastern plaza features a fifteen-meter pyramidal temple. The walls of the upper shrine are partially preserved, and its north and south facades are finished with finely dressed stone blocks. A considerable part of the south wall was destroyed by a rather large looters' trench, which must have been dug a long time ago, as we concluded from a Carta Blanca beer bottle found nearby; it had been decades since this beer had last been sold in southeastern Mexico.

While examining the plaza we spotted a stela lying, mostly buried, on the ground at the foot of the pyramid. From the two hieroglyphs on its upper side, only the date 3 Ahau of the 260-day cycle was discernible. Octavio, Gaspar, and Crescencio carefully released the stela from the earth and raised it, but they found no relief images on its back or sides. It was unusual that both glyphs on its front were carved into the surface very close to the bottom—so close that they would have been barely visible had the stela been upright and lodged in the ground. It was not impossible, we thought, that the stela had been smooth at first and both hieroglyphs were carved into it only after it had fallen over. If so, this would have been yet another example of a monument being altered. Such modifications, previously identified in Chactún, indicate that the communities living there after the period of florescence ascribed these monuments a different significance.

North of the two plazas with the largest buildings is a flat area, probably another plaza. Its northern side features an acropolis with three temples. Triadic compounds like this almost always originate from the Preclassic period. On this acropolis, too, we discovered some ceramic fragments of the Late Preclassic Sierra Rojo type. In general, the surface sherds led us to conclude that the site was particularly important during the Preclassic and Early Classic periods.

While finishing the work in Tamchén, we also continued to clear the dirt trail toward the second site targeted that season because Ken Jones, our main sponsor, had announced he would be joining the team, and we

Figure 37.1. The stela in Tamchén.

wished to show him both sites. The trail along which we camped while working in Tamchén led southeast. However, it was clear from aerial photographs that it passed relatively far from the site we were searching for. The nearest point was about four kilometers away, and we would be able to drive our vehicle only to that point, which meant we would have to set up camp there and then get to the site on foot. Wouldn't it be too difficult to walk four kilometers every day, carrying water and all the equipment, and then return? This was a serious question, but I had to put it aside for the time being. We should see the site first—it might not be that big, and we would be able to finish work in a few days.

The final stretch of trail was increasingly impenetrable and had clearly been abandoned long ago: some trees had a diameter of more than twenty centimeters, and our chain saw roared incessantly alongside our machetes. A bajo we crossed was approximately seven hundred meters wide and caused us special concern because just one rainy night had turned several stretches of the otherwise completely dry terrain into a quagmire. After two weeks of tireless clearing, we finally reached the spot where our trail came closest to the site. The day before, Ken Jones and his colleague Dan Griffin had arrived. Dan is an American living in Mexico and, being an excellent photographer, partners with Ken on their archaeological projects.

38

In the Maw of a Monster

We left the dirt trail and started cutting a path west through the forest. A few coatis were leaping in the nearby trees and peered down at us with curiosity, and a bit later a troop of howler monkeys gathered above us: they typically ignore people, but this time their combative demeanor and barking howls suggested we were not very welcome.

On the first day Ken and Dan volunteered to lead the team and managed to get through the first two kilometers, so it was not until the afternoon of the second day that we arrived at our destination. The terrain started rising after we crossed a large bajo, and we finally set foot on a plaza rimmed on the east side by an oblong mound and on the north by a pyramid with partially exposed walls. This was the first group of buildings, but it was clear from the aerial photographs that there was a second, larger one to the west.

Descending from the elevated terrain of the East Complex, we reached the prominence with the second architectural group in less than half an hour. Enrique and Ken followed the north edge of this group, whereas Atasta and I headed straight and ascended between two buildings onto an expansive plaza. The remainder of the group split up and searched for monuments. The plaza was surrounded by mighty oblong mounds, but there were no exposed walls to be seen, and no stelae or altars. After we had covered the entire plaza, each on his own side, we met again and briefly stopped.

"What do you think? They're big, but . . ." I said.

". . . actually nothing special," Atasta finished my thought. He was not impressed either. We had gotten used to scenes like this over the years: monumental architecture, no doubt an important center, but no exposed architecture, no stelae with inscriptions. . . .

Engaged in our thoughts, we were alarmed by shouting coming from the west. We responded, and the call was returned. It was impossible to make out the words, but no one wastes energy yelling unless they have a good reason. Had Enrique and the others found something more exciting than we had?

Figure 38.1. The zoomorphic portal of Structure II at Chicanná.

Figure 38.2. The zoomorphic portal at Lagunita, looking northeast. A wooden lintel is partially preserved above the eye socket.

Heading in the direction of the voices, we arrived at a second plaza, but the growth there was very thick, so we turned right and found the path that Enrique and Ken had cleared. We traced the base of a platform that contained multiple buildings and turned south at its northwestern corner. Soon we saw them, standing on a steep slope above us.

"Come on up!" Enrique waved his hand energetically, as Ken grinned victoriously. Other members of the group arrived, reverting to their native language in the excitement and creating a chorus of celebration.

The scene awaiting us justified the elation. We were literally looking down the gaping maw of a fanged monster staring at us with huge, menacing, bulging eyes. A richly decorated facade was penetrated by a doorway with jambs decorated with protruding curved and pointed stones, some of which were still covered in a layer of stucco, and large sockets on both sides with spiral decorations representing eye pupils. This was a typical zoomorphic portal of the kind particularly common in the Río Bec and Chenes architectural styles.

Many facades of this type have been discovered at other sites; some of the best-preserved ones are at Chicanná, Hochob, Hormiguero, and Tabasqueño. A supernatural being with a gaping maw is depicted on these portals as a highly stylized stone mosaic and from three sides at the same time: the frontal view is complemented by profiles next to the doorway jambs. The lintel and the jambs are dotted with upper-jaw fangs, eye sockets and a protruding nose are placed over the lintel, and the lower jaw is represented by a low sill in front of the entrance, which is likewise edged by stone fangs. Adjacent to the jambs, the monster is further depicted in both side views, with eye sockets and fangs in the upper jaw of the gaping maw.

Opinions remain divided as to the identity of the deity that such portals represent, but there is unanimous agreement that these are symbolic entrances to the underworld. Fertility gods had connections not just with rain and corn but also with the earth: life-giving crops grow in the earth, which is why the underworld was the site of the mythical origin of corn; the dead are buried in the earth and therefore played an important role in the fertility cult; and under the earth there is water, without which nothing grows. In Mesoamerican beliefs, hills, which were the abode of the gods of water, fertility, and abundance, had a significant role. Many indigenous communities still perform rain rituals on hilltops. The belief that hills collect water is rooted in fact: water gushes forth from hillside springs, and hilltops are where clouds start to gather. Mesoamerican temples may be considered artificial hills, and their entrances mimic caves, which are natural gateways to the underworld; beginning in the Preclassic period such entrances were depicted as the gaping maws of the earth deity. In agrarian societies every farmer is well aware that water is no less important than earth, so it is no surprise that gods or goddesses representing the earth also control water and fertility. On their buildings and carved monuments the Maya would often depict a grotesque, half-skeletal head of a monster representing a hill or the earth, but in many ways this is so similar to Chaac, the god of rain and thunder, that it is hard to tell them apart. Earth and water deities, depicted not just in Mesoamerica but also elsewhere in the world as frightening, monstrous beings, reflect the reality that is patently obvious in agrarian societies: the earth swallows everything but is also the giver of everything; it devours and decomposes but also creates new life from seeds. Water is just as indispensable: it makes crops grow but may also bring destruction; thunder and lightning portend beneficial rain but sometimes bring devastating storms.

Maya rulers, just like the rulers in other ancient states, personified major deities. Not only did such personification magnify the rulers' power

Figure 38.3. The north side of the zoomorphic portal at Lagunita.

Figure 38.4. The south side of the zoomorphic portal at Lagunita.

and justify their authority; the rulers also took divine responsibility on Earth. A note by the Spanish chronicler Francisco López de Gómara from the sixteenth century is very instructive: during an enthronement ceremony the Aztec ruler had to swear to make the sun move with its light, to make clouds rain, to make rivers flow, and to make the ground produce crops. If the Aztec ruler had the duty to control such important phenomena—preserving the universal order and providing for the people's prosperity—he must have been seen as the personification of a powerful deity. That the Maya adhered to the same beliefs and practices is evident from emblems of gods that embellish the rulers' gear, and from their names: the names of Itzamná the creator, Chaac, and other deities form part of the names of many rulers.

And this is precisely how we may interpret Maya zoomorphic portals: they usually decorate entrances to temples or palaces, but in our case it was clearly the entrance to the center of the city, a consecrated zone of the ruling elite who maintained balance in nature and therefore deserved their privileges. With the help of magical rituals and gifts to the gods and ancestors, they ensured abundance and averted misfortune caused by the destructive tendencies of fickle and often menacing divine forces.

Finding such a portal was not surprising, for they are one of the most prominent characteristics of the Río Bec architectural style common not far to the south. But there are few examples as well preserved as this one: the lintel with the top front part of the monster had collapsed, but the rest of the facade was in good condition and the lower jaw was probably hidden beneath the layer of debris, on which we saw multiple stone fangs and other decorative elements that had fallen off.

After the first comments and expressions of enthusiasm, it occurred to me: "This could be Lagunita!"

I told the crew that my Austrian colleague Karl Herbert Mayer had mentioned a site by this name several times: he told me that the American archaeologist Eric von Euw had visited it decades ago but never published his discovery. All he left behind were a few drawings that are kept by the Peabody Museum at Harvard University, and one of the things they depict is a zoomorphic facade.

"Karl Herbert has these drawings and he's sent them to me; I have them on my computer. We'll check them at camp this evening to see if this is Lagunita. But as I recall, some of the drawings also contain monuments with inscriptions. Let's look around to see if we can find a stela or an altar."

The sun was already low, and we did not have much time to explore the site that day. The zoomorphic portal faced west, where the terrain descended steeply; this clearly used to be a stairway that rose from the west to a high platform supporting the building with the gaping monster. We entered through the maw into an expansive plaza surrounded by monumental buildings. The walls of one of them were preserved to a significant height and there were a few vaulted rooms inside. To the east was another, larger plaza—the same one that Atasta and I had already walked through—but nowhere did we come across any stelae or altars.

At camp that evening, I turned on the computer before Magda served dinner, and everyone stood anxiously around the screen. I uploaded the photos of the facade taken a few hours ago and searched for the scanned drawings that Karl Herbert Mayer had sent me. They showed a few stelae and altars with partially preserved figural motifs and hieroglyphic inscriptions, and one was a sketch of a zoomorphic facade; a comparison of the details in the drawing and in our photos dispelled any doubt: we had found the facade that Eric von Euw had sketched years before.

"So, this is Lagunita!" Ken concluded. "But where are the stelae and altars?"

"It really is strange that we haven't seen any monuments," I replied. "Might looters have taken them all? But I suppose we didn't check everything today."

After dinner, Ken and I talked for a long time over inexpensive Mexican rum. He was naturally very pleased to participate in such a major discovery.

Ken and Dan had to conclude their visit, so I took them to Xpujil. Atasta meanwhile realized that he had lost his GPS device the previous day. While the rest of the team returned to work in Tamchén, Atasta, Enrique, and Gaspar returned to Lagunita to find the missing GPS. They had no luck finding the device, but they did find all the stelae and altars that Eric von Euw had sketched decades before.

39

The Story of Lagunita

Karl Herbert Mayer, whom I have known for many years, lives in Graz, Austria. Although studying the Maya culture is only a hobby, he is an expert and enjoys great respect among professionals in this field. He mentioned Lagunita to me on several occasions, encouraging me to try to find it again during my field explorations. He sent me von Euw's drawings, but the information about the location of the site was very incomplete.

Eric von Euw, who worked on the Corpus of Maya Hieroglyphic Inscriptions (CMHI) project at the Peabody Museum for several years, first met Karl in April 1980 in Mexico City. During their conversation, von Euw showed Karl his drawings of a number of unpublished monuments, which included the stelae and altars he had documented approximately two years prior at the site in Campeche called Lagunita. Many years later, Karl obtained—with the permission of the legendary Ian Graham, director of the CMHI project at the time—copies of numerous drawings kept by the Peabody Museum, including those that von Euw had sketched in Lagunita. Karl attempted to find Lagunita several times during his frequent trips to the land of the Maya, but with no luck. All he knew was that it was somewhere near Xpujil, but he could not find any locals who could tell him more. It had also been a while since anyone knew the whereabouts of Eric von Euw, who had long since abandoned Maya archaeology. Eventually, Karl's American colleague Lee Jones tracked him down in 2009 and called him on several occasions to obtain more information regarding his discovery of Lagunita. Von Euw told him he had been there in 1977 or 1978, accompanied by two locals. The nickname of one of them was "El Negro," and he could not remember the other's name. From the archaeological site of Chicanná along the Escárcega–Chetumal road they headed north mounted on horses and within eight hours reached an aguada where *ramón* trees grew. In his estimation, the distance between Chicanná and the aguada was between ten and twelve kilometers, and from there to the ruins they walked about two and a half kilometers.

When they attempted to find the two men who had accompanied von Euw, Lee Jones and Karl Herbert Mayer learned that "El Negro" had died and the other man had moved away, but they received help from Nicolás Feldman, a tour guide living in the village of Valentín Gómez Farías east of Becán. Together, they set off north and found some hitherto unknown ruins, which they named Kichpampak, but they did not find Lagunita.

Karl would keep me up to date on the situation. Based on what von Euw had said, Lagunita should be about fifteen kilometers north of Chicanná. However, this was too vague to be helpful: both the distance and the northerly direction were only estimates. Considering the probable degree of error, we would have to comb several square kilometers of the overgrown terrain, which could take days or weeks. Although some years ago we were lucky enough to find Altamira, all other experiences told us that we could not afford to just wander around, as it could prove expensive as well as completely fruitless. As we had done during previous field seasons, this year, too, we preferred to rely on aerial photographs, which helped us discover two sites. We realized that one of them was Lagunita only when we came across the decorated monster-mouth facade and compared it to von Euw's drawing.

While we came from the east, Eric von Euw and his companions had come from the south. As they traveled on horses, the paths they followed must have been cleared and comfortable enough. Karl Herbert Mayer and his assistants came from the south as well, but since the paths had again become overgrown after the area became part of the protected Calakmul Biosphere Reserve in 1989, and since there was no longer anyone around who knew the area, their search was not successful. Fortunately, however, these circumstances favored Lagunita in that—being well hidden—it stayed safe from looters. As we would subsequently establish during a detailed examination of the site, none of the very few looters' trenches were fresh; apparently no one had set foot there in a very long time.

I reported our discovery to Karl as soon as possible, and he further notified the American archaeologist Joseph W. Ball, one of the greatest experts on Maya ceramics. Ball, who had studied the ceramics of Becán years ago and expressed great interest in our area, soon provided an interesting new tidbit: Eric von Euw had not been the first archaeologist to visit Lagunita.

Joe Ball remembered one day in 1972 in Mérida, the capital of the state of Yucatán, when he had dinner with Ian Graham and Jack D. Eaton. Eaton was the archaeologist who discovered Chicanná in 1969 and later carried out excavations there, but he also surveyed the surrounding area. According to Ball, at that dinner Eaton mentioned several sites he had visited, including Lagunita, and said that one of the men accompanying him was called "El Negro." Eaton, who had been employed by the Middle American Research Institute of Tulane University in New Orleans in the United States, had a falling-out with the institute around 1974 and left—along with all his field notes—and any trace of him was lost. Joe Ball made very serious attempts to locate Eaton. As he put it in a private communication to Karl Herbert Mayer: "Several search agencies were able to find a number of Jack D. Eatons in Texas and Florida, some even about the right age (early to mid 80s now, I would estimate), but none proved to be our man. For all intents and purposes, Jack Eaton has vanished from the face of the earth, along with his precious notes and records."

Ball assumed that Eaton had visited Lagunita in 1968 and later reported it to Ian Graham. If he also mentioned monuments with inscriptions, that may have been the reason Graham—as head of the epigraphic project—thereupon commissioned Eric von Euw to revisit the site.

And now we were there. We realized we would have to make a detailed record of the portal, stelae, and altars, as well as map the whole urban core with a total station. This was going to be a lot of work. Would we have to walk all the way from camp on the dirt trail every day for the coming weeks?

40

A New Acquisition

With no other solution on the horizon, we started fixing the footpath toward Lagunita: to make it shorter and less exhausting, we wanted to clear it better and straighten any unnecessary bends.

It was clear from aerial photographs that there was an aguada just south of the footpath, about a kilometer and a half east of the site. If that was the aguada that Eric von Euw had passed a long time ago with his companions, and if the site was named after it, it should have water: depressions that do not retain water throughout the year are referred to by the locals as aguadas, while *lagunita* is a diminutive of *laguna*, a term for a lake that does not dry up. I suggested that Atasta check it out and gave him the coordinates. When we arrived at an appropriate point during the clearing work, he and Enrique veered south off the footpath. They returned several hours later.

"Nothing, dry," Enrique said, his words emphasized by his despondent look.

Atasta nodded earnestly before pulling a camera from his backpack, turning it on, and handing it to me. "This is what it looks like."

I had seen plenty of dry aguadas with tall grass and brush; I took the camera languidly, but my mood changed in an instant.

"What?! This is what it looks like?"

The photo showed a lake filled with water! That was one leg-pulling I could not be angry about. Enrique responded to my elation with a thunderous smile, while Atasta remarked smugly, "It is big, quite beautiful."

"This one never dries out, and the water is very clear," Enrique added.

So, my hope was not in vain. This must be the little lake that von Euw had mentioned and that gave the nearby *reinado* the name Lagunita.

The discovery meant that our water supply problems would not be as bad as feared, but our worries were not over yet: if we were to make camp on the dirt trail, we would have to walk eight kilometers every day, adding to the already strenuous work on the site. It would be ideal if we could set up camp somewhere near the lake. But how to transport all the equipment there and ensure regular provisioning?

As we were throwing around ideas in the evening trying to find the best solution, Enrique remarked, "If we had a *cuatrimoto*, everything would be much easier."

"A *cuatrimoto*?" It now dawned on me as well. What Enrique had in mind was a quad bike or all-terrain vehicle (ATV). Most people in the West use them for entertainment or sport, but here people know their practical value: this "toy" can get through pretty much any terrain, and it can even be loaded up with cargo.

"For a quad it would be enough to clear a narrow trail among the trees and we could make camp closer to the site," Enrique continued.

"What about the cargo, all the equipment?"

"We could load up everything, we'd just have to do multiple runs."

"And the generator? It's large and heavy."

"We'll strap it on, no problem," Enrique said with the voice and demeanor of one who knew. Miguel and Cristóbal immediately concurred.

"Do you know someone who has one? And how much would a rental cost us?" I was thinking out loud before it occurred to me: the Calakmul Biosphere administration had several ATVs!

The following morning, I ascended the walls of the upper temple of the tallest pyramid in Tamchén, the only place where it was possible to get a mobile phone signal. I called the director of the biosphere, the engineer José Zúñiga Morales. We had met the previous year, and this year we had already collaborated on a proposed UNESCO listing of the southern portion of the biosphere as a mixed natural and cultural property. He had asked me to help with the cultural aspects of the proposal since it was

Figure 40.1. Loading up an ATV during the move.

our expeditions that in previous years had discovered almost all the archaeological sites on the territory that was to be inscribed on the World Heritage List (I did not know back then that the inscription would be approved in June 2014 at the UNESCO conference in Doha, Qatar). Pepe Zúñiga responded to my request without hesitation: he would lend us not one but two ATVs.

That was such a relief, as we would now be able to camp much closer to the site. We picked a good spot along the footpath we had cleared out, under tall trees, just half a kilometer north of the lake. We were still a kilometer and a half from the site, but any point farther west would be less appropriate since there the terrain started to descend into a bajo—and in any case going farther would take us away from the water.

Using the first chance we had—when we went shopping in Xpujil—we brought in the ATVs and moved camp after completing work at Tamchén. First, we took all the equipment and food to the end of the cleared trail and unloaded it, and then Enrique took the three-tonner a good two kilometers back and left it on the other side of the seven-hundred-meter-wide bajo: if we were to be surprised by a major downpour—and there had already been an unseasonal amount of rain in the past few weeks—this bajo could turn into an insurmountable obstacle for the three-ton truck. Finally, we transported the equipment to the new camp with the ATVs, which required multiple runs.

Enrique masterminded the operation, and as he had done many times before, he showed yet again just how capable and resourceful he was. To strap down the cargo, we bought two old tractor inner tubes and cut them into strips: the rubber strips were far superior to ropes because they did not eat into the cardboard boxes, and they could be tightened much more. We also had to be mindful of balance as we distributed the goods

Figure 40.2. The generator arrived at camp safely as well.

on the front and rear racks. What I worried about most was the almost one-hundred-kilogram power generator, but it made it to camp safely as well: the men strapped it on tightly and leaned against it at several tricky sections to make sure it did not tip the vehicle over.

The ride itself was particularly demanding. To make it fit for the ATVs, we broadened the path a bit, straightened out some unnecessary bends, and cleared it more thoroughly: we had to remove all the stubs of cleared undergrowth that could puncture the tires, and the trunks of many trees that we could step over but could not drive over. And yet the drive was anything but comfortable or smooth: we wound among large trees we did not want to cut down—and could not, since this was a protected biosphere—and the ground was reticulated with innumerable roots. On top of that, the path crossed all manner of rocks that used to form dry stone walls for fields, the remains of ancient homes turned into mounds large and small, and artificial terraces. Such traces of ancient life, which revealed that the expansive territory around the urban core of Lagunita had been very densely settled, were scattered everywhere and could not be avoided.

All this made the ride a unique experience. The ATVs roared and bounced around, and the driver had to grip the handlebars tightly so the wheels hitting the roots and stones would not pull the bars from his hands and thus redirect the vehicle into the nearest tree. We also had to be mindful of the cargo, which was loaded on the front and rear racks and could have ended up strewn on the ground if the vehicle hit a tree. Many rounds were required for the actual move, which lasted two days, but the traffic on the path remained quite regular later as well: as always, we occasionally brought provisions from Xpujil with the pickup, which remained parked at the end of the dirt trail, from where the goods had to be shuttled to camp by ATV. Even though Enrique was the main driver, I learned the ropes as well and concluded that compared to this obstacle-course slalom, which required absolute concentration, the most challenging adventure park was just child's play.

Although we were cautious, we had to patch flats several times; unable to avoid many bumps against rocks and vegetation, we tore up the plastic skid plates on the frame and frequently had to fix them and jury-rig them together with wire. Fortunately, we did not have any major accidents.

We also cut a comfortable enough trail from the camp to the lake to bring water on the ATVs. The size of the oval lake changes depending on

Figure 40.3. The lake east of Lagunita.

the abundance of rainfall; while we were there it measured roughly one hundred meters across. To be able to scoop up clean water, we carried out the usual task of laying down a simple structure of thin tree trunks across the muddy banks, and nearby we set up a station for laundry and washing up. We could be outright wasteful with water there, and that way we did not have to bring so much to camp. True, the romance of showering by the lake was spoiled by swarms of horseflies or, depending on the time of day, mosquitoes, so everyone also had their own space for personal hygiene at camp. Nevertheless, the proximity of a permanent source of fresh water was, in that situation, a veritable luxury. The first chance they got, the men even procured fishing tackle because, along with a crocodile that occasionally appeared on the banks, there were many fish, making a welcome addition to Magda's menu.

The camp was pleasant despite featuring an inordinate number of scorpions, which were as abundant as they had been the year before in Chactún. We also encountered some nasty kissing bugs and the occasional coral snake. In the last few days, as the rain intensified, frogs proliferated; they became almost too comfortable at camp and drowned out our evening conversations with their croaking concertos.

Figure 40.4. Our cook Magda with her "range" at camp Lagunita.

Atasta had had to leave before we relocated camp: he had made ar-
rangements with the group of Canadian archaeologists to participate in
their exploration in Yaxnohcah. He was replaced by Arianna Campiani,
an Italian architect who had lived in Mexico for several years to dedicate
herself to archaeological work and complete her PhD on Maya architecture. She was now the one helping Aleš with mapping, and she also
documented the zoomorphic portal and other architectural details. To
make measurements, the prisms had to be placed at hundreds of points;
virtually the entire site had to be combed through. No wonder, then, that
among the things the men came across during this work was also Atasta's
lost GPS device.

41

The Known and Unknown Maya

The urban core of Lagunita comprises three groups of monumental buildings erected around four large plazas and a few smaller courtyards. The zoomorphic portal on the western edge of the Northwest Complex most likely designated the main entrance to the administrative and religious center. We were searching for signs of a causeway that must have led to the portal from the west, but all we found was a flat, perhaps artificially leveled space with visible cut stones and several lower structures; due north were two oblong mounds—the ruins of a ball court. The position of the ball court near the posited causeway was reminiscent of the West Complex in Chactún: the ball court there was also at a lower elevation, outside the main concentration of buildings, and running parallel to it was a *sacbé* leading to the Southeast Complex.

The Northwest Complex of Lagunita, which has two plazas, is the largest and is built on elevated terrain. We had not gone south during our first visit because the terrain descends there, the vegetation is thicker, and we had not imagined that a few dozen meters farther on there would be another large plaza with major buildings. That is why at first we had not found any of the stelae and altars that Eric von Euw had drawn. They were

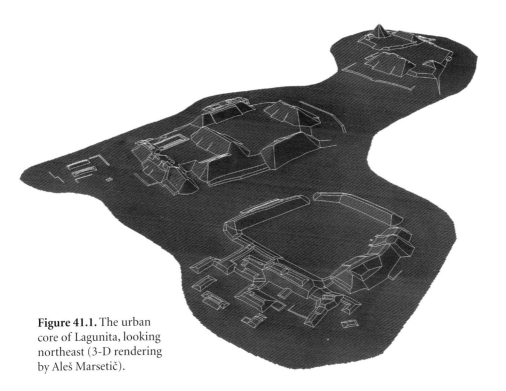

Figure 41.1. The urban core of Lagunita, looking northeast (3-D rendering by Aleš Marsetič).

found only when Atasta, Enrique, and Gaspar were unsuccessfully searching for the lost GPS device.

The building bordering the Northwest Complex on the eastern side has one stairway that provided access from the plaza, and the remains of a second stairway are visible on the eastern side. A path or causeway probably led from there to the largest and westernmost building of the East Complex, because that building, about one hundred meters away, has stairways on both sides as well. In the lower terrain in between we found two undecorated stelae lying on the ground that had probably stood on the side of the causeway. The East Complex is built on a natural prominence, which was artificially modified to give the impression of an acropolis with two levels. The pyramidal temple rising from the platform on the north side reaches a height of over fifteen meters above the natural terrain and is the tallest building in this group; on the north slope of the ruin an exposed part of the facade with finely dressed stones is preserved.

The potsherds we found on the surface indicated that Lagunita had already been settled in the Preclassic period, from the middle of the first millennium BC onward, but it reached its apogee in the Late Classic period.

Figure 41.2. Enrique and Gaspar next to Stela 6 in Lagunita.

Aside from five carved relief stelae and three altars that Eric von Euw had sketched, we found a handful of plain, undecorated monuments. The inscriptions on the stelae and altars were pretty badly damaged, and all Octavio could make out were a few calendar glyphs. The most interesting find was Stela 2 with the date 9.14.0.0.0, 6 Ahau 13 Muan, which corresponds to December 1, AD 711. The Long Count date was not entirely preserved, but Octavio was able to reliably reconstruct it from other calendrical data. Because the dates in Chactún, ten kilometers north, correspond to the years 731 and 751, we can infer that both sites reached their climax in the first half of the eighth century. A coincidence?

Probably not. All dates carved into stelae in Oxpemul range across a fairly narrow time frame, from AD 731 to 830, whereas the accompanying texts indicate that the rise of Oxpemul was precipitated by the demise of the Kaan dynasty. As mentioned before, Calakmul, where the dynasty had its seat in the Late Classic period, was defeated by the Tikal army in

AD 695. This severe blow must have badly weakened the rulers of Cal-akmul, who experienced another—this time final—defeat in AD 736. It must have been these events that allowed constituent parts of the territory under Calakmul control to free themselves from its yoke, with local rulers starting to erect their own monuments.

We were naturally excited about the zoomorphic facade in Lagunita, as it was the best-preserved piece of architecture we had found. But the find was not particularly unexpected: such portals are an outstanding charac-teristic of sites not far to the south, where the Río Bec architectural style predominates. We were more surprised that we did not come across other signature elements of this style. Instead of palaces finished with finely cut stone and mosaic decorations, Lagunita as well as Tamchén and Chactún boast voluminous buildings distributed around large plazas, numerous pyramidal temples, and stone monuments with inscriptions. In Becán, Chicanná, Hormiguero, Xpujil, and other sites of the Río Bec type, on the other hand, the architectural complexes are typically smaller and have fewer buildings, stelae with inscriptions are rare, and palaces with slen-der, nonfunctional towers are favored over pyramidal temples. Although Chactún and Lagunita reached their apogee in the same period as the sites in the Río Bec area, they bear a much stronger resemblance to the Petén tradition, which was widespread elsewhere in the central lowlands.

What is the meaning of the special features that make the Río Bec ter-ritory stand out in the Late Classic period? How are we to interpret the use of similar architecture around one hundred kilometers to the north, in the Chenes area, but in Chactún, Lagunita, and Tamchén, which are in between, the new fashion did not take hold? To what extent do these regional differences reflect the political organization, trade routes, and other connections between the individual territorial units at that time? These are questions we currently cannot answer.

And what do the monuments that were once erected and later broken in half and relocated signify? Instances of this are especially numerous in Chactún, although in Lagunita, too, Octavio determined that one of the stelae had been reshaped by trimming at some point. Thus far, we had discovered only three dates carved on stelae: two in Chactún and one in Lagunita, all from the first half of the eighth century. We can suppose that this was the period of florescence when local rulers raised stone monu-ments in exaltation of their power, which may have coincided with the downfall of Calakmul and the Kaan dynasty. If so, their glory was short-lived. In nearby Becán, where extensive excavations were carried out years before, analysis of ceramics revealed that for several decades after the middle of the eighth century, the population decreased and many buildings were abandoned. It was not until the ninth century that new types of ceramics emerged, probably brought by newcomers. If our three cities underwent a similar series of events, that would explain why so many erected stelae were broken, reshaped, relocated, or even turned upside down. Examples of secondary use such as this are known from other sites in the Maya lowlands as well; however, it remains unknown what exactly occurred, what happened to the people who first erected the monuments, and where the newcomers came from. This all took place in the final decades before the utter demise of the Classic Maya culture in the central and southern lowlands, a period that is still poorly understood.

Among the other riddles posed by Chactún, Lagunita, and Tamchén are certain features that were previously completely unknown. First, the Maya typically wrote in two columns, from top to bottom and from left to

Figure 41.3. Altar 2 in Lagunita has an unusual, nail-head shape.

right, and thus inscriptions on monuments generally have an even number of columns. Stela 2 in Lagunita, however, has only three columns and an incomplete Long Count date. Although it is possible to reconstruct the date from other available information, it is unusual that the number of days is missing. Second, while most Maya altars are cylindrical and some cubical, two altars in Lagunita have an unusual "nail-head" shape, with a longer and narrower bottom section that was probably lodged in the ground, and a broader upper part. Third, in Tamchén, dozens of *chultuns* are scattered in the urban core, and although some are collapsed or filled in with material that has accumulated over the centuries, others still extend ten meters—sometimes more—into the ground. Whereas *chultuns* are common at Maya sites, the two peculiarities of those at Tamchén are their far greater depth and their high concentration within the civic and ceremonial center of the ancient settlement. Finally, Chactún is the only known site where stone monuments were found with motifs modeled in stucco. These are featured not only on Stela 1, which is the most notable because of its large hieroglyphs, but also on Stela 14 and the otherwise severely damaged fragment of another monument.

Were Tamchén, Lagunita, and Chactún indeed so special in the Maya world, or do the above-mentioned features seem unusual, even unique, simply because we are not familiar with their neighboring sites? The latter explanation sounds more reasonable if we keep in mind that a vast area to the north has yet to be explored archaeologically. Perhaps it holds the answer to numerous questions that still trouble us. In recent decades Maya archaeology has progressed in giant leaps; however, certain hardly accessible areas remain terra incognita, and a great deal that is still unknown can be resolved only by future research.

42

Deluge

Unable to truly sleep, I tossed and turned in bed all night. The heavy rain, which had been pouring down incessantly since the afternoon of the previous day, pounded against the tin roof, occasionally turning into a thunderstorm that raged across the land, with bolts of lightning piercing the sky and deafening claps ringing in my ears.

I was in a cabin at Rick and Diane's hotel. I got up at the crack of dawn and drove off to Chetumal. It was June 2, 2014, and our work in Lagunita was nearing an end. In order to pay my workers, I had to go to Chetumal to get money because there was no bank in Xpujil. Breakfast was the last thing on my mind, as I wanted to return to camp that same day and was wondering how the team was doing in the heavy rain.

On the way to Chetumal the rain subsided slightly. A little before the village of Nicolás Bravo I ran into a line of vehicles stopped on the road. Upon approaching and coming to a stop myself I realized why: approximately seventy meters of the road were flooded. Or better put, a lazy river was running across the road that had not been there before. I was considering my options when one of the men standing on the edge of the road called, "This one can get across." He was pointing at my pickup. "The body's quite high. A similar one has just made it."

I had just thanked him for the encouragement and hopped back into the truck when a young woman came running over to me. She was loaded down with a few bags and had a daughter, about five years old, holding on to her hand:

"Could you take us along? Please, señor! I urgently need to get to Chetumal. I came in that van but it can't get across."

I opened the door and helped them both get in. I switched on the 4WD and boldly entered the water. It was getting deeper and the water was almost up to the door, and although I had the gas pedal all the way down, the truck was still losing speed. It crossed my mind now how rash I had been to take the mother and child: I had put them in danger too. I rapidly switched into first gear, advanced to the middle of the new watercourse and, after passing its deepest point, could finally feel the vehicle pick up speed again.

"We've made it across," I said to my passengers with relief. However, it was too soon to celebrate. Only a few kilometers down the road, on the other side of Nicolás Bravo, another line of vehicles awaited us. It was immediately apparent that the situation was far more hopeless: we were faced with another river bisecting the road, only this one was more than 150 meters wide. Even the larger trucks, two of them tractor trailers, did not dare attempt to cross.

I joined a few men who were standing next to the vehicles ahead of us, talking while helplessly observing the situation.

"That bus there drove in a few minutes ago," one of them said, pointing. "But the water carried it off to the edge of the road. It was lucky it didn't tip over."

The bus was sitting in the water a hundred meters ahead of us. It was tilted to the side, apparently right on the edge of the embankment.

We considered what could be done and which bypass roads one could possibly take, but any such endeavor would also be very risky. If this main paved road was flooded, what could one expect on minor roads, which only connect small villages?

What now? I was trapped between two rivers running across the road and again noticed black, threatening clouds rapidly piling down from the east after a short interlude.

I had to go back; there was no other way. I had overcome the first barrier once already, so I should be able to do so again.

"The water must have gone down a bit there by now," someone was saying, trying to make us both feel better. "There's been hardly any rain for about two hours."

But when we got back it was clear that his prediction had been too optimistic. The water had not subsided the slightest bit. My two passengers were still with me, as they had no other choice. Heartened by my previous success, I again boldly drove into the water, only to realize a moment later that my decision had been too hasty: a huge tractor trailer had just entered the stream on the other side and was bearing down on us. If I turned the steering wheel too much I would slide off the road, which I could not see anyway. The woman sitting next to me was crying, "We're gonna crash! We're gonna crash!" and her daughter joined in with audible weeping. I stepped on the gas pedal and gently maneuvered the wheel left and right. Fortunately, the large truck, too, turned slightly and passed me on my left, missing us by only about a meter. Huge splashes of water surged over us, gushing from under its wheels so violently that the pulsing waves almost brought us to a stop. In first gear, I pushed lightly on the clutch, thus preventing the engine from stalling, until—a few endless seconds later—the pickup overcame the resistance of the mass of moving water and accelerated past the flooded section.

The woman gradually calmed down, and the high pitch of her voice lowered; however, she would not stop talking and thanking God. I joined in. Was it luck or divine providence that saved us? I do not know, but it would be presumptuous to think we had made it out of danger simply due to my abilities.

In Xpujil I stopped at the bus station. My passengers got off, saying they would stay with relatives for now. I needed to know the situation on the road to Escárcega, which was the second-closest place with a bank, 150 kilometers to the west. I managed to locate a bus driver who had just arrived from there and was headed to Chetumal. He had been informed that the Chetumal road was underwater and said he would have to make a detour of more than a hundred kilometers through the town of Peto in the state of Yucatán. But he assured me that the road to Escárcega was fully passable.

I headed off to Río Bec Dreams Hotel, where Diane, whom I had called a few minutes earlier, was expecting me with breakfast. She had been getting ready to leave for Chetumal to run some errands, but my story convinced her that simply wasn't going to happen today. Half an hour later I was back on the road, this time going in the opposite direction. It was raining again, and some kilometers before Conhuás I noticed that the engine temperature was rising. There was enough water in the radiator, the fan was working, and the V-belt was on tight. Could it be that the fan clutch was malfunctioning, and thus the fan could not reach the required speed?

I called Ciriaco. His village of Constitución was not far away, a little over twenty kilometers. There must be a car mechanic there. To my good fortune, Ciriaco was not in Uxul with the German team but in Escárcega, shopping. He arranged for his friend Pancho to wait for me in Constitución. Pancho was not exactly a professional mechanic but knew his way around an engine. Although he could not locate the problem, he did organize a solution: I would leave the pickup there for a mechanic to check out, while someone else drove me to Escárcega. He thought of Víctor, another man from the village, who had a car and was also the brother of one of our men, Enrique. We found his father first and he immediately sent for Víctor, who soon arrived and was willing to help without a moment's hesitation. I guess Enrique hadn't said anything bad about me.

We drove off to Escárcega, where I withdrew the money, and we returned to Constitución. It rained the entire time. The mechanic did indeed conclude that the fan clutch was broken. Without the necessary part on hand, he was not able to fix it, but he thought I should be able to get to Xpujil if I didn't go too fast. Indeed, I did manage to make it; I arrived a little before five in the afternoon and caught a car repair service just before it closed. A mechanic got the clutch off quickly enough, but I couldn't relax just yet: although Pata de Jaguar (Jaguar Paw), the main hardware and spare parts store in Xpujil, carries many different items, it is always a problem to find parts for my imported pickup. The salesman took the old clutch and, without saying a word or giving me any hope, disappeared into the storeroom. Despite all my troubles since waking up, it proved to be my lucky day after all: the man returned with the right part, which was soon locked into place.

It was too late to get back to camp, so I spent the night at the Río Bec Dreams Hotel and hit the road early the following morning. While I was driving, various chaotic thoughts buzzed around in my head. I had more than enough reason to be concerned. The rain had stopped only last night. What shape was the dirt trail in? How had they handled everything back at camp? Had they finished the work? Had there been any accidents? While making measurements a few days ago they had encountered a poisonous Mexican moccasin, and after a rain even more such creatures come out . . . .

I switched on the four-wheel drive and the reduction gear, veered off the road, and plowed into the mire, which was abundant even at the beginning of the trail. The water crossing the trail one kilometer on looked critically high, but my truck was able to handle it. Perhaps it wouldn't be too bad after all?

I got over the few elevations that followed smoothly. The first bajo was flooded but it was short and had little water, so no trouble there either. The next one was longer and the water somewhat deeper. I stopped to take a better look, but I couldn't see where the winding trail might emerge from the waters. I took a run-up, stepped on the gas, and somehow got across. My pickup seemed invincible, but only for a few moments. The upcoming inundated bajo was several hundred meters long. The engine roared and the pickup bounced up and down, skidding from left to right on the boggy terrain. My constant, wild turning of the steering wheel barely managed to keep me on track and avoid the trees along the way, as great gushes of muddy water splashed the windshield. Every now and then the truck sank dangerously deep and seemed about to die; the engine was choking, yet the water just kept on going . . . .

Miraculously, the truck did not give up. It conquered all the flooded sections, even those that had seemed hopeless. It was only then that I fully grasped the importance of the right kind of tires: the year before I had bought new ones, a type especially appropriate for muddy terrain. In my experience, my previous—all-terrain—tires would not have gotten me far. The pickup did have a winch, but had I gotten stuck in the quagmire, using it would have been extremely difficult by myself, particularly because in the bajos there are few trees capable of supporting a cable to pull out a vehicle.

I arrived at the spot where our three-tonner was parked. A tarp covering it protected equipment that had already been loaded: they must have started packing up and moving things already. But why did they tie the tarp onto the trees in such a manner that it blocked my path? Because there was nowhere else to put it up? Or were they trying to stop me from going farther? In only a few meters the largest bajo began, and the water in it almost reached the three-tonner, although it was on higher ground, so the entire seven-hundred-meter stretch of the trail across the bajo had to be deep underwater. Should I untie the ropes and try anyway?

Pondering this, I heard an engine. In a moment or two Enrique appeared around a curve on an ATV loaded with stuff. The trail resembled a creek and the vehicle, half-submerged, gradually swam out of it.

The tarp obstructing my way was indeed a message.

"The bajo is completely filled with water. You would not be able to make it across," Enrique said.

"Where is everyone else?"

"They're on their way, on foot. Cristóbal is driving the other ATV."

They did appear soon, wading through the water, each carrying as much as they could. They were soaking wet but still in good spirits—just another adventure. Cristóbal arrived as well. The two ATVs were a true blessing and had been for weeks: with them, no barrier was impassable.

As they soon explained, the day before, they had finished work in Lagunita, and Enrique had already brought some equipment to the truck. Early this morning they broke down the camp and set off. Since I had not returned the day before, they expected me today, but in any case—even had I not showed up—they had to head for the hills as soon as possible; here, too, it had been raining incessantly and streams of water had already started flowing through the camp.

The question remains, though, how they would have made it out by themselves with the three-tonner. I told them that the way back was going to be anything but simple. We would see how far the truck would get in the mud and then we would tow it with my pickup, which we would attach to something with the winch cable.

We loaded everything onto the two vehicles, covered them as it began to rain again, and prepared everything to leave. We waited a little longer for Cristóbal, who had returned to camp on one of the ATVs to get some remaining stuff, which we then loaded as well, and set off.

In the first few hours we made relatively good progress. Although the three-tonner following behind me got stuck in almost every pool of muck, we managed to winch it out with the pickup each time. Our first attempt without the winch was not successful, which was no wonder. The one-and-a-half-ton pickup simply could not haul the fully loaded three-tonner out of the mire. Luckily, the previous year I had bought a good winch with four-ton pulling power. We uncoiled the cable and tied it to a tree a sufficient distance ahead of us, or around several smaller trees. Good tires, the four-wheel drive, and the winch aided the slow yet steady progress of the pickup and the three-tonner tied to it. Enrique, who was driving the three-tonner, had his foot pressed moderately on the gas pedal, so that the back wheels of the truck provided at least some traction despite constant slippage, thus making less pulling power necessary.

Progress was slow. At every longer flooded section we had to give the winch a break so as not to overheat its electric motor; furthermore, once the cable had coiled enough and thus become shorter, it had to be untied, unwound, and tied to another tree farther away.

After a few hours I got the feeling the winch was losing power, and then, in the middle of another mudhole, the truck's motor cut out and would not restart. Was the battery dead? Evidently. I had jumper cables, but they were too short to reach the battery of the three-tonner behind me. Besides, if the winch had been draining the battery that much, we would not get too far pulling the three-tonner.

The situation was dead serious. It was well past noon already, yet we still had eight kilometers to go before reaching the road. The men were sloshing through water and mud without end—there might be a poisonous snake anywhere. Something needed to be done. Soon. Could the army come to our rescue? Perhaps I could call them. There was no reception where we were, but we would often get some bars on top of the pyramid in Tamchén.

We made a plan and each went about our individual tasks. Tamchén was a few kilometers back. Gaspar and I hopped on an ATV, drove back on that stretch of trail, and then reached the pyramid on foot. I was soon able to contact the commander of the Xpujil base on his cell phone; he had given me his number at the beginning of the season when I stopped by his office. He was not at the base but promised to help if a Hummer could be found that was not already providing assistance elsewhere in the flooded areas. He suggested that I also call the major who was in charge of the base in his absence. While I could not get the major, I did manage to contact Pepe Zúñiga, the director of the biosphere. I asked him to go over to the military base in person and ask for help. Furthermore, I asked him to also send someone from the biosphere administration, as they were the only ones who knew which trail to take. Pepe Zúñiga promised to do everything in his power. And he did.

Gaspar and I returned to the rest of the team, who had in the meantime moved the battery and the most essential equipment from the three-tonner into my pickup. Since we could not just wait for help—we did not even know whether it was coming—we decided to continue on our way

Figure 42.1. At first, the towing went well . . .

in my pickup and both ATVs and leave the big truck behind for the time being, as it could not move at all without being towed.

I was a lot less worried now. If my pickup got stuck, all of us together would be able to pull it out. But it proved its worth again; we did not need to use the winch at all. We were only a couple of kilometers from the road when our path was suddenly blocked by a Hummer.

Salvation! The military was here, ready for action and accompanied by Ernesto from the biosphere administration, whom I had known for several years. We immediately came up with a plan: Enrique, Cristóbal, and Crescencio would return to the truck with the soldiers, also taking one ATV, and I would drive the others to Xpujil and then return to help where necessary. Miguel would drive the other ATV and return it to the biosphere.

I made it through to the road without any major trouble and arrived in Xpujil just as it turned dark. Miguel returned the ATV and then joined the others from my truck in front of a store, where we bought tequila: we were all soaked and cold, except for Magda and Arianna, who had been riding in the cab. Magda and I went to buy some roasted chickens, beer, and other drinks for the soldiers and our colleagues still struggling in the jungle, while I instructed the others to take a taxi to Río Bec Dreams Hotel, where Diane—whom I had just called—was expecting them. The brave Magda said she would come with me since someone would need to serve the food. We took off, heading back the same way. A little before the turn-off onto our dirt trail we saw the other ATV coming toward us carrying Ernesto and the driver of the Hummer.

"We're going to the base to get the jack," the driver said. "We got stuck. Or do you have one?"

That's just great. The Hummer's stuck—and they don't have a jack.

"Yes, sure, I have two, actually."

"And you have a winch too! Great, you'll pull us out." The driver's excitement was growing by the second, while my good mood was melting like snow in summer. Now *I* was supposed to pull out the Hummer? The vehicle that had come to rescue our truck?

Still, I had no other choice. Soon after turning onto the dirt trail, I noticed that the light coming from my headlights was fading. At first we thought the battery was low, as it had already been greatly strained by the use of the winch. But no. Apparently, the alternator was dead.

The Hummer was sitting deep in water and mud only about one or two kilometers from where we had bumped into one another some hours ago. When we reached it, the light from my headlights was so weak that we first had to charge the battery. The soldiers moved it into the Hummer, where they had two batteries, and while mine was charging, everyone enjoyed the food Magda and I had brought. Enrique was getting quite irritable, having worked hard all day without a bite to eat. Now his mood improved a little. Unfortunately, the battery still had not charged sufficiently. When we moved it back into the pickup and tied the cable onto the Hummer the latter did not budge an inch.

It was already about nine o'clock. Over the radio, the lieutenant in charge called the base for help, and about an hour and a half later another Hummer with a crew arrived. First the soldiers cleared out a *desecho*, a bypass track, onto which one Hummer would pull the other. The maneuver succeeded and took a little more than an hour; however, at that point it was clear that we would not be going back to our three-tonner. All our efforts were dedicated to getting out of the mud and returning home. During the following hours the entire crew of almost twenty soldiers plus our team had their hands full pulling one or the other Hummer out of the mud, as they were to get stuck many more times. Occasionally, we would also have to recharge my battery.

Although I had always considered the military Hummer to be ideal for such circumstances, I now had to revise my opinion. It was obvious that it could not handle such extreme conditions.

We finally made it through to the road and arrived in Xpujil at about four in the morning. Naturally, I thanked the soldiers for their efforts, although I still had the exact same problem I had approximately fifteen hours ago when I called the commander.

We arrived at Río Bec Dreams Hotel and unloaded the equipment into my cabin, while rain was still pouring from the sky. There was no one waiting for us. Why would they be? They could neither help nor know whether we were coming at all. Enrique called his brother Víctor and asked him to come pick them up. I paid everyone and waited with them for Víctor to arrive. We were exhausted, completely drenched, speechless, defeated. The farewell was quite sad. We did agree, though, that I would call them once we were rested and we would think of a solution, although at that moment I did not have the faintest idea what that solution might be.

I went into my cabin, dug up a bit of tequila, and poured some into a glass. I was tired, but worries kept me awake; the situation seemed hopeless. We had left behind equipment of all sorts—the borrowed generator, the tripod for the theodolite—many people had left their clothes, and Octavio had even forgotten his wallet. And of course the truck—a rental! —was still out there, embedded in water and mud. How long before we could get it out? I could not wait forever; I would have to pay the men to take care of it. What would the total cost be?

While I was pondering all this, the night gradually turned into day and someone knocked on my door. Miguel and Gaspar entered. They had stayed up waiting until three in the morning, they said, and then they had gone to bed. Diane had taken care of them as well. They listened to my story and offered to help however they could. I naturally did not doubt their willingness to help: just like the others, they, too, had demonstrated on numerous occasions not only their commitment to work, but also selfless friendship. I thanked them and paid them their earnings.

"It's almost morning. We'll just go out on the road; we'll surely get some transport."

We said our goodbyes. Sleep finally came. I woke toward noon. As I entered the restaurant I found Aleš, Octavio, and Arianna sitting there. Diane was also already around somewhere. During breakfast I summarized our futile efforts of the previous night.

No one was in the mood for joking, which otherwise would have been the norm.

43

Saved

The battery was not completely dead, so I was able to drive to Xpujil. An auto electrician replaced the alternator, which solved the first problem. He also switched out the battery from the three-tonner and replaced it with mine, now fully charged. After that I started inquiring among my acquaintances about our options for getting the truck out. I found a young man who had a 4WD tractor; a nice guy, but he could not guarantee success.

"A Tree Farmer would be more effective. There are two in Zoh Laguna."

A Tree Farmer? I had just spoken to Ciriaco, who had also mentioned this vehicle. But he said it would be expensive to bring one in from any distance, because it moves slowly and uses a lot of fuel. And now it appeared there were two in Zoh Laguna, a village less than twenty kilometers from our dirt trail. Besides their Xpujil office, the Calakmul Biosphere administration also had an office in Zoh Laguna; surely they knew something about these machines?

The friendly Pepe Zúñiga helped me out again. The following day he arranged a meeting with two men: one of them had his own Tree Farmer, while the other was in charge of the one owned by the village. The condition of the latter was doubtful, as it had a leaky radiator, but the first one was in good shape. I asked the owner how much such an undertaking would cost us and when we could begin.

"No, no, now it's not possible," he said.

Ciriaco had not been too optimistic, and I certainly did not expect an immediate solution. The man would most likely say we needed to wait at least a couple of days for the water to subside, if it stopped raining in the first place.

"Today it's already too late, it's one o'clock," he continued. "But we could do it tomorrow morning if you'd like."

"Tomorrow morning?" I asked in surprise and disbelief. "Do you think that will be possible?"

"It will, it will," he assured me.

The man must know what he's talking about, I thought to myself, full of new hope. He must be aware what the terrain looks like after so much rain.

We agreed on a price and the time when the vehicle and driver would be ready. I called Enrique and told him the plan.

"OK," he said. "I'll be at your hotel at seven. I'll bring Pancho along; he's good with repairs, in case we need anything."

The following morning, we packed the battery for the truck and some food and headed off. At nine o'clock we met up with our potential savior and his machine on the road north of Zoh Laguna, near the beginning of our trail. A Tree Farmer skidder is a heavy-duty vehicle used predominantly for hauling logs. Its wheels are huge and it has a winch in the back and a plow in the front. It hardly needs a path, as it can literally drive through a forest, knocking down trees as if they are nothing. It was not a coincidence that Zoh Laguna had two of them—until recently, logging had been its most important industry.

The driver of the skidder followed my pickup onto the dirt trail. I left my truck one kilometer from the road, before the stream crossing the trail. There was even more water than two days ago. This would be the first challenge for the Tree Farmer, I thought to myself; Enrique also shook his head skeptically. The Tree Farmer had no place for cargo and the cab was big enough for only the driver, so the rest of us squeezed behind the cab, around the winch. The driver, a good-natured middle-aged man, immediately set off. Several spots on the vehicle were quite rusty, and the thick wire mesh protecting the cab was bent out of shape in many places; it must have received a great many heavy blows in its life. The engine clattered

Figure 43.1. . . . and then, the Tree Farmer had to come to our rescue.

and creaked with a tremendous roar, while the enormous tires with their prominent tread sank more than halfway into the water and mud. Yet they retained traction without the slightest slippage, and so, slowly but steadily, we made it to the other side.

Only now could we relax: this monster was clearly up to the task. A few hours later we arrived at the truck. The Tree Farmer turned around, knocking over a few trees growing along the trail with its plow. The driver unwound the thick cable from the winch and we tied it to the truck. Then we inserted the battery and Enrique got behind the steering wheel. The Tree Farmer started slowly, the cable tightened, and the truck began to move; Enrique stepping on the gas did not contribute much to this success. Before every stretch of solid terrain Pancho disconnected the truck, which allowed the vehicles to go faster, and hitched it again when towing was unavoidable.

By three in the afternoon we had already made it to the road. I handed the driver his payment, shaking his hand and thanking him. He grinned and said, "Not at all." His efforts were clearly not out of the ordinary to him, but I felt as if he had saved my life.

Upon our triumphant return to the hotel we were greeted—naturally—with excitement. Our problems had not been forgotten, but now the whole world seemed different, somewhat brighter, despite the heavy clouds still hanging low in the sky. Only yesterday the entire situation had seemed hopeless, but now we had overcome this problem as well.

And, most importantly, no one had been bitten by a snake, no one had been injured; we were all alive and healthy.

•　•　•

This is how the ninth field season of archaeological surveys in southeastern Campeche finished on June 6, 2014. Only two decades ago this area had been almost unknown, archaeologically speaking, yet today we can say with certainty that in the heyday of the Classic Maya culture it was very densely populated and punctuated by several important political centers. Furthermore, the discovery of early, Preclassic sites resulted in interesting new insights. It has long been known that large cities such as El Mirador and Nakbé existed in the first millennium BC in the much better explored northern Guatemala lowlands; with their monumental architecture they had been deemed the earliest expression of Maya statehood. However, it is now clear that similar development occurred simultaneously in the neighboring areas to the north, where large urban centers, such as Mucaancah and Yaxnohcah, also arose during that same early period. Certain characteristics of architecture and urban layouts in southeastern Campeche reveal contacts with neighboring regions in northern Guatemala and northwestern Belize, while shedding light on trade networks and other connections in different periods. Furthermore, the distribution of major centers reflects the degree to which their locations were conditioned by the natural environment, as well as, to some extent, the territorial political organization, for which a plethora of new data has been obtained from hieroglyphic inscriptions.

Our discoveries have provided a great deal of new information but have also posed new questions—as is typical in science. Although Chactún and Lagunita were on the rise, it seems, in the Late Classic period, their characteristics do not match our expectations. What were their relations with their contemporaries, who created, not too far to the south, very different settlements and their own unique architectural style? Why did their rulers discontinue, after a short period of glory, the erection of monuments to their memory? Furthermore, who would later break those monuments in half, move them, and turn them upside down—and why? Were such events just an overture of a great crisis that caused the demise of this once-powerful civilization?

Our narrative ends here, but the search continues. We have covered a vast area rich in archaeological heritage, of which we knew barely anything before. We have discovered the remains of numerous, once-flourishing but now long-abandoned settlements and have attempted to decipher the mute speech of stones. However, all this is only the first exploratory phase. Since our visit, many ruins have reverted to their solitary lives, keeping many secrets to themselves that only patient future excavations will bring to light.

Moreover, we still do not know what is hidden in the jungle to the north of the areas we explored. That extensive territory remains unpenetrated but is undoubtedly promising for future research. It is also there that we will have to seek answers to some of our unresolved questions.

Further Reading

Adams, Richard E. W.
   1999   *Rio Azul: An Ancient Maya City*. Norman: University of
           Oklahoma Press.

Brady, James E., and Keith M. Prufer eds.
   2005   *In the Maw of the Earth Monster: Mesoamerican Ritual
           Cave Use*. Austin: University of Texas Press.

Coe, Michael D.
   1999   *The Maya*. New York: Thames & Hudson.
           Demarest, Arthur
   2004   *Ancient Maya: The Rise and Fall of a Rainforest Civilization*.
           Cambridge: Cambridge University Press.

Estrada-Belli, Francisco
   2011   *The First Maya Civilization: Ritual and Power Before the
           Classic Period*. London & New York: Routledge.

Gendrop, Paul
   1998   *Rio Bec, Chenes, and Puuc Styles in Maya Architecture*.
           Lancaster: Labyrinthos.

Graham, Ian
   2010   *The Road to Ruins*. Albuquerque: University of
           New Mexico Press.

Hammond, Norman
  1994   *Ancient Maya Civilization*. 5th ed. New Brunswick, NJ:
          Rutgers University Press.

Leifer, Tore, Jesper Nielsen, and Toke Sellner Reunert
  2017   *Restless Blood: Frans Blom, Explorer and Maya Archaeologist.*
          New Orleans: Middle American Research Institute, Tulane
          University – San Francisco: Precolumbia Mesoweb Press.

Martin, Simon, and Nikolai Grube
  2000   *Chronicle of the Maya Kings and Queens: Deciphering the
          Dynasties of the Ancient Maya*. London: Thames & Hudson.

Mathews, Jennifer P.
  2009   *Chicle: The Chewing Gum of the Americas, from the Ancient
          Maya to William Wrigley*. Tucson: The University of Arizona
          Press.

Nondédéo, Philippe
  2003   *L'évolution des sites mayas du sud de l'Etat du Campeche,
          Mexique*. BAR International Series 1171 (Paris Monographs
          in American Archaeology 12), Oxford: Archaeopress.

Ruppert, Karl, and John H. Denison
  1943   *Archaeological Reconnaissance in Campeche, Quintana Roo,
          and Peten*. Carnegie Institution of Washington Publication
          543, Washington.

Sánchez Nava, Pedro Francisco, and Ivan Šprajc
  2015   *Orientaciones astronómicas en la arquitectura maya de las
          tierras bajas*. Colección Arqueología, Serie Logos, México:
          Instituto Nacional de Antropología e Historia.

Sharer, Robert J., and Loa P. Traxler
  2006   *The Ancient Maya*. 6th ed. Stanford: Stanford University
          Press.

Šprajc, Ivan
- 2008 ed., *Reconocimiento arqueológico en el sureste del estado de Campeche, México: 1996-2005*. BAR International Series 1742 (Paris Monographs in American Archaeology 19), Oxford: Archaeopress.
- 2015 *ed., Exploraciones arqueológicas en Chactún, Campeche, México*. Prostor, kraj, čas 7, Ljubljana: Založba ZRC. Available at: http://iaps.zrc-sazu.si/sites/default/files/pkc07_sprajc.pdf.

Šprajc, Ivan, Atasta Flores Esquivel, Saša Čaval, and María Isabel García López
- 2014 *Reconocimiento arqueológico en el sureste del estado de Campeche, México: temporada 2007*. Prostor, kraj, čas 4, Ljubljana: Založba ZRC. Available at: http://iaps.zrc-sazu.si/sites/default/files/pkc04_sprajc_0.pdf

Stephens, John Lloyd
- 1841 *Incidents of Travel in Central America, Chiapas and Yucatan*. 2 vols. New York: Harper & Brothers.
- 1843 *Incidents of Travel in Yucatan*. 2 vols. New York: Harper & Brothers.

Stuart, David
- 2011 *The Order of Days: The Maya World and the Truth About 2012*. New York: Three Rivers Press.

Thompson, J. Eric S.
- 1994 *Maya Archaeologist*. Foreword by Norman Hammond. Norman: University of Oklahoma Press.

Webster, David
- 2002 *The Fall of the Ancient Maya: Solving the Mystery of the Maya Collapse*. London: Thames & Hudson.

Index

200; mentioned, 129, 155–156, 173; present-day, 125–126; as reference point, 223

Villahermosa camp, 126–127, 163–166, 164p, 189–190, 195, 206, 209, 228

virgin water, 99

Wakná, 5

water: for bathing, 28, 105, 138, 142, 280; in caves, 99; cenotes (sinkholes), 23; chultuns (cisterns), 106p, 107, 261–262, 287; crocodiles and, 28, 83; ensuring a supply of, 126; fresh, sources of, 23–24; lack of, 28, 135, 243, 276–277; potable, 31, 105, 138, 141; purchasing, 91, 102, 195; rainwater, collecting, 55p, 59; rationing, 138; from roots of trees, 133, 133p; sources of, 133, 133p, 140, 141p, 188, 190; transporting, 141, 225, 243, 276–277, 279–280; trapping, 140, 141p; virgin, 99

water cisterns, 106p, 107, 287

water deities, 268

water hazards, 137

water purification, 138

waterways, 23–24, 105

weapons, 85

Xochicalco, 98

Xpujil: architectural complexes, 285–286; architecture nearby, 232; area south of, 23–25; bank in, 288; cold beer in, 79; errands in, 153, 154; getting to, 290; help from, 67, 79; Hotel El Mirador, 205; mechanic in, 299; medical care at, 88–89; mentioned, 30, 96, 101, 164, 170; military headquarters, 82–84; El Mirador Maya, 64–65; naming of, 22; rain in, 258; as reference point, 232, 239,

272; settlement of, 22; shopping in, 22, 39–40, 199, 277–279, 289, 291; tire repair services, 243; waiting in, 158–159; water from, 243

Xpujil barracks, 90

Xpujil chiclero, 136

Xpujil clinic, 199

Xpujil commander, 92, 118, 153, 171

xulab, 82

Yamá, Martín (Don Martín) (mechanic), 40, 157–158, 163

Yaxchilan, 248

Yaxnohcah (First Big City): architectural structures, 200; camping at, 168; checking out, 204; excavating, 231; field workers, 281; illustrated, 129i; mapping, 163, 165p; naming of, 131; peripheral architectural groups, 155–156, 204, 206, 212, 214–215; pyramids, 155–156, 206, 212, 214; surveying, 166; trail cross section, 128p

Yucatán (state), 2

Yucatán Peninsula: animal life, 24; caves, 97–100; Christianizing the, 184–185; geography, 4, 23; languages of the, 19; paving the, 19; people of the, 112–113; rainfall and groundwater, 23–24; settlement of the, 4–5; snakes, 63; tropical forest of the, 2; typical landscape, 3p; vegetation, 24

Yuknoom Ch'een II, 214

Yuknoom Yich'aak K'ak,' 70

zapote trees, 16

Zavodnik, Metod, 237

Zoh Laguna, 40, 96, 158, 233, 299–300

Zúñiga Morales, José (Pepe Zúñiga), 276, 277, 294, 299

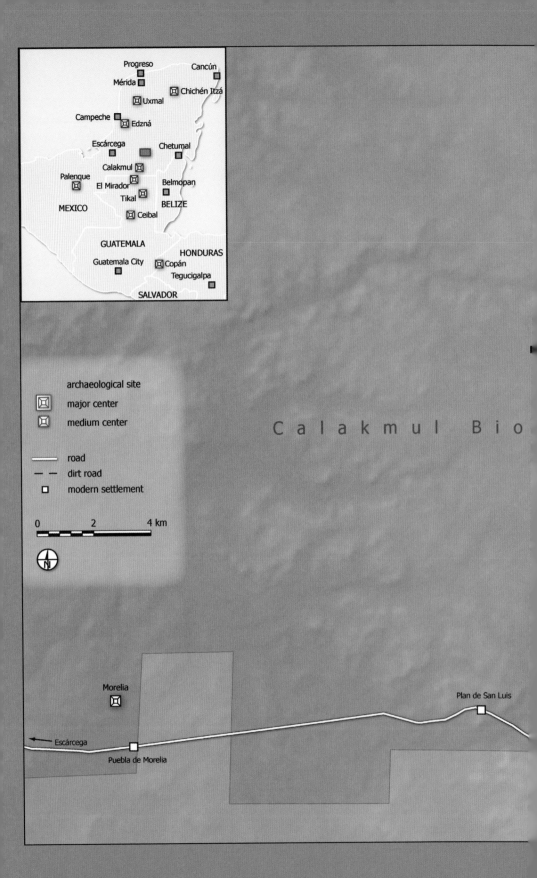

Progreso

Cancún

Mérida

Chichén Itzá

Uxmal

Campeche

Edzná

Escárcega

Chetumal

Calakmul

Palenque

El Mirador

Belmopan

MEXICO

Tikal

BELIZE

Ceibal

GUATEMALA

HONDURAS

Guatemala City

Copán

Tegucigalpa

SALVADOR

archaeological site

☒ major center

☒ medium center

—— road

– – dirt road

☐ modern settlement

0   2   4 km

N

C a l a k m u l   B i o

Morelia

Plan de San Luis

← Escárcega

Puebla de Morelia